Musics Lost and Found

'Folk song is the heart's home town' – Japanese proverb

'My mother would never spin in silence. She would always sing as she spun' – a villager in Podserednieje

'First a musician must tune himself. Then he must tune his instrument. Only then can he tune the listener' – Turgun Alimatov

'Tuvan music is like loose snow, and overtones are like a spray of snow' – Valentina Süzükei on the importance of timbre

'The day has rested and the night is ready for work. Two seas have served each other – the bright blue of the sky and the vigilant black of the earth. The moon has risen above the stars to plough the rows of clouds. Above is life that moves the mind and heart, below is a world of effort. The peasant awakes, the plough takes heart and encourages him, tearing the field, piling up waves of soil to right and left. The whole team is breathing heavily, the oxen are murmuring, the men are shouting, the breeze is whistling, the flowers are whispering, the brook is plashing. Meanwhile the plough-wheel creaks and whimpers … The dark and light of the peasant's life, his labour and his hopes, give birth to our beautiful song' – Komitas on a nocturnal ploughing song in Armenia

Musics Lost and Found

Song Collectors and the Life and Death of Folk Tradition

Michael Church

AGA KHAN MUSIC
PROGRAMME

THE BOYDELL PRESS

First published 2021
The Boydell Press, Woodbridge

ISBN 978 1 78327 607 3

The Boydell Press is an imprint of Boydell & Brewer Ltd
PO Box 9, Woodbridge, Suffolk IP12 3DF, UK
and of Boydell & Brewer Inc.
668 Mt Hope Avenue, Rochester, NY 14620–2731, USA
website: www.boydellandbrewer.com

A CIP catalogue record for this book is available
from the British Library

The publisher has no responsibility for the continued existence or accuracy of
URLs for external or third-party internet websites referred to in this book, and
does not guarantee that any content on such websites is, or will remain, accurate
or appropriate

This publication is printed on acid-free paper

To the keepers
of the traditional
flame

Contents

Illustrations

The author and publisher are grateful to all the institutions and individuals listed for permission to reproduce the materials in which they hold copyright. Every effort has been made to trace the copyright holders; apologies are offered for any omission, and the publisher will be pleased to add any necessary acknowledgement in subsequent editions.

Acknowledgements

GREAT THANKS ARE due to my publisher Michael Middeke whose support for the project has been generous and unwavering, and to Ingalo Thomson for her super-meticulous editing of this book. And I am profoundly grateful to my dear friend Joyce Arnold, whose picture editing has given each chapter an illuminating extra dimension.

Others who have been generous with their help include Debra Boraston, Radek Boschetty, Patricia Braun, Natasha Buss, Cara Chanteau, Gill Dunbar, Jean During, Hilary Finch, Jo Frost, Nick Gold, Stephen Griffin, Howard Hannah, Todd Harvey, Ira Jacknis, Steve Jones, Nikolas Labrinakos, Nicholas Reed Langen, Theodore Levin, Ginny Macbeth, Terry Miller, Maria Nefedova, Fairouz Nishanova, Serge Noelranaivo, Laudan Nooshin, Bayan Northcott, Mark Pappenheim, Sally Reeves, Realdo Silaj, Theo Spyrou, Monika Walenko, Nick Wall, Jeremy Warren, Richard Widdess, and the ever-helpful staff of the London Library; Chapter 25 was first published in *Songlines* magazine.

Boydell & Brewer acknowledges with gratitude the support of the Aga Khan Music Programme in the publication and illustration of this book.

Author's note

THE MAIN TEXT of this book was finished just as Covid-19 surfaced; in a coda to the Introduction, I have sought to relocate my argument in the context of the post-coronavirus world. Covid's long-term effects are as yet incalculable, but, aside from those, I have aimed to tread a realistic path between cautious optimism and outright pessimism, in my portrait of traditional music's present and future prospects.

If some chapters of this book come over like extended pieces of journalism, that is because journalism is my primary calling. There are no footnotes: with Covid forcing libraries to close, it has been impossible to source all page numbers. But every printed quote from a published source has been drawn from one of the titles in the relevant chapter's Further Reading list; the other quotes are from personal communications to me. Some of the later chapters are based on my own research, but for many chapters I have leant gratefully on research by other writers. Prominent among these has been Theodore Levin, whose work in Russia and Central Asia has greatly expanded our knowledge of music in those regions. Certain works – notably John Szwed's *The Man Who Recorded the World* and Steve Roud's *Folk Song in England* – have been of key importance, while my chapter on Theodor Strehlow would have been unthinkable without the aid of Barry Hill's ground-breaking biography *Broken Song*, which has rescued its elusive subject from near-oblivion. For the chapter on drumming I am indebted to my dear friend Hisako Shiina, who has patiently schooled me in Japanese culture.

Michael Church, London 2021

1 Ulzhan Baibussynova (born 1973), a Kazakh bard celebrated for her 'black' vocal timbre.

Introduction

It HAD TAKEN months of planning to corral five charismatic bards for a Christmas recording session in the snow-bound Kazakh city of Almaty, but things went well. Some tracks they wanted to re-record, others I wanted redone, but finally we were all satisfied, and toasted our communal triumph. Then the singers dispersed to their villages, to start their traditional New Year week of non-stop inebriated revelry.

I went for a walk in the snow, to mull things over. Back in my hotel room, I settled to listen again to the products of our labour, and turned on my machine …

Nothing! The digital tape, which two hours earlier had been full, was blank. I called my producer in London, who said I must have walked through a magnetic field, maybe under a power cable, which had wiped the tape. These were pre-mobile days, and by now the singers were God knows where. Lost beyond recall, as was their wonderful Kazakh music.

Throat-slitting moments like this will be familiar to all collectors of songs in the wild: such mishaps come with the territory, but it's a territory which acts on its denizens like a drug, even on part-time bit-players like me. But there's no uniformity in the compulsions which have driven the collectors in this book, in which 'song' can denote a style as well as a melody. The reasons for their chosen path reflect everything from simple patriotism to convoluted personal psychology, and quite often pure chance.

When the French Jesuit priest Joseph Amiot set sail for Beijing in 1751, he surely had little idea as to what he might do there, beyond learning enough Chinese to save some souls for Christ: the massive tome he compiled on Chinese classical music over the next forty years, which scholars still consult today, was an unplanned by-product. When the teenaged Moldavian prince Dimitrie Cantemir was imprisoned in Constantinople as a political hostage in 1689, no one could have predicted that he would put down roots, fall in love with the arcane intricacies of Ottoman music, and become its chief exponent and chronicler.

Colonial curiosity, sometimes tinged with guilt, drove song collectors visiting the beleaguered Native Indian communities of nineteenth-century America, but most found their music bewildering. It took the experience of Alice C. Fletcher – falling ill while doing fieldwork, and being nursed (and sung) back to health by the Omaha Indians whose culture she had been studying – to reveal the musical insights available to a researcher with empathy.

Meanwhile it was a casual challenge, light-heartedly issued over dinner, which prompted the Reverend Sabine Baring-Gould – lyricist of 'Onward, Christian soldiers' – to devote much of his life to song collecting in Britain's West Country. Cecil Sharp's accidental discovery of his vocation resulted from looking out of a window one Boxing Day, and seeing a group of Morris men singing and dancing in the snow.

Patriotism has been the spur behind much song collecting. Domna Samiou grew up in a shanty town for Greek refugees from Turkey, and Greek folk music became her crusading passion, leading her to found, and fill, its national archive in Athens. Komitas Vartabed healed the wounds of his orphaned childhood in an oppressed Armenian-Christian community by collecting and championing the folk songs he'd heard in infancy. Mily Balakirev, who collected what became known as the 'Song of the Volga Boatmen' in Nizhny Novgorod, was one of several patriotic Russian composers who enriched their works with melodies gleaned from the people. Angry Hungarian patriotism was Béla Bartók's primary motive for his folk-song research, before he settled into the scientific and didactic mode of his maturity.

Some collecting has been a response to horrifying circumstances. The most heroic collector of Nazi death-camp songs was the Polish singer-songwriter Aleksander Kulisiewicz, who survived three years in Sachsenhausen and devoted the rest of his life to performing the songs he had memorised from Jewish fellow-prisoners. There was a clandestine Jewish choir in Sachsenhausen whose members told him that, if he survived, he should preserve their memory by singing their songs to the rest of the world. That became his mission; his 3,000-page typescript of death-camp songs – many collected from survivors of other camps whom he sought out after the war – is now lodged in the Washington Holocaust Memorial Museum.

But collecting can also take unexpected forms. Working with rough sleepers under the arches of London's Waterloo station in 1971, the British composer Gavin Bryars chanced to hear, and record, an old man singing an improvised religious song whose first line was 'Jesus' blood never failed me yet'. Back home, Bryars worked it into a loop and gave it a simple orchestral accompaniment, and then turned it into an LP. The man died before he could hear what Bryars had done with his singing, but the piece remains eloquent testimony both to his spirit, and to what can be made out of an unpretentious little piece of field recording.

* * *

This book may not be a formal history of song collecting, but with its chronological structure it is in effect an informal one. Kulisiewicz might well have merited a chapter, as might many other collectors. For the field is

2

vast – every student of ethnomusicology dreams of discovering lost musics – and this selection is necessarily arbitrary. Some figures were obvious candidates – Sharp, Bartók, the Lomaxes – but others are people of whom readers may not have heard: they are here because of the extraordinary stories they embody, and the musical worlds they have brought to light. Readers should not feel guilty if they skip the theoretical musicology in Chapters 2, 4, 5, and 17; other chapters are an easier read.

Some of the collectors in this book predate the birth of what became known as ethnomusicology; others have resisted that academic label as limiting and over-prescriptive. Ethnomusicological orthodoxies come and go, and the latter half of the twentieth century saw the high priests of the discipline overreach themselves in claiming that a one-size-fits-all set of principles could be applied to all music everywhere; Alan Lomax's messianic belief in the universal applicability of his home-made system of song-classification was a case in point. And there is some truth in the taunt that sociologically oriented 'ethnos' are often interested in *everything but* music.

Other members of that ilk, however, are the song collectors of today, combining scientific rigour with a deep love for the music they pursue: one thinks of Bruno Nettl and Native Americans, Simha Arom and the Pygmies, John Baily and Veronica Doubleday in Afghanistan, Steve Jones in Chinese villages. These people are not deterred by the fact that they are working against the clock, as Richard Widdess's thirty-year study of the *bhakti* tradition of devotional Hinduism poignantly demonstrates.

In *dapha* rituals in the Newar city of Bhaktapur in the Kathmandu valley, antiphonal chants are supported by drums, cymbals, and trumpets; performances are interwoven with the city's sacred geography. This may be a small corner in the grand scheme of things, but as Widdess unpicks its intricacies it becomes fascinating. He hopes to help preserve this communal art form by putting a spotlight on it, but admits it may soon disappear. 'If that happens,' he says, 'I hope to have done a small service to Newar culture, by recording for posterity an important part of its musical history.' Recording for posterity is the key.

All the collectors in this book have been romantics with a scientific, taxonomic bent. All have acted as a bridge between cultures. All have treasured rare melodies and styles, as naturalists treasure endangered flora and fauna. All have championed folk music.

* * *

But what *is* folk music? Louis Armstrong's apocryphal assertion that all music is folk music, because 'I ain't never heard no horse sing it', won't quite do. When the eighteenth-century Prussian philosopher Johann Gottfried Herder coined the term *Volkslied*, everyone knew what he meant. Traditional songs everyone knew and could sing, songs which expressed the soul of a people; village music, a peasant art. Its social essence was captured by Leon Trotsky in his manifesto *Literature and Revolution*. 'You may count up the alliterations in popular proverbs, classify metaphors, count up the number of vowels and consonants in a wedding song,' he wrote in 1924.

> But if you don't know the peasant system of sowing, and the life that is based on it; if you don't know the part the scythe plays, and if you have not mastered the meaning of the church calendar to the peasant, of the time when the peasant marries, or when the peasant women give birth, you will have only understood the outer shell of folk art, but the kernel will not have been reached.

In 1954 the International Folk Music Council published a definition which is still serviceable: 'Folk music is the product of a musical tradition that has evolved through the process of oral transmission.' The term could apply, it said, to music by individual composers, provided it had been 'absorbed into the unwritten living tradition of a community'. It would not cover composed popular music which had been taken over ready-made by a community, and preserved unchanged, 'for it is the re-fashioning and recreation of the music by the community that gives it its folk character'. One point the IFMC might have made, but didn't, is that folk music can be a highly sophisticated art.

Should we classify as folk music 'Silent night', composed by an Austrian pastor, translated into 230 languages, and charming when sung in Arabic with accompaniment on the oud? What about 'Danny Boy', written by an Englishman, set to an ancient tune collected from an Irish street fiddler, and now the unofficial anthem of all Irish Americans? Consider the trajectory of 'You'll never walk alone', born as a Broadway show tune in 1945 and now adopted by football clubs in every clime. What about 'Waltzing Matilda', first published as sheet music in 1903, now Australia's most loved bush ballad? And what about the gospel song which became the quintessential protest anthem, 'We shall overcome'? Surely yes to all these, and an emphatic yes to 'Amazing grace', originally written (without a tune) for use in the Anglican church, but now sung everywhere to a tune by the American composer William Walker. The words of 'Ilkla Moor baht' at' are thought to have been composed by a Yorkshire chapel choir on an outing, but the tune was taken from a Methodist hymn, so classifying that song presents more of a conundrum. What about 'My way', 'Every time we say goodbye', 'Somewhere over the rainbow', Paul McCartney's 'Yesterday', Bob Dylan's 'The times they are a-changin'', and all the material Dylan has mined from the *American Songbook*? Shouldn't pop classics which have entered the global bloodstream deserve to qualify at least as honorary folk music?

But the term is now laden with extraneous connotations. This is partly thanks to the fact that in the 1970s the record industry found the adjective 'folk' was a useful label to pin on up-and-coming young singer-songwriters. But it's also thanks to an intellectual shift in academe. The old idea of an immutable musical corpus is giving way to the idea of an endlessly mutable art; the primacy of collecting is being replaced among scholars by the primacy of interpretation. And new forms of folk music are emerging all the time – on the internet, in clubs forging new musical identities, and in cities where populations are in flux. Writing in *The Cambridge History of World Music*, Timothy Cooley defines today's task for researchers as being no longer to discover and document songs 'as a botanist might look for new species of plant life', but to interpret what they hear as 'inventive ... expressions of human creativity'. Cooley's research principle can be retrospectively applied, but since most of the collectors in this book predate his ideas, I am using 'folk music' in the old-fashioned, quasi-botanical sense. And also in the European sense, because in some societies the distinction between folk music and art music is not made. In much of Africa and Asia – and also in Georgia – people simply talk of 'traditional' music. In this book I treat the adjectives 'folk' and 'traditional' as being more or less synonymous.

* * *

If the collectors whose lives are chronicled here have been people in a hurry, it's for fear that their chosen music might evaporate before they managed to fully document it. That fear is the leitmotif of this book, and, seen in the context of traditional genres, it's well-founded. The music of Bach, Beethoven, and Brahms is a vibrantly living tradition, reinvented by successive generations, sustained by armies of amateurs, and consumed in concert halls, coffee bars, and through headphones. Cutting-edge musical experiment is everywhere in rude health; jazz, despite the fact that its greatest exponents are dead, thrives in pubs and clubs; gospel and the blues sing on; rock and pop constitute a self-contained and self-perpetuating universe. But traditional music, and folk song in particular, is being eroded across large swathes of the globe, most markedly in Europe and the USA.

This book will indicate the scale of this global deficit, which has been triggered by Westernisation, urbanisation, and industrialisation. To that unholy trinity should be added the decline of religion in some places, and the loss of a shared ideology in others; religion and a shared value system have always been the glue that holds traditional music together.

Most of the work songs which Alan Lomax collected in Spain and Italy in the 1950s are sung no more. The same applies to the work songs which Komitas found in rural Armenia, and which Cecil Sharp and Percy Grainger collected in England a century ago. These songs are gone, because the reasons for their existence – the trades they accompanied – are gone. And after the death of the village comes the death of the songs marking its calendrical and life-cycle events; there comes, in short, the death of local music. This rule holds for all villages, everywhere.

Colin McPhee, who rescued certain Balinese forms from the brink of extinction, said his aim had simply been to 'prolong the past'. Alice Fletcher, whose work celebrated the music of the Omaha Indians, said that since the Omaha had 'ceased to exist as a tribe' her business had perforce become the archaeology, rather than the anatomy, of music.

War, persecution, and the coronavirus are currently taking an ever greater toll as they shatter communities beyond repair. Many countries spring to mind, but at present particular focus might be on Syria, Libya, and Yemen, which for eight centuries were home to that refined art form, *muwwashshah* song.

* * *

But we shouldn't oversimplify: the prospect is not one of unrelieved gloom. In any village where communal life goes on more or less as it has for centuries, traditional music will be found. This holds for much of Africa, India, China, and Indonesia. Some countries have thriving choral traditions, notably in the Balkans and Northern Europe; most Europeans sing carols at Christmas, celebrating the chaste simplicity of 'In dulce jubilo', 'Lullay my lyking', and the Coventry Carol, thus maintaining a tradition unbroken since the fifteenth century. In Georgia, complex three-part songs are routinely sung both in church and round the dinner table; pretty well every Georgian over fifty can negotiate their angular harmonic shifts, no matter how much alcohol they've drunk, because this music is hard-wired into them.

Folk music has its own momentum, and nourishes itself in an infinity of ways. Buskers are an increasingly significant presence in the musical life of cities. New work inspires new songs: baggage-handlers for Amazon in Genoa, whose forefathers sang as they humped fish, have devised new songs to speed their parcels. Ad hoc village ensembles pop up everywhere: somebody has an accordion, someone else a sax, someone wants to sing, and they're off. Migrants carry their music in their baggage; viz. Jewish musicians and the global spread of klezmer. Uzbek *shashmaqom* transplanted itself to Queens, New York, when Uzbek communities migrated there in the 1990s; there's a well-embedded Québecois population in New England, thanks to the French-Canadians who settled there in the nineteenth century, but their spirited *chanson* tradition is

2 Cover photo for the inaugural album from Buena Vista Social Club,
which in 1998 sold a million copies and won a Grammy.

now distinctively American, rather than being a clone of the tradition those
settlers left behind. Think of the exuberant migrations of tango which Astor
Piazzolla set in motion after rescuing the form from its traditional restraints.
And songs themselves can migrate: 'Auld Lang Syne' is now as much a part of
Chinese social life as it is of Britain's.

Commerce may accidentally prolong the life of folk music: think of your
local ice-cream van's 'Simple Simon' (aka 'Yankee Doodle') chimes. Record
companies can do the same, bringing unknown ensembles to the world's
attention like Orchestra Baobab, Taraf de Haidouks, and Buena Vista Social
Club. Musicians may popularise forgotten instruments, as did Kathryn Tickell
with the Northumbrian pipes, Wu Man with the *pipa* lute, and Kodo with
taiko drums. Pop stars may put old songs into orbit the way Paul Simon did –

taking his cue from a galaxy of British folk singers – with the eighteenth-century English ballad 'Scarborough Fair'. And even nursery-song CDs can play their part. That's why you may hear mothers regaling their toddlers with 'Row, row, row your boat' and 'What shall we do with the drunken sailor' in swimming-pool changing rooms, and their children replying with 'Twinkle twinkle little star'.

It's often argued that cross-cultural fusions are now the folk music of the future, and, given the speed with which musics can transplant themselves round the globe, there has to be some truth in that. The best fusions may come like a will o' the wisp, viz. the Don Kipper ensemble melding the heterogeneous sounds from the clubs and bars of their particular corner of north London: klezmer, samba, Senegalese *mbalax*, and assorted Balkan styles. But those fusions which are arbitrarily willed by producers, rather than being the spontaneous result of social shifts, have little life beyond the moment of their creation.

Meanwhile ambitious institutional strategies have been devised to shore up traditional music. UNESCO's list of 'intangible cultural heritage' musics is a crusading survey of the styles under threat of extinction. The aim is admirable, but the effects are of questionable value. Some countries use the list to bolster their claims to disputed ethnic territory; think of China, with its appropriation of Tibet and Uyghur Xinjiang. And although a UNESCO accolade confers prestige, it brings no financial support, so it doesn't alleviate the lot of struggling musicians. It is at least to UNESCO's credit that it has moved beyond the museum-culture approach: leading practitioners are now encouraged to pass on their skills and experiment with new forms. This policy also underpins a visionary system set up by the Aga Khan Trust for Culture, whereby, in a network of schools across Central Asia, instrumental and vocal masters teach children traditional styles.

And as the AKTC has demonstrated with a series of Central Asian discs, recording is a major weapon in the conservationists' armoury. 'Cylinder projects', in which old recordings are transferred to new technology, are another means by which the folk music of the past is being repatriated to the people whose heritage it is. Groups like the Moscow-based Pokrovsky Ensemble are systematically reviving endangered Russian forms; the British singer-arranger Belinda Sykes and her Joglaresa ensemble have recreated, through historically informed guesswork, Andalusian musics lost centuries ago. Such initiatives, however, only scratch the surface of the problem. Overwhelming anecdotal evidence suggests that much of the world's local traditional music is now under threat of extinction.

* * *

To speculate on the future of a tradition, we need to look at its past. We need to see how it has emerged, how it has thrived, and what might make it wither. To grow and develop it will need both social stability and time, maybe centuries; it will need a communal sense of purpose, a shared religion or ideology, and, most important, participation by everyone. Take away any one of these elements, and the music may go into a decline.

The story of English folk music is a case in point. Its documented history starts in the early sixteenth century with the carols collected by a grocer's apprentice named Richard Hill, and with the ballads, each roughly printed on one side of a sheet of paper, known as 'broadsides'. Passed from hand to hand and pinned on alehouse walls, these pop songs of the day fed an insatiable public demand for songs in both cities and the countryside. In the eighteenth century, pleasure gardens were a prime focus for song, and in the nineteenth century its spread was boosted through music halls and pub concert-rooms and private parlours. Cecil Sharp may have been dewy-eyed in his description of the typical English village in the nineteenth century as 'a nest of singing birds', but there was a song for everything, and everybody sang; communal singing in a rural Northamptonshire pub is most evocatively described in Flora Thompson's *Lark Rise to Candleford*. In the early twentieth century people still routinely sang at work, in the pub, on coach trips, and at weddings. Soldiers, sailors, and miners were the repository of a vast treasury of songs, as were Gypsies and travellers; now, rendered passive by records and the radio – by the substitution of recorded and broadcast sound for live music – they have fallen silent. British folk music may still be heard in pubs and clubs, but it's increasingly concert fare performed by professionals: museum-culture, for which the concert hall is the end of the road. Moreover, software is now displacing those professionals themselves. Who needs many pairs of clever hands, when the same effect can be achieved with two clicks of a mouse? This story has been replicated across the whole of Europe and much of the USA.

All music needs its eco-system in order to survive, and its loss is comparable to that of a biological species, or of a spoken language. As the expression of a particular society, of a particular way of thinking and feeling, a music is a living organism which, if it withers, may not be capable of resuscitation.

Does this matter, in an age when we can call down every conceivable form of music from the sound cloud? As Ben Ratliff has shown in his book *Every Song Ever*, the creative control which listeners can now exert over their material offers limitless possibilities: no other generation has enjoyed such an *embarras de richesse*.

But the loss we are concerned with in this book most certainly does matter, and not just because all forms of music, and classical music in particular, have vernacular roots and periodically draw sustenance from them. It matters because we may be approaching what could be described as local traditional music's 'end of history'. Worn-out and irrelevant forms may not be replaced by new ones, because the conditions required for that process – community and kinship networks and the aforesaid shared religion or ideology – no longer obtain, and may never obtain again. Since time immemorial, communities have produced their own music: is humanity now losing that capability? If it is, no loss may be immediately apparent. But there may be a gradual realisation that a barely sensed but mysteriously significant musical underpinning has gone, leaving an ache like that from a phantom limb. There's a human parallel to the plight of the Australian song-bird whose species is now so numerically depleted that it has forgotten its own song.

This is the pessimistic view: the loss of what has been described by the globe-trotting sound recordist Ian Brennan as 'the original worldwide web'. We must hope that traditional music's capacity to adapt, absorb, and recreate itself will go on surprising us. But will it?

Coda

The completion of this book coincided exactly with the emergence of Covid-19, and the ink had scarcely dried on what I had thought was the final sentence of the Introduction when music furnished its own answer to that question.

While wreaking horrifying destruction in countries with rudimentary or non-existent healthcare systems, the global convulsion also exposed the fragility of society in every developed country, and served as a reminder that we are all brothers and sisters under the skin. While panicky governments dithered, armies of volunteers rushed to fill the void in everything from health provision to social welfare; vast reserves of unsuspected altruism reflected a rebirth of the idea of community, as millions became caring neighbours. And poets too: the tributes read out to dead friends and family often possessed great eloquence. People began to question the principles by which they had lived.

Sound pollution diminished in parallel with atmospheric pollution. Lockdown had a profound effect on how people listened. Empty streets and skies meant they could savour birdsong and the sound of silence. But the damage to live music was immediate, and devastating. All concerts were cancelled for the foreseeable future; it would be years before performers could pick up the threads of their shattered professional lives, if they ever managed to do so. It became clear that social distancing would make concert life economically unworkable in its traditional form.

Yet the musicians' own response to the crisis was, like the actors' response, remarkable. Overnight, en masse, they migrated online, professionals and amateurs coming together to play and sing in a communal affirmation of belief in live performance.

Everyone started streaming. Solo instrumentalists offered a daily snatch of Beethoven or Chopin from their living rooms; duos presented Schubert songs. Cellist Yo-Yo Ma set up a website called #SongsofComfort from which he sent out melodies on Twitter, Instagram, and Facebook, which were viewed millions of times. Pianist Igor Levit streamed Satie's provocative piece *Vexations* in its twenty-hour entirety, dedicating it to raising awareness of the plight of freelance artists everywhere. Other musicians – like the seven prodigiously gifted Kanneh-Mason siblings in Nottingham – began serenading their neighbours in the street.

Some musicians took advantage of this moment to revive their flagging careers: Lady Gaga convened a galaxy of faded rock stars for an online concert broadcast round the world and entitled 'One World: Together at Home'. Variously dubbed 'the WiFi Woodstock' and 'the Living Room Live-Aid', the event was one of many designed to persuade philanthropists to open their wallets.

But this was also a grass-roots movement. Ordinary families armed with webcams turned into Von Trapps, posting their own renditions of showbiz classics. The young British saxophonist Jess Gillam set up a 'virtual scratch orchestra' to which all-comers were welcome, regardless of their level of competence. Each player downloaded a part, filmed themselves playing it in time to a click-track, then uploaded the results back to Gillam, who did a mix with her producer prior to playing the piece live on Instagram. As Gillam explained, her original dream had been to have hundreds of people playing simultaneously, connected by the internet, 'but the technology just can't cope. The lag is too great, even for a small group to play together.' Professional orchestras adopted the click-track strategy for virtual performances of major works.

The most exciting aspect of this new communal creativity lay in the choral sphere, as if in acknowledgement that choral singing is exceptionally beneficial for physical and psychological health. The *Times* critic Richard Morrison, who runs a north London church choir, decided to record one final sing – with the choir observing a two-metre social-distancing rule – on the eve of the lockdown taking effect. 'We decided we would use the most high-tech equipment available to us – someone holding up a mobile phone – to film something that we could send to members of our congregation as a kind of musical "stay well till we meet again" greeting,' he wrote. They recorded Phineas Fletcher's seventeenth-century hymn 'Drop, drop slow tears' in Orlando Gibbons's exquisite setting. As the video was of decent quality, Morrison put it on Twitter, and the response from other choirs was heartfelt, with the Munich Bach Choir emailing them to say 'we listen to you with tears streaming down our faces'.

Those were early days, and choirs on every continent followed suit in what came to seem like a global equivalent of the Prisoners' Chorus in *Fidelio*. One of the most unexpected projects came in Holy Week from a community of Benedictine nuns in the south of France who posted seven thousand hours of their chant. In a neatly symbolic gesture, the a cappella group Stile Antico celebrated the first forty days of the British lockdown with a virtual rendition, from their living rooms, of Thomas Tallis's forty-part motet *Spem in alium*. Meanwhile the television choirmaster Gareth Malone launched his Great British Home Chorus. His original inspiration was the Italians singing on their balconies, but his intention was to give homebound people everywhere a cheerful weekly focus. His singers downloaded sheet music and rehearsed via YouTube; 300,000 people tuned in for the first online session, learning to sing 'You are my sunshine'. Malone's next project – a very moving one – was to co-write and co-perform songs with front-line health workers, some of whom had themselves been stricken by the virus.

The quirkiest British response came from the song collector and folk singer Sam Lee, who led his audiences into the woods for 'nightingale concerts' where he mingled folk song with birdsong. He saw unexpected virtues in a suddenly stilled world. 'Necessity,' he said, 'has made Mother Nature the mother of invention.'

But reactions to the pandemic could also be thought-provoking. In a medically shocking demonstration of faith in the power of traditional music, Easter worshippers at the cathedral in Tbilisi were seen queuing up to kiss an icon, then sharing the Host from the same unwiped spoon, and claiming with shining eyes that they would be protected from all infection by their ancient hymns.

At the height of the pandemic in London, with the death toll rising alarmingly, shoppers queuing outside my local supermarket were serenaded one Sunday morning by a man obsessively singing 'Many more are gonna suffer, many more must die'. If his revivalist zeal was striking, so was the fact that his home-made chant had a pleasing musical form. Was this evidence – admittedly very primitive – of that self-renewing quality which people had feared folk music was losing? More sophisticated evidence came with the new-minted pandemic lyrics which showbiz professionals applied to traditional melodies.

But what also came over loud and clear was the proprietary affection in which those melodies were held. As an aged folk singer declared, before delivering a Cornish miners' song on Radio 3's morning news programme, 'We must keep the old songs alive.' Britons seemed to be doing that, particularly with their rediscovered passion for carols at Christmas and with their eager participation in the sea-shanty craze on Tiktok.

As we go to press in March 2021, the economic and political portents for the world as a whole are profoundly disquieting; the quality of life as we knew it before Covid-19 will never be recovered. But there are bright spots in this global tragedy, with its myriad attendant smaller tragedies. The campaigns to combat economic inequality and to modify climate change have in some places been galvanised. Localism and 'small is beautiful' have become governing principles in the way societies organise themselves; it's a fair bet that the new spirit of community will in many places endure.

Moreover, it looks as though the pandemic will provoke changes in live music which will be more fundamental – and more healthy – than any we have seen so far. As the novelty of streaming wore off, people began to realise how deeply they craved the immediacy of live events with an audience, and to hell with acoustic 'perfection'. One of the most exhilarating London events in the summer of 2020 took place in a multi-storey car park in downtown Peckham: it may have been open to the winds, and to the noise of trains and traffic, but in other respects the acoustic was generally felt to be invigorating.

Just as significant was the realisation that the old business models for live performance – particularly those for opera and orchestral tours – would never again be viable. It became clear that, rather than striving to re-establish a pre-pandemic economic 'normality', a more local and more nimble approach was needed, in which new audiences could be reached, and traditional ones engaged minus the old aura of exclusivity.

One other heartening result of the pandemic may be that folk music gets a new lease of life – always assuming that fears of spreading the virus through choral singing can be convincingly allayed. We hope this book will serve as a reminder of the healing continuity which folk music has always represented, particularly for societies under stress.

Sources

Bardic performances salvaged from a partial repeat of Michael Church's abortive recording session in Almaty can be heard on *Songs from the Steppes: Kazakh Music Today* (Topic Records). Richard Widdess's *Dapha: Sacred Singing in a South Asian City* offers an intimate account of music and society in the Kathmandu Valley; the BBC World Service's *Songs from the Depths of Hell* is a vivid portrait of Aleksander Kulisiewicz; Timothy Cooley's essay on folk music is published in *The Cambridge History of World Music*. Flora Thompson's

Lark Rise to Candleford has a charmingly atmospheric description of a pub sing-song in 1880s Northamptonshire. The New England version of Québecois *chanson* is recorded in *Mademoiselle, voulez-vous danser?* (Smithsonian Folkways). Don Kipper's recording of their local North London music is on *Seven Sisters* (TUG). Ben Ratliff's *Every Song Ever* is a virtuoso display of lateral musical thinking; Ian Brennan's *How Music Dies* is a breathless tour of his field-recording experiences in every corner of the globe. The essays in Tim de Lisle's *Lives of the Great Songs* approach the question of longevity from a different and revelatory angle. Ulzhan Baibussynova can be heard on *Music of Central Asia Vol. 4: Bardic Divas*. In *Search: Journal for New Music and Culture*, Ivan Hewett's essay 'The Vanishing Discipline: The Threat to Musicology' shows how the social sciences are driving the music out of ethnomusicology.

Bibliography, recordings, and films

Brennan, Ian, *How Music Dies (or Lives)* (New York: Allworth Press, 2016)

Cooley, Timothy J., 'Folk Music in Eastern Europe', in Philip V. Bohlman, ed., *The Cambridge History of World Music* (Cambridge: Cambridge University Press, 2013), 352–70

De Lisle, Tim, *Lives of the Great Songs* (London: Penguin, 1994)

Ratliff, Ben, *Every Song Ever: Twenty Ways to Listen in an Age of Musical Plenty* (New York: Picador, 2016)

Roud, Steve, *Folk Song in England* (London: Faber, 2017)

Thompson, Flora, *Lark Rise to Candleford* (Oxford: Oxford University Press, 1945)

Trotsky, Leon, *Literature and Revolution* (Chicago: Haymarket, 2005)

Widdess, Richard, *Dapha: Sacred Singing in a South Asian City* (London: Ashgate, 2013)

Mademoiselle, voulez-vous danser?, Smithsonian Folkways SFWCD 40116

Music of Central Asia Vol. 4: Bardic Divas, Smithsonian SFWCD 40523

Seven Sisters, Don Kipper, TUGCD1114

Sing We Yule, Joglaresa, JOG007

Songs from the Steppes: Kazakh music today, recordings by Michael Church, Topic Records TSCD929

Stravinsky: Les noces, Pokrovsky Ensemble, Electra Nonesuch Explorers 7559 79335-2

The Songs from the Depths of Hell, BBC World Service documentary, 2019

Why it all began

SONG COLLECTING TOOK wing in eighteenth-century Europe under three impulses: political, colonial, and economic. 'Through music our race was humanised; through music it will attain greater humanity,' wrote the Prussian philosopher Johann Gottfried Herder (1744–1803). When he coined the term *Volkslied* – 'folk song' – it was to exemplify the soul of a people; folk song would be the quintessential expression of Romantic nationalism, and its character would reflect the character of a nation. The concept didn't operate in terms of rich or poor, educated versus peasantry; it embraced everyone. Herder argued that it was a patriotic duty to collect *Volkslieder* as devotedly as he himself did, before they disappeared.

The second impulse behind the new vogue was colonial curiosity: what did the music of the subjugated peoples – and the hoped-for Christian converts – actually sound like? The Swiss theologian Jean de Léry (1534–1611) wrote about the music of Brazil, using musical notation and describing antiphonal singing between men and women; Captain James Cook (1728–1779) described the music and dance of Pacific islanders. Jean-Jacques Rousseau's *Dictionnaire de musique* (1768) was the first book to deal with the 'diverse musical accents' of other lands, giving samples of Swiss, Iranian, Chinese, and Canadian Amerindian music. The most graphic colonial account came from the Scottish explorer Mungo Park (1771–1806) on his journey along the Niger River. Repeatedly attacked by tribesmen, and several times imprisoned by their suspicious rulers, he was at one point taken in, fed, and lodged with great generosity by the women of a Malian village, who allowed him to watch as they spun cotton and sang through the night. 'They lightened their labour by songs,' he wrote,

> one of which was composed extempore; for I myself was the subject of it. It was sung by one of the young women, the rest joining in a sort of chorus. The air was sweet and plaintive, and the words, literally translated, were these: 'The winds roared, and the rains fell. The poor white man, faint and weary, came and sat under our tree. He has no mother to bring him milk; no wife to grind his corn' – Chorus: 'Let us pity the white man, no mother has he' etc etc. Trifling as this recital may appear to the reader, to a person in my situation, the circumstances were affecting in the highest degree. I was oppressed by such unexpected kindness; and sleep fled from my eyes.

What's striking about Mungo Park's notes on public performance in Mali is the continuity they reveal between music then and music now. He lists the instruments, including the *kora* harp, the *balafon* wooden xylophone, the flutes, bells, shells, gourds, and several types of drum. And he gives a detailed account of the role of the *jali* – professional praise-singer and local historian – and of the Muslim chanters who travel about the country 'singing devout hymns, and performing religious ceremonies, to conciliate the favour of the Almighty, either in averting calamity, or ensuring success in any enterprise'. These itinerant bards 'are much employed and respected by the people, and very liberal contributions are made for them'. Extraordinary: he might have been describing musical life in Malian villages today.

Meanwhile the third impulse underlying the song-collecting movement was the desire to make a profit, as with the trade in songbooks and broadside ballads in seventeenth-century London.

Now read on ...

Bibliography

Park, Mungo, *Travels in the Interior Districts of Africa* (London: John Murray, 1816)

1

From broadsides to Child ballads

Songs of the British people

To 'BALLAD' SOMEONE in seventeenth-century London meant to libel them in a song: ballad-singers were often on the wrong side of the law. Singers in the employ of the rich, or serving their municipalities as 'waits', were well-paid and legally protected. But in 1597 'wandering minstrels' with no licence to perform were officially condemned to be whipped till they bled, 'burnt through the gristle of the right ear with a hot iron', and sent to a house of correction.

Yet the country was awash with printed songs. They were pasted up on walls in city streets and taverns, and were sold in every market and at every fair; trade was particularly brisk at public executions. These were the penny-dreadfuls of the day.

Printed in bold 'blackletter' type on one side of a folio, these song sheets were known as broadsides, and the diarist Samuel Pepys was an avid collector of them. So were those who saw in them a commercial opportunity; songbooks became a profitable business. Most were filled with popular tunes by contemporary composers, with John Playford's *English Dancing Master* going through eighteen editions. As the leading authority on British folk music Steve Roud observes, it's worth remembering that in seventeenth-century London, musical literacy among the poor was high: Mr Pepys's servant boy and all Mrs Pepys's maids were sight-readers and instrumentalists.

The first songbook with antiquarian ambitions was published by Thomas Percy in 1765 as the three-volume *Reliques of Ancient English Poetry*, but its genesis was accidental. Percy was a cleric who eventually became a bishop, but he was also a well-connected poet and man of letters. While visiting a friend he noticed a sheaf of papers 'lying dirty on the floor, under a bureau in the parlour', which maids were using as firelighters. This turned out to be a miscellany of old songs and poems, albeit damaged and incomplete. He took it home and knocked it into shape. Two similar collections had recently been published without exciting interest, but friends including Samuel Johnson encouraged Percy to publish his. The poet William Shenstone, another of those friends, urged him to include additional songs culled from libraries, but to rewrite

A Jeſt;

Or, Maſter Conſtable.

To the Tune of, the *Three Pilgrims*.

A Pretty jeſt I ſhall declare,
Which I not long agoe did hear
Of one who did intend to jeere,
  Maſter Conſtable.

I hope there's none wil matter make
Of that that I intend to ſpeake,
Of a buſy man who ẏ place did take,
  Of a Conſtable.

For I hope each wiſe man wiſer is,
Then to think he is touch'd in this,
For thinking ſo, he thinks amiſs,
  'Twas a buſy Conſtable.

For this is but a merry Jeſt,
Which will I hope, no man moleſt,
For I no grudge beare I proteſt,
  To any Conſtable.

Then pray you let this poor man paſs
For he for money ſings alas,
Let none then ſhew himſelfe an aſſe
  Like this Conſtable.

He as his Office did direct,
To ſet his watch was circumſpect
And nothing therein did neglect,
  Like a Conſtable.

Alſo when any paſſed by,
He did examine them ſtrictly,
Obſerving with diſcretions eye,
  A wiſe Conſtable.

At length it chanc'd ẏ one came neer
And he demanded who goes there
You know not (ſaid he without fear
  Maſter Conſtable.

Come hither that I may you ſee,
And now what are you ſhew to me,
No Man nor Woman replyed he,
  Maſter Conſtable.

Where have you been then aſhed he
That you thus croſly anſwer me,
Know you not the authority
  Of a Conſtable.

Yes I know your authority,
And I have been for certainty,
Where you would have been glad to be
  Maſter Conſtable.   (be

Then ſaid the Conſtable, ſome end,
Will come hereof, but ſay my friend,
Whither to goe doe you intend,
  VVhy good Conſtable·

I am going thither where   (eats
you dare not goe for your right
What you are ſet upon the jeere
  ſaid the Conſtable.

What is your name pray tel me that
Who dare ſo boldly to me prate,
Be briefe, and truth to me relate,
  Said the Conſtable

Twenty ſhillings I am nam'd
I thereof need not be aſham'd,
Although by you I may be blam'd,
  maſter Conſtable

Sir, that hereafter we ſhall ſee
But in the mean time tell to me,
Where your dwelling place may be,
  Quoth the Conſtable

Out of the Kings dominion I,
Doe dwell ſaid he aſſuredly,
As my Neighbours can teſtiſie,
  maſter Conſtables

But in the Kings dominion you
Are now my friend, and you ſhall rue
That ſtill croſs language you renew
  To a Conſtable.

3 A seventeenth-century broadside ballad portraying the Master Constable as a self-important busybody.

anything he deemed inelegant; 'mere historical merit', said Shenstone, was 'not a sufficient recommendation for inclusion'. The published results were enthusiastically greeted by Wordsworth, Coleridge, Scott, and Burns, but others regarded them as fraudulent. Percy's nemesis arrived in the form of a choleric republican named Joseph Ritson, who excoriated the paternalistic tamperings of (now bishop) Percy to a point where, publicly humiliated, he was forced to quit the song-collecting game.

Yet it was Percy's example which induced Ritson to collect and publish anthologies of his own, starting with *A Select Collection of English Songs* in 1783; this was followed by collections of songs from the north-east and Scotland, which themselves drew on collections made by an Edinburgh clerk named David Herd. Yet Herd's *The Ancient and Modern Scots Songs, Heroic Ballads, Etc*, published in 1769, had taken texts from Percy: so circular was this chain of borrowings. But by also taking words from the mouths of working people, Herd had broken new ground. He was the first British collector to do this.

As time went on, Ritson's attitudes became increasingly extreme. In Walter Scott's sardonic view, 'whenever presented with two copies of a traditional song or ballad, Ritson perversely chose the worse as the most genuine.' But as the song-collecting craze migrated north of the border – Scottish crofters and farm hands were busy readers – Ritson too was attracted by the pastoral simplicity of Scots song. This he found infinitely preferable to what he called the 'more of art than of nature' character of its English equivalent. The difference, he said, was like comparing a 'beautiful peasant, in her homespun russet' with the 'fine town lady, patched, powdered, and dressed out, for the ball or opera, in all the frippery of fashion'.

And it was Ritson's work which fired Robert Burns's enthusiasm for song collecting, inducing him to launch a project entitled *The Scots Musical Museum* designed to register 'every Scotch air worth singing'. But Burns too has had his detractors: the Marxist ballad-historian Dave Harker has stigmatised him for his attempt to please bourgeois taste, and for feeling obliged to apologise for the 'inelegant and vulgar' dance tunes he included. And he bowdlerised 'indelicate' texts like everyone else.

By the end of the eighteenth century Walter Scott and his circle were making all the running. As a romantic Tory with reactionary political views, Scott had a predilection for lost causes such as those of Queen Mary and the Jacobites, and, as Harker puts it, paid more attention to 'the Fairies of Scotland' than to peasants and the common people. But Scott prospered mightily: his *Minstrelsy of the Scottish Border* (1802) – plus subsequent collections – sold like hot cakes.

Meanwhile one of his acolytes, a ferociously Tory Glaswegian law-officer named Robert Motherwell, published *Minstrelsy Ancient and Modern*, but Motherwell did at least believe in the faithful transmission of texts by 'the unlettered and the rude', and in the importance of collecting songs 'from the lips of "the spinsters and knitters in the sun"'. The role of an editor, he said, was to fillet out what was genuinely 'ancient' from later accretions. But his motive was less social inquiry than a passionate conservatism. As he wrote in his introduction, workers had 'departed from the stern simplicity of their fathers', and had 'learned with the paltry philosophers, political quacks, and illuminated dreamers on Economick and Moral science, to laugh at the prejudices, beliefs, and superstitions of elder times'. Song collecting was now going on in many parts of England, with Davies Gilbert and William Sandys scouring the West Country, and John Bell in Newcastle meticulously classifying his findings, at one point collecting a 'last dying speech' – a popular genre – printed on a page made from the skin of an executed murderer.

* * *

The most unexpected English collector of the early nineteenth century was the volatile John Clare, like Robert Burns a 'ploughman poet', and also by turns a cobbler, clerk, and soldier. His father was a 'thresher and local wrestler' who could sing entertainingly all night in the tavern, and Clare himself sang and played the fiddle. Following Ritson's example, he published every Northamptonshire tune he managed to hoover up in *A Collection of Songs Airs and Dances for the Violin* (1818). These included ballads like 'Black-eyed Susan', mysterious counting-songs like 'Green grow the rushes O', and nursery rhymes like 'Oh dear, what can the matter be?'.

Clare was particularly intrigued by the music of the Gypsy fencers and hedge-setters he worked and drank with, as his journal attests: 'Finished planting my ariculas – went a botanising after ferns and orchises [*sic*] and caught a cold in the wet grass. Got the tune of "Highland Mary" from Wisdom Smith a gypsey and pricked another sweet tune without name as he fiddled it' ('pricked' being his term for notating). But he was congenitally averse to classifying his songs, thus making it impossible to tell where his found material ended and his poetic recreations began. 'New song inspired by old' was a typical title; scholars have given up on such conundrums as 'Song taken from my mother's and father's recitation & completed by an old shepherd'.

Clare's poetry could reveal a world of beauty in a snowdrop, and his love for the oral tradition was coupled with an obsession with its fragility. 'I commenced some time ago with the intention of making a collection of old Ballads,' he wrote in a draft preface, and with a headlong lack of punctuation.

But when I had sought after them in places where I expected [to] find them, viz the hay field and the shepherds hut on the pasture – I found that nearly all those old and beautiful recollections had vanished as so many old fashions and those who knew fragments seemed ashamed to acknowledge it as old people who sing old songs only sung to be laughed at – and those who were proud of their knowledge of such things knew nothing but the senseless balderdash that is brawled over and sung to County Feasts Statutes and

4 A portrait of the poet John Clare by William Hilton in 1820.

Fairs where the most senseless jargon passes for the greatest excellence and rudest indecency for the finest wit.

British song collecting was meanwhile being revolutionised from America. In 1860 the first part of an eight-volume study of British ballads was published. Its author, Francis James Child, was a remarkable polymath whose research on Chaucer and Spenser still informs scholarship today, and who as professor of English at Harvard set about compiling what he intended to be the definitive collection of British vernacular ballads. He drew on published sources, starting with Percy's *Reliques* and Motherwell's *Minstrelsy*, and moving on to printed broadsides. Working under the guidance of the Danish folklorist Svend Grundtvig, he expanded what was eventually published in full as *The English and Scottish Popular Ballads*. Impeded by a psychological block, he couldn't bring himself to write his promised introduction to this magnum opus, but for decades it was holy writ, and to a considerable extent remains so today; each of the 305 'Child Ballads' is still known by the number he gave it.

Some of them go back to medieval times. The manuscript of 'Judas' dates from the thirteenth century, and a version of 'A Gest of Robyn Hode' was printed in the late fifteenth century, but the origins of most can't be traced further back than 1600. Despite Child's respect for evidence, however, debate still continues over the validity of his work. One limitation lay in the fact that his primary interest was in words rather than tunes. As the American collector Phillips Barry pointed out: 'The fieldworker knows that the ballad is a living organism, tune and text together, the spirit and the body. When the spirit is gone, what is left is a dead thing.' Child also came under fire for unquestioningly following the Romantic notion of spontaneous creation by 'the people' rather than by individuals; he has been attacked for academic arrogance, and his theory about the ballads' origins was indeed provocative.

'The popular ballad is not originally the product or the property of the lower orders of the people,' he wrote. 'Nothing, in fact, is more obvious than that many of the ballads of the now most refined nations had their origin in that class whose acts and fortunes they depict – the upper class.' The lower orders, he believed – on the basis of a sketchy knowledge of medieval culture – would simply not have been capable of such refinement, and he likened their song to 'veritable dunghills in which, only after a great deal of sickening grubbing, one finds a very moderate jewel'.

Due recognition for the songs of those lower orders would have to await the arrival of Cecil Sharp and his friends. And recognition for the songs of their urban descendants would only come with the British folk-song revival of the 1960s.

Sources

Leslie Shepard's *The Broadside Ballad* is richly informative; Dave Harker's erudition in balladry makes *Fakesong* required reading, but his unrelenting Marxist bias demands the counterbalancing perspective of Steve Roud's massive and judiciously even-handed history, *Folk Song in England*, on which this chapter draws. Jonathan Bate's biography of John Clare sets the ploughman-poet's song collecting in its wider context.

Bibliography

Bate, Jonathan, *John Clare: A Biography* (London: Picador, 2003)
Harker, Dave, *Fakesong: The Manufacture of British 'Folksong', 1700 to the Present Day* (Milton Keynes: Open University Press, 1985)
Roud, Steve, *Folk Song in England* (London: Faber, 2017)
Shepard, Leslie, *The Broadside Ballad: A Study in Origins and Meaning* (Newton Abbot: David & Charles, 1973)

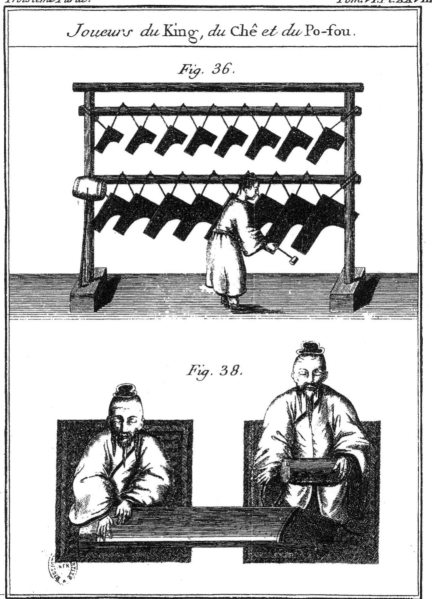

5 An illustration of chime-players from Amiot's *Mémoire sur la musique des Chinois, tant anciens que modernes.*

2

Orientalists from France

Jesuit priests in Beijing,
Salvador-Daniel in Algiers

EUROPEAN MUSICAL EXPLORERS had China in their sights three centuries before the era of recording; prominent among them were Jesuit priests. And the influence of their discoveries could be far-reaching: by introducing the *sheng* mouth organ to Europe in 1777, Father Joseph Amiot paved the way for the invention of the harmonica and the accordion. Chinese musicologists, who beat their European counterparts in the race to solve the mathematics of equal temperament, were in many ways ahead.

The Jesuit project was to win souls for Christ, but in China they realised they would only achieve that by going native. One of the first of these explorer-missionaries was an Italian named Matteo Ricci (1552–1610), who wore the traditional silk robes of the Confucian literati and was one of the first Western scholars to speak and write Mandarin; his intellectual feats included translating Euclid into Chinese, and mapping the world in Chinese characters. It was this cultural immersion that earned him the honour of being, in 1601, the first European allowed to enter the Forbidden City of Beijing. The clavichord with which he charmed the reclusive emperor Wan Li was his hook to engage the monarch's interest in both Western music and the religion of which that music was the expression.

Ricci was an omnivorous diarist, and although he didn't make a formal study of Chinese music he did observe it, even if his reaction was lordly disdain. While living in Nanjing he witnessed a rehearsal for a Confucian ceremony in which priests played 'elegant' music, as opposed to its raucous 'banquet' counterpart. 'The priests who composed the orchestra were vested in sumptuous garments,' he noted,

> as if they were to attend a sacrifice, and after paying their respects to the Magistrate they set to playing their various instruments; bronze bells, basin-shaped vessels, some made of stone, with skins over them like drums, stringed instruments like a lute, bone flutes and organs played by blowing

into them with the mouth rather than with bellows. They had other instruments shaped like animals, holding reeds in their teeth, through which air was forced from the empty interior. At this rehearsal their curious affairs were all sounded at once, with a result that can be readily imagined, as it was nothing other than a lack of concord, a discord of discords.

Ricci concluded that even the Chinese themselves didn't like this stuff: 'One of their sages said on a certain occasion that the art of music known to their ancestors had evaporated with the centuries, and left only the instruments.'

Intermittent bouts of xenophobia, and friction between Beijing and Rome, meant the expatriate missionaries could never feel secure, but respite came with the accession in 1668 of the intellectually curious Emperor Kangxi, who employed Jesuit priests as his astronomers, mathematicians, engineers, artists, doctors, and makers of the mechanical toys which were the top status-symbol of privilege. As he was also fascinated by European music – filling his palace with the harpsichords which foreign visitors had brought – he kept his court musician and duet-partner Father Teodorico Pedrini (1671–1746) close by him. He reportedly excused Pedrini's lack of Chinese by saying that 'harpsichords are tuned with the hands, not with the tongue', and he commissioned him to complete a major encyclopaedia of music theory entitled the *Luluzhenyi*, or *A True Doctrine of Music* (1713). Dealing first with Chinese theory, then with European, this book represented a summation of all the musical knowledge in Beijing at the time.

Meanwhile, back in Paris, the Jesuit historian Jean-Baptiste Du Halde was collating missionary reports on every aspect of Chinese life; in 1735 he published his findings in *Description géographique, historique, chronologique, politique et physique de l'empire de la Chine et de la Tartarie chinoise*. But when it touched on indigenous music, the consensus among his informants was damning. 'They like to think they invented music,' Du Halde wrote scathingly of the Chinese, 'but if so, it must have degenerated, because it's so imperfect that it scarcely merits the word, so far as we can judge from some of their melodies which I have notated to give some idea of them.' The banality of the examples he prints leads him to devote most of his allotted space to the Chinese admiration for Western melody, and for the miracle of Western notation.

Forty years later, however, another French Jesuit priest published an account of Chinese musical theory and practice which was so magisterially accurate that it's still consulted by scholars today. *Mémoire sur la musique des Chinois, tant anciens que modernes*, by Jean-Joseph-Marie Amiot (1718–1793), was the fruit of decades of close observation, and formed part of a multi-authored series of *Mémoires* on Chinese civilisation published in Paris between 1776 and 1789. As a gifted flautist and harpsichordist, Amiot had been invited by Emperor Qianlong (1711–1799) to join his staff of music teachers. This emperor, like his grandfather Kangxi, loved both European and Chinese music, and with typical thoroughness commissioned a 120-volume supplement to the *Luluzhenyi* which covered the music of the Qing dynasty. By this time, as Lam Ching Wah has noted in *Chime* magazine, the musics of East and West were peacefully co-existing in the Chinese capital. The Mass

6 Jean-Joseph-Marie Amiot, *c.* 1790.

in celebration of the arrival of new missionaries was sung to the sound of Chinese instruments, and the mechanical clock in the Beijing church played both Chinese and Western melodies.

Amiot was a prolific and versatile scholar, and his works ranged from a Manchu dictionary to a French translation of Sun Tzu's sixth-century BCE treatise *The Art of War*. But unlike Ricci, he had an empathy with Chinese music which steadily deepened in the course of his forty-year sojourn in Beijing. And in a monograph entitled *De la musique moderne des Chinois* he laid out with winning charm what he saw as the contrast between Eastern and Western music. A European composer, he writes, applies himself first of all to the fundamental bass, 'from which he draws all the chords for the other parts'. But in China 'there is neither bass, nor tenor, nor treble, everything is unison, but that unison is varied according to the nature and capacity of each instrument. The composer's skill, the beauty of a piece, and the whole art of music, lies in that variation.'

Trying to induce Chinese listeners to take pleasure in European music would be pointless, he continues:

> As disciples of what is natural, they would consider they were moving away from the rules of nature, if, in order to pleasantly titillate the ear, they presented it with a multiplicity of sounds that it finds wearisome. 'Why play several different things at the same time?' they ask. 'Why play them so fast? Is it to show off the lightness of your mood, and the nimbleness of your fingers?'

If that is your aim, he writes, 'we will readily admit that you surpass us. But if it is simply as recreation for yourselves and to please us, we think you are taking the wrong course.' His next sentence has an oddly prophetic ring for the Darmstadt generation: 'Your concerts, especially if they are rather long, are violent exercises for those who perform them, and small tortures for those who listen. After all, it is inevitable that European ears are built differently from ours.' Then comes the *coup de grâce*: 'You like things that are complicated; we are fond of things that are simple. In your music, you often run until you are out of breath; in ours, we always walk at a serious and measured pace. Nothing tells one more about the genius of a nation than the music it appreciates.'

This was Amiot in broad-brush descriptive mode. But Amiot the scholar was the soul of analytical rigour. *Mémoire sur la musique des Chinois, tant anciens que modernes* is a gracefully readable tract in which, after apologising for its profusion of technical Chinese terms, and after noting that Chinese listeners were left cold by his performance on the harpsichord of Rameau's suites *Les sauvages* and *Les Cyclopes*, he gently leads the Western reader through China's fastidiously organised sound-system.

But first he castigates those *savants* – including France's leading music-theorist Rameau – who have missed the point of his previous study of Chinese music. They have failed, he says, to see that the division of the octave into twelve semitones was a Chinese invention, and they have not understood that the musical discoveries by the Egyptians and Greeks – including those by Pythagoras himself – were predated by those made in China (though, as Lam Ching Wah points out, modern research suggests that the mathematical achievements of the Babylonians are probably the common source for acoustical theories developed in both Europe and China). To make his points crystal clear, Amiot tells his readers that he has sent back to Paris four instruments on which they can test his theories: a seven-string *qin* zither, a *qing* chimestone, a *sheng* mouth organ, and a bamboo pipe embodying China's imperial pitch-standard.

Then he gets down to business, citing sixty-nine specialist Chinese sources as well as major histories, and beginning with China's categorisation of eight types of instrument according to the materials from which they are made: animal skin, stone, metal, clay, silk, wood, bamboo and gourd. He then looks at the mystical connection between this classification and the cabalistic songs known as the eight trigrams; the three lines in each of those represent the three principal kingdoms of nature – animal, vegetable, and mineral. Each instrumental category is then broken down into sub-categories – for example, types of drum, with a short history of each. His discussion of the stone category leads him to describe the discovery, in 32 BCE, of an ancient *qing* consisting of sixteen stone slabs which were found at the bottom of a pond, and also of the discovery of a set of sixteen jade slabs presented to the Emperor in 247 CE, and still perfectly in tune.

He then turns to the twelve fundamental semitone pitches known to the Chinese as *lü*, which are divided into two groups of six according to the principles of *yang* and *yin* (here he invites the common reader to skip, if the going gets tough). He lists the name and related symbolism of every note: thus the first of the *yanglü*, *huangzhong*, stands for the eleventh moon, the time of the winter solstice, and the beginning of the astronomical year, while the second, *taicou*, symbolises the first moon, and the beginning of the official year, a time when nature's growth begins; and so on. All these terms are equated with the 'twelve terrestrial branches' which, with the 'ten celestial stems', make China's traditional cycle of sixty years. Later sections of the book are devoted to scales, tunings, and to the question of whether the Chinese had counterpoint; Amiot rounds out his account with diagrams, charts, and drawings.

Such a book, backed by the digital tools now available to researchers, would have been an impressive achievement even today; that it should have been written in the mid-eighteenth century, by a French priest who had to begin by teaching himself Chinese from scratch, is extraordinary. Yet while Du Halde's breezy survey was translated into several languages, Amiot's monumental study of Chinese ceremonial music only had currency among a tiny community of Orientalist scholars; as European interest in China switched to trade, Amiot's work receded into the shadows.

* * *

But orientalism lived vigorously on among French artists and intellectuals: in the nineteenth century its focus shifted to the Middle East under the influence of the proto-Communist Comte de Saint-Simon. Among the count's disciples was the composer Félicien David, whose campaign to promote musical Orientalism attracted other musicians to the cause. And one of those musicians, Francisco Salvador-Daniel (1831–1871), was to carve out a niche as France's first musical Arabist, though he became better known thanks to his heroic and tragic demise.

He was taught to play the piano and violin by his organist father, and by his bandmaster uncle to play wind instruments. He studied at the Paris Conservatoire, failed to make a career as a composer, worked as a dance-music arranger, and got a job as an orchestral violinist.

When the Saint-Simonians were banned in France, Félicien David went to Egypt to study that country's music. Salvador was inspired to go further, setting up in 1853 as a violin teacher in Algiers. There he also became director of a choral society, and professor of music at the Ecole Arabe. But his real purpose was research into the indigenous music. He scoured Algeria and made collecting trips to Tunisia, Egypt, Morocco, Malta, and Moorish Spain; he left Algiers with four hundred Arab songs in his bag. Moving to Madrid, he became a musical polemicist under the pen-name Sidi-Mahabul and gave salon concerts. Moving to Lisbon, he published an essay on Middle Eastern instruments followed by his magnum opus, *La musique Arabe, ses rapports avec la musique Grecque et le chant Grégorien*, in which he sought to overturn prevailing anti-Arab prejudice.

Returning to Paris, he began to introduce the music he'd collected to a European public. He published a *Messe Africaine* for piano, and works for orchestra and male-voice choir based on melodies he'd collected. As his biographer Henry George Farmer wrote, 'Salvador stands in relation to the Arabs as Grieg does to the Norwegians, or Borodin and Musorgsky to the Russians.' Salvador began composing an Arabic opera in which Berlioz encouraged him; he set up as a teacher, conductor, and evangelist for the music of the Middle East. Unwinding with friends, he liked to play desert music on the instruments he'd brought back from Algeria, getting people to accompany him on an ancient harpsichord.

He was a flamboyant figure, and it was inevitable that he should get caught up in the practical socialism blowing through Paris in the 1860s: as a champion of *la musique sociale*, he marched in step with his friend the painter Gustave Courbet in dedicating his work to social change; he gave concerts for the poor, and wrote for revolutionary journals. This radicalism alienated him from the musical establishment, and he was forced to resume work as an orchestral violinist. During the German siege of Paris in 1870 he was wounded in the October Rising, and when the proto-Marxist Commune was established in 1871 he figured prominently, first in demonstrations and then in street battles.

The Paris Conservatoire had been turned into a hospital during the siege, and when the Commune reopened it, Salvador was the natural choice for its vacant post of director. His first act was to summon the staff and beg them to swear loyalty to the revolution, and to a democratic system of teaching; only a handful agreed, but he continued undaunted. He also continued to fight in what was now a civil war. The end came for him when the inhabitants of a Parisian district opposed to the Commune denounced him – and the group of fighters he was leading – to some soldiers of the regular army. Defiantly puffing on his pipe, and straightening his flowing silk cravat, he indicated the spot at which his executioners should aim, and died on his own barricade.

La musique Arabe was published in 1863, and became a standard work. Farmer's translation – retitled *The Music and Musical Instruments of the Arab, with an Introduction on how to appreciate Arab music* – was the first book on the subject in English, and its tone was welcoming to novices: Salvador was aware of the prejudices he had to confront. For example, the eighteenth-century British traveller Lancelot Addison found that the Moors had 'very harsh and sawing voices'. Guillaume-André Villoteau, who studied Arab music while serving in Bonaparte's Egyptian campaign, found it 'revolting to the ear', while the Canadian traveller Thomas MacGill thought the music in Tunisia 'barbarous … the braying of an ass is sweeter than their softest note, whether vocal or instrumental.'

'Like everyone else,' Salvador began,

I at first recognised in [Arab music] only a frightful medley, devoid of melody or measure. However, when I had become habituated to it … a day came when I could distinguish something resembling a tune. I tried to set it down but without success, the tonality and the measure always evading me. I could distinguish many series of tones and semitones but it was impossible to assign them to a starting note or tonic.

Moreover, he couldn't relate the rhythms to the tunes, though he could see that those rhythms underpinned dance. 'There was an interesting problem in this difference of sensations, and I tried to fathom it.' He got to know Arab musicians, questioning and imitating them until he could pass as an Arab musician himself. Finally he was able to declare triumphantly, 'I now revel in Arab music.'

His analytical findings include one which is surprising. 'I have never been able to discover in Arab music those third and quarter tones which others claim to find,' he wrote. This flew in the face of the abundant historical evidence, as found in the treatises of medieval theorists like al-Farabi and Safi al-Din al-Urmawi, who posited a scale of seventeen tones per octave. It's unlikely that that microtonal sound-world would have entirely disappeared by the time Salvador was doing his research. Was his ear at fault, or did he just register what he wanted to hear? In other respects, however, his conclusions chimed perfectly with the Arab music we know today.

He noted the structure of the North African *nuba* suite, which begins with an instrumental prelude. He recognised the tetrachordal basis on which Arab melodies were built, and he relished the Arab use of heterophony, several voices embroidering on a melody, each in their own way. Above all he loved Arab improvisation, a procedure he saw as 'reigning as supreme and absolute mistress over all singers and players from Tangier to Alexandria'. This, he believed, was cognate with a tradition from the eighth-century European monasteries: 'These trills, accents, and abbreviations which adorned the music of the time of the most pious King Charlemagne were the same among the Arabs, who have still kept them.' And he was a super-observant listener: 'The suppression or addition of a note, sometimes the mere interposition, suffices to impart a fresh melodic idea, another accent, and one which prepares in a novel and graceful manner the return to the fundamental note.'

Salvador did admittedly take the fashionable Darwinian view – which Arab musicologists at the Cairo conference in 1932 endorsed to their own detriment – that Arab music, lacking the harmony which Guido d'Arezzo's eleventh-century invention of notation had made possible, was simply music in a less evolved state. But what set Salvador apart – and what makes his ideas relevant today – was his awareness that the Arab sound-world possessed a melodic richness which European music, despite its harmonic complexity, had lost. He contrasted European music's two modes, major and minor, with the fourteen Arab modes, each subtly distinguished from the others by its mood and colouring.

But as he observed, medieval European music had itself once employed twelve modes, before these were narrowed down to two. He believed that in the music of the Arabs he had discovered a missing link with Europe's musical past, which could be used to introduce new dimensions into the European music of the present with improvisation, and with the expanded palette of modality.

Félicien David and his friends, he wrote, had well-meaningly harnessed Arab melody to the European harmonic system:

> We, on the contrary, would like the application of a system of harmony appropriated to the scale of each mode, without altering the character of the melody. Here lies, in our belief, the source of a new wealth of harmony, the use of which could be combined with those which we have already. Just as the minor mode has a special harmony, so ought each of the other modes we have mentioned.

'This musical archaeology may be of some interest,' was Salvador's modest summing-up. 'I believe I have traced out a path for others to take up.' Those taking that path include many avant-garde Western composers today.

Sources

For a bird's-eye view of the Jesuits' musical activities in seventeenth- and eighteenth-century China, *Rhapsody in Red* by Sheila Melvin and Cai Jindong does the job. Du Halde's survey is perfunctory, but Jean-Joseph-Marie Amiot's great study *Mémoire sur la musique des Chinois, tant anciens que modernes* is both illuminating and delightfully written. Lam Ching-Wah's commentary on Amiot in *Chime* magazine sets him helpfully in context. Meanwhile the nearest thing to a biography of Francisco Salvador-Daniel is Henry George Farmer's memoir included with his translation of Salvador-Daniel's key treatise: *The Music and Musical Instruments of the Arab, with an Introduction on how to appreciate Arab music.*

Bibliography

Amiot, Jean-Joseph-Marie, *Mémoire sur la musique des Chinois, tant anciens que modernes* (Paris: 1779)

Du Halde, J. B., *Description géographique, historique, chronologique, politique et physique de l'empire de la Chine et de la Tartarie chinoise* (Paris: 1735)

Lam Ching-Wah, 'A Highlight of French Jesuit Scholarship in China: Jean-Joseph-Marie Amiot's Writings on Chinese Music', *CHIME: Journal of European Foundation for Chinese Music Research*, nos. 16–17 (2005), 127–47

Melvin, Sheila and Cai Jindong, *Rhapsody in Red: How Western Classical Music Became Chinese* (New York: Algora, 2004)

Salvador-Daniel, Francisco, *The Music and Musical Instruments of the Arab, with an Introduction on how to appreciate Arab music*, translated by Henry George Farmer (London: William Reeves, 1914)

7 Dimitrie Cantemir, from the first edition of his Latin work *Descriptio Moldaviae* (1716).

3

Going native in Constantinople

Dimitrie Cantemir, the happy hostage

DIMITRIE CANTEMIR WAS an unlikely toiler in the music-exploring vineyard. Born in 1673, he was the son of a minor noble in the principality of Moldavia: that little Balkan state, now divided among Romania, Moldova, and the Ukraine, was then plagued by marauding Tartars, rapacious boyars, and by the annual extortion of money and labour by the Ottoman Empire, to which Moldavia was a vassal state. When Dimitrie was twelve his father was appointed Prince of Moldavia: the downside to this was that, following tradition, one of the prince's sons had to live permanently under guard in Constantinople, as a guarantee that Moldavia would not rebel against the Ottoman yoke.

First Dimitrie's elder brother was the hostage, then it became sixteen-year-old Dimitrie's turn. But he got on so well with his Turkish captors that he was soon able to exchange his hostage status for that of a diplomatic envoy. Constantinople was at that time the heart of Islam, and a cultural melting pot; Christians were made welcome and allotted their own sector of the city, and Dimitrie was allowed to roam wherever he wanted. As he was a polyglot polymath, that meant the freedom to roam through the city's libraries, including the one at the Grand Seraglio which was normally forbidden to non-Muslims, and he studied there for twenty years. His writings in Latin, Turkish, and French covered subjects ranging from science, philosophy, and Greek-Orthodox mysticism to cartography, Peter the Great's Russia, and the decline of the Ottoman Empire, about which his forecasts were prophetic. He became renowned across Europe as a political commentator, and his admirers included Gibbon, Burke, Byron, and Victor Hugo; his claim to be of Tartar descent provoked Voltaire to declare that the multiplicity of his talents suggested he must have been descended 'from the race of Pericles, rather than that of Tamburlaine'. His son recorded his austere daily routine: rising at five, smoking a pipe over a bowl of coffee, studying till midday and then, after lunch and a siesta, working on until seven in the evening.

But Dimitrie was also a musician, and he fell in love with the sound of the long-necked *tanbur* lute, which in his view 'flawlessly reproduced' the flow of the human voice when bowed, and had a particular expressiveness when plucked. The fact that the Ottomans regarded music as an occupation for the lower orders meant that virtually all the court musicians were of Greek, Jewish, or Armenian origin, and Dimitrie took tuition in playing the *tanbur* from two Greek masters. After a fifteen-year apprenticeship he fledged as a virtuoso, becoming affectionately known as Kantemiroglu. 'Nobody in Constantinople could play better than him,' wrote a chronicler of the time.

And Dimitrie fell in love with Turkish music. 'It may seem strange to Europeans,' he wrote, 'that I should celebrate the musical taste of a nation reputed to be barbarous. I even dare to suggest that Turkish music is much more perfect than that of Europe, and also that it is so hard to understand that you will find scarcely three or four people who really grasp the principles and delicate qualities of this art.' By this he meant Turkish classical music, and he applied himself to study *makam*, the system on which it was based. As the American scholar Robert Labaree puts it, the word makam variously denotes a system encompassing composition and performance, the entire repertoire of Turkish classical music, and also a single mode which is part scale, part melodic template, and part aesthetic rule-book. There are 120 of these modes, each with its own character and colouring. Moreover, the art form depends on a high degree of metrical and tonal complexity: while a whole-step in the West is divided into two semitones, in Turkish *makam* it's divided into nine equal parts, and the *tanbur* has over forty adjustable frets. The rules governing the structure of a *makam* piece are commensurately complex; the creative possibilities contained within the confines of a single makam are limitless.

By the time Cantemir had arrived in Constantinople, the Ottoman 'science of music' was already sophisticated, thanks to the Mediterranean culture which the Turks had inherited through the Christian Byzantines; this culture had brought them pre-Christian Greek music theory. This theory could handle the structure of scales and the mathematical tuning of intervals, but it didn't include a notation which could indicate rhythm or metre. By using a combination of Turkish and Arabic symbols, Cantemir created a workable notation, but through his *Book of the Science of Music* his contribution to Turkish musical culture went further. Written in Turkish and dedicated to the Sultan, this was both a theoretical treatise and as complete a collection of Turkish compositions – 355 in all – as he could find and transcribe; some dated from previous centuries, others were contemporary, while nine were compositions by Cantemir himself.

Turkish music had long needed an underpinning which would allow it to free itself of Persian influences, and this book with its newly invented notation – European notation would have been powerless to render Turkish music's subtle tonal refinements – perfectly fitted the bill. Cantemir's aim was a scientific rigour and the application of logic, that being the thing which in his view distinguished human song from birdsong, 'no matter how great [the latter's] sweetness and beauty'. He even drew a medical analogy: 'In the same manner in which dissections are carried out, we have explained the canon, and decoded its rules.'

From that day to this, Turkish *makam* has always been a preserve of the cognoscenti, but some of the melodies Cantemir collected became popular in nineteenth-century Constantinople; one had already surfaced in the ballet music of Mozart's *Die Entführung aus dem Serail*. Today, thanks to the Spanish musical explorer Jordi Savall, Cantemir's work is enjoying a sudden renaissance.

Savall's musicological researches have taken him many times round the Mediterranean, and one of those trips took him to the Turkish metropolis. The CD which he and his Hespèrion XXI ensemble have entitled *Istanbul: Dimitrie Cantemir* draws on the *Book of the Science of Music* to recreate both the instrumental music of the seventeenth-century Ottoman court, and the bardic music which ordinary Turks would have enjoyed. Savall's perennial aim has been to repair – symbolically through music – the damage done in the sixteenth century to multi-faith harmony in the Mediterranean lands, and for him the ethnic diversity of old Constantinople is a perfect case in point. The ensemble's *makam* performances are interlarded with traditional Armenian music, and with the music of the Sephardic communities which had settled in the Ottoman Empire after their expulsion from Spain. When the instruments play *makam* together, it's in unison, since Turkish music, like all the traditional musics of the Middle East, is basically monophonic. But to listen to the improvised solo *taksim* (preludes) on the *lira*, *ney*, *oud*, *kanun*, *santur*, *tanbur*, *duduk*, and *kemence*, is to enter a garden – and here the cliché really fits – of fragrant musical delights.

Sources

The books by Scarlat Callimachi and Stefan Lemny give the basic facts about Dimitrie Cantemir's life, but the liner notes to Savall's CD *Istanbul: Dimitrie Cantemir* are more informative.

Bibliography and recordings

Callimachi, Scarlat, *Demetrius Cantemir* (Bucharest: Meridiane, 1966)
Lemny, Stefan, *Les Cantemir: l'aventure européenne d'une famille princière au XVIIIe siècle* (Paris: Complexe, 2009)
Istanbul: Dimitrie Cantemir 1673–1723, Hespèrion XXI, directed by Jordi Savall, Alia Vox AVSA9870

The birth of ethnomusicology

It was the Zuni and the Hopi, the Sioux and the Passamaquoddy, who first prompted field recording in America. In the mid-nineteenth century, the emergent science of anthropology found its home-grown focus in the indigenous tribes which had been decimated by disease, robbed of their land, and targeted for obliteration through everything from forcible 'civilisation' to outright genocide. The grisly climax of the undeclared war which had raged for decades between the USA and its Indian communities was the massacre at Wounded Knee in 1890 where 150 men, women, and children of the Lakota tribe were butchered by whites who were fearful of the shamanic – yet essentially pacific – Ghost Dance movement. Thereafter, with most of the tribes confined to reservations, it was generally assumed that Darwinian evolution would ensure their culture's demise.

Enlightened whites, including some of the soldiers who had been waging war on them, did what they could to ameliorate the Native Americans' lot; they were driven by a combination of guilt and curiosity to celebrate Indian culture, and Indian music in particular. But that celebration was uphill work, given that many shared the views of a prominent 'authority' on American-Indian culture named Richard Irving Dodge. For him 'the singing of the Indian consists in the monotonous repetition of a few half-guttural, half-nasal sounds (notes they can scarcely be called, as they form no music), varied by an occasional yell.'

This was the spur for the pioneering work of Alice C. Fletcher ...

8 Alice Fletcher with her interpreter James Stuart (left) and Chief Joseph at the opening of the Nez Perce Reservation in 1890.

4

The Song of Approach,
the Pipes of Friendship

Alice Fletcher and the Omaha Indians

THE FIRST MAJOR champion of Native Indian music – and the first American fieldworker in the ethnomusicological sense of the word – was Alice C. Fletcher, a self-taught anthropologist whose initial trip into Omaha territory fired her to such a degree that she devoted the rest of her life to pro-Indian activism. She had met the Omaha singer Francis La Flesche at a Boston literary society in 1879, and he became her lifelong informant and collaborator. But as she made clear in her book *A Study of Omaha Indian Music*, which she published in 1893, the path of true love did not initially run smooth. At the first few festivals she attended she registered nothing beyond 'a screaming downward movement that was gashed and torn by a vehemently beaten drum'. The sound was distressing, she said, until she realised that everyone else was enjoying themselves, and that the distress was simply her own. She began to listen more intently, and to note down what she heard, but the process was 'crude and full of difficulties, difficulties that I afterward learned were bred of preconceived ideas … generally accepted theories concerning "savage" music. The tones, the scales, the rhythms, the melodies that I heard, which after months of work stood out more and more clearly as indisputable facts, lay athwart these theories and could not be made to coincide with them.' For a long while she was tempted, she said, more to distrust her ears than her theories.

But then she was taken ill, and for months lay at death's door.

> While I was thus shut in from the rest of the world, with the Indians coming and going about me in their affectionate solicitude, they would often at my request sing for me. They sang softly because I was weak, and there was no drum, and then it was that the distraction of noise and confusion of theory were dispelled, and the sweetness, the beauty and meaning of these songs were revealed to me. As I grew stronger I was taught them, and sang them with my Indian friends, and when I was able to be carried about, my returning health was celebrated by the exemplification of the Wa-Wan ceremony with its music.

She was taken to a mud building covered in flowers, placed on a throne of skins, and serenaded with the Song of Approach (which they had taught her), and with strains on the Pipes of Fellowship. Only then did she fully understand both Omaha music and its place in daily life. 'There is not a phase of life that does not find expression in song,' she wrote later. 'Religious rituals are embedded in it, the reverent recognition of the creation of the corn, of the food-giving animals, of the fructifying sun, is passed from one generation to another ... Song nerves the warrior to deeds of heroism, and robs death of its terrors ... The old man tunefully evokes those agencies which can avert death.' She also noted that a song could be bought, and thus become personal property, 'but the purchaser would never claim to have composed it'.

Working with pencil and paper, and requesting endless repetition by singers so that she could get the detail down, she transcribed several hundred Omaha songs, as well as songs of the Dakotas, Otoes, Poncas, and Pawnees, and her commentaries have a poetry of their own. One song suggests 'the eagle stirring, and lifting itself from the nest, as the wind blows the branches of the trees'; another suggests 'sunshine, birds and verdure, and a fleet, happy movement'; yet another evokes 'the eagerness of the warrior, and suggests the tremulous movement of the leaves just before a thunderstorm'. She writes illuminatingly about what the casual listener would dismiss as mere nonsense syllables like scat singing. Most of the songs 'are furnished almost wholly with syllables which are not parts or even fragments of words, but sounds that lend themselves easily to singing and are without definite meaning; yet when a composer has once set syllables to his song, they are never changed or transposed, but preserved with as much accuracy as we would observe in maintaining the integrity of a poem.'

But she remains intensely aware of the gulf between herself and the people whose culture she is investigating. In contrast to Europeanised society with its complex layers of convention, Indian society, she writes, has an openness and simplicity: 'There are no secrets, no hidden tragedies, no private sorrows in the tribe; everything is known and seen by everybody.' Yet she too takes a Darwinist view of Indian music. It has as much emotional power as European music, she argues, but its limitations are intellectual. Where the food supply was dependent on the hunter, where the armed fight for survival was constant,

> where the language of the people had never been reduced to writing, and where there was no possible training of the mind in literature or art, these songs stand as a monument, marking the limit which the Omaha Indian's environment placed upon the development of his mental life and expression. The Omahas as a tribe have ceased to exist; therefore there can be no speculation upon any future development of Omaha Indian music.

Her business, she declares, is 'the archaeology of music', and it is indeed in this spirit that today's musicologists trawl through her transcriptions, and listen to the cylinders on which she recorded.

For she had hit on a problem which was bothering many ethnologists – the inadequacy of Western notation as a transcription tool. 'I am sorry,' she said in a lecture, 'that it is impossible for me to exemplify for you the Indian scale. It could only be done with the violin. There is no notation in common use that would make it feasible to describe it.' Edison's invention of the phonograph in 1877 therefore arrived with perfect timing. Following the redoubtable Jesse Walter Fewkes, who made the first-ever ethnographic field recordings with some Passamaquoddy Indians in 1890, Fletcher and La Flesche also took advantage of the new device.

* * *

Fletcher's research had set a benchmark for American ethnomusicology, with its emphasis on fieldwork rather than armchair-theorising in the German academic style. But her focus was on the social context, and, not being a trained musicologist, she felt the need for technical advice on musical matters. So she invited a music-theory specialist named John Comfort Fillmore to help with her transcriptions. Fillmore came out of the European Romantic tradition, but he did at least recognise that, in terms of rhythm and emotional power, Indian music had special qualities.

Bruno Nettl's later description of Plains-Indian vocal technique made clear the challenge Fillmore was faced with: 'It is characterised by a great deal of tension in the vocal organs ... an effort to sing as loudly as possible, and pulsation in the lower tones. Strong accents, glissandos, and as a result intonation which is probably less stable or fixed than other musical areas, as well as ornamentation and shouting before, during, and after songs, are the main results of this tension.'

Fillmore's transcription method was as follows: 'First, to listen to the singer attentively without trying to note down what he sings. This gives me a good general idea of the song.' Then he noted it down phrase by phrase. 'Then I sing it with him, and afterwards by myself, asking him to correct any errors in my version.' But he was still working with the European tuning system, and in European staff notation. And this flew in the face of ground-breaking research by the British phonetician Alexander Ellis in his celebrated study of 'the scales of various nations'. Based on the instruments housed in British museums, this had led Ellis to declare in 1885 that 'the Musical Scale is not one, not natural, nor even founded necessarily on the laws of the constitution of musical sound so beautifully worked out by Helmholtz, but very diverse, very artificial, and very capricious.' Thus was opened a path by which ethnomusicologists could escape from the constraints of Eurocentric tonal thinking.

Herman Helmholtz had proposed the existence of a universal, 'natural' scale based on Western musical perception, and that was much more to Fillmore's taste. Asserting that all societies possessed a 'latent harmonic sense', and that melody would everywhere evolve into harmony (as opposed to more sophisticated melody), he proceeded to clean up what he heard. He reduced Indian songs to a pentatonic major or minor, and ascribed anything which

9 Piegan Indian, Mountain Chief, with ethnologist Frances Densmore, listening to recording for the Bureau of American Ethnology in 1916.

didn't fit to what he deemed the Indians' 'primitive' and 'savage' pitch-perception. 'I am profoundly convinced,' he wrote, 'that the Indian always intends to sing precisely the same harmonic intervals which are the staple of our own music, and that all aberrations from harmonic pitch are mere accidents due … to imperfect training, or rather to the total lack of it.' Although the Indians sang in unison, with Fletcher's blessing he added chords and harmonies to the transcriptions. And as the American musicologist Helen Myers has pointed out, he was not above arbitrarily shifting a pitch up or down a semitone, 'to ensure its proper position in Western functional harmony'. He announced his intention to spare himself 'the useless labor of enumerating all the specific varieties of scale to be found in these songs, regarding it as a wholly irrelevant matter'.

The matter may indeed have been vexatious – musicologists still have trouble analysing Plains vocal style – but it was anything but irrelevant. Fillmore's stance put him very much on the wrong side of history, as the psychologist Benjamin Ives Gilman, whose transcriptions for Fewkes were done without any key or time signature on a 45-line staff, asserted at the time. This, however, was when people were eagerly looking for globally unifying theories, so Fillmore's seductive notion of a 'natural harmonic sense' won him powerful adherents, particularly when he could glibly argue that 'the Navaho howls his song to war gods directly along the line of a major chord; Beethoven makes the first theme of his great "Eroica" symphony out of precisely the same material.'

One of his adherents was Frances Densmore, who, fired by Fletcher's example, gave up her career as a pianist in order to devote her life to collecting the songs of the Sioux before they vanished; her most celebrated coup was to surreptitiously notate a tune which the Apache chief Geronimo was humming while he fashioned an arrowhead at the 1904 St Louis World's Fair. Another of Fillmore's adherents was Franz Boas, and he deserves a chapter, which now follows, to himself.

Sources

Alice Fletcher's *A Study of Omaha Indian Music* is an engaging memoir, detailing her induction into this tradition, and providing a poetic commentary on songs for which she also gives Fillmore's piano arrangements; Fillmore's own commentary is included, and Helen Myers's general introduction places the debate on Indian music in its current academic context. Frances Densmore's *The Study of Indian Music in the Nineteenth Century* provides a perspective from the 1920s, and in Bruno Nettl's 'North American Indian Musical Styles' (published in 1954) it is brought further up to date.

Bibliography

Densmore, Frances, 'The Study of Indian Music in the Nineteenth Century', *American Anthropologist*, vol. 29, issue 1 (1927), 79–86

Fillmore, John Comfort, 'Report on the Structural Peculiarities of the Music', in Alice C. Fletcher, *A Study of Omaha Indian Music*, introduction by Helen Myers (Lincoln, NE: University of Nebraska Press, Bison Books, 1994)

Fletcher, Alice C., *A Study of Omaha Indian Music*, introduction by Helen Myers (Lincoln, NE: University of Nebraska Press, Bison Books, 1994)

McNutt, James C., 'John Comfort Fillmore: A Study of Indian Music Reconsidered', *American Music*, vol. 2, no. 1 (Spring 1984), 61–70

Nettl, Bruno, 'North American Indian Musical Styles', *Memoirs of the American Folklore Society*, vol. 45 (1954)

5

'I am now a true Eskimo'

Franz Boas and first principles

IT'S IRONICAL THAT the man who conferred academic respectability on the art of song collecting, and on the science of its analysis, should have done so almost as an aside. For Franz Boas's main claim to fame is as the father of American anthropology. But his life was long enough – 1858 to 1942 – to allow the pursuit of a remarkable range of intellectual objectives. To appreciate his musicological achievements, it helps to trace the serpentine journey by which he arrived at them, even though that journey may seem at times irrelevant to his musical work. If this chapter dwells heavily on his character, it's because that character shaped his ideas.

He was brought up in the Prussian garrison town of Minden, where his father Meier was a textile merchant; his mother Sophie, who shared the utopian dream of Germany's early Communists, was the dominant force in their assimilated Jewish household, imbuing in her children a love of learning, and of natural history in particular. Franz's elder sister Toni became a professional pianist. He too learned the piano, but with humbler ambitions: 'I want to learn the playing of music,' he wrote to his sister, 'only insofar as it allows me to appreciate it.'

Sophie had set up a Froebel kindergarten in which Franz was enrolled at four, where each pupil had to sow, water, and care for their own personal flower-bed. When he was six his favourite book was *Robinson Crusoe*, and although a sickly child he began to prepare himself for travels of his own: eating food he didn't like to accustom himself to the imagined privations of Africa, and running in the snow to train for Arctic conditions.

As a teenager he immersed himself in mineralogy and the study of mosses, fungi, and ferns. 'It became clear to me,' he wrote, 'that true science consists not in describing single plants, but in a knowledge of their structure and life, and in the comparison of all classes of plants with one another.' When still in his teens he traced the geographical distribution of plants in the Minden region, and devised his own system of plant classification; dissatisfied with what he called 'simple learning', he strove to penetrate to the 'fundamentals

10 Franz Boas posing as Hamats'a, a supernatural figure in Kwakiutl myth,
as he emerges from a 'secret room'.

of things'. He complemented this quest with an intensive study of mathematics, physics, and medicine, and of Latin and Greek classics in their original languages, plus Goethe, Schiller, and Kleist; Nordic sagas were a particular passion. In his last year at the Gymnasium he dismissed medicine as being merely a 'descriptive' branch of science, and not worthy of his time. He'd come successfully through the most rigorous educational system in Europe, and was determined to excel. 'If I do not become really famous,' he confided to Toni, 'I do not know what I will do. It would be terrible if I had to spend my life unknown and unregarded.' This vaulting ambition may have been attributable to the cultural aspirations of assimilated German Jewry, but it also indicated the originality of a pioneering genius.

Socially diffident, but now physically strong, he enrolled at Heidelberg University to study mathematics and the natural sciences. As a young man-about-town he also took fencing lessons, which came in handy in a dispute with neighbours over his piano-playing. A duelling challenge was issued, which he accepted; badly cut on the head, he gave as good as he got. This was the first of a number of duels he would fight as member of a student guild; the aim was to cut the opponent's face, and Boas's features became scarred for life. He moved on to Bonn where, besides drinking and duelling, he formed a piano trio, became a Wagnerite, and went deeply into the fashionable new science of 'psychophysics' before finally reverting to his teenage love, geography.

Going on to study at Kiel, he had his first encounters with the anti-Semitism unleashed by the so-called Berlin Movement. Chancellor Bismarck's crackdown on liberalism centred on those universities with large numbers of Jewish students, and Boas's pugnacity with the sabre made him a provocative target. 'Unfortunately,' he wrote to his father on one occasion, 'I bring home again a few cuts, even one on the nose. I hope you won't concern yourself too much about it, but with the cursed Jewish situation this winter, one could not come through without quarrel and strife.' He always made light of his injuries, later joking to his children that the scars were the result of an encounter with a bear on Baffin Island.

German Polar explorations had fired his teenage imagination, and Baffin Island became the focus of his first geographical foray in 1883. His typically extensive preparations included the study of Arctic languages, cartography, photography, anthropological measurement, and astronomical orientation. Embarking on an exploration with one local assistant and a team of dogs – and armed with guns, ammunition, and tobacco for barter – he planned to make a detailed study of customs in one Inuit region, which he would also map over the space of a year.

Dressed in animal skins, enduring frostbite, and dependent for food on the seals and caribou he managed to shoot, he was lucky to survive his journey across the ice-cap. But he bonded so successfully with his Inuit hosts – administering rudimentary medicine, and taking an avuncular interest in their families – that after nine months he could write, 'I am now a true Eskimo. I live as they do, hunt with them, and belong to the men of Anarnitung [a harbour in Cumberland Sound].' The geographical research he did on Inuit migration customs made a significant contribution to academic debate, but what fired him more was the idea of documenting a culture which was already starting to disappear.

There were some odd congruences between the student culture he had grown up in and the Inuit culture he began to study. Writing home from an igloo – his letters were picked up by passing Scottish whalers – Boas expressed both the cultural relativism which would become his watchword and his hostility towards the constraints of tradition. The more he saw of Inuit culture, he wrote, the more he realised that 'we have no right to look down on them. The fear of tradition and of old customs is deeply implanted in mankind, and in the same way as it regulates life here, it halts all progress for us.' He declared that as a student he would have fought a duel with anyone who had damaged one of his photographs, thus confirming the cultural congruence between his superstitious Inuit hosts and his own innate superstition.

* * *

Boas may have loved music from infancy, but it was a long while before he homed in on it as a subject for study. When he did, however, it was to lay down analytical ground-rules which ethnomusicologists still follow today.

Music was just one element of his research trip to Baffin Island, but in his ground-breaking monograph *The Central Eskimo*, published in 1888, he transcribed Inuit folk tales and songs for games, work, shamanism, and ceremonial occasions. He even described how the drivers of sled dogs musically summoned their animals, and sang to them as they pulled on the reins. 'Every man has his own tune, and his own song,' he observed. Drums, rattles, and jew's harps were the usual accompaniment; there was much throat singing, and although many songs were on just one note, a polyphonic effect was produced by the contrast, not of melodies, but of textures.

Installed in 1885 as a curator at Berlin's Royal Ethnological Museum, he had his first encounter with the Indians of America's north-west coast who were to become the subject of his later investigations. A touring group of Bella Coola Indians from British Columbia had come to perform in Berlin, and Boas transcribed their songs; he went to Victoria to study Chinook songs, and to Vancouver for Kwakiutl ones.

The Kwakiutl had an elaborate range of ceremonies: 'potlatch' feasts which could last for a month and involved orgies of gift-giving and non-stop theatrical song-and-dance, and the *hamatsa*, an ecstatic ritual in which the community reclaimed boys who had been undergoing teenage initiation by having to survive for weeks among spirits in the wild. The songs for these events, and for love and mourning, used falsetto and fast vibrato; the complex Kwakiutl rhythms have been likened to the steady yet broken beat of the sea. At the 1893 World's Columbian Exposition in Chicago, Boas was able for the first time to record those Kwakiutl songs with a phonograph.

In 1902, appointed as a curator at the American Museum of Natural History in New York, Boas devised a crazily ambitious exploration, with an army of researchers, of the cultural and musical correspondences between the north-eastern territories of Asia and the westernmost regions of North America. He believed those correspondences were so numerous that they indicated a cognate origin, even if that had been long in the past. After all, shamanism was still flourishing on both sides of the Bering Strait, and ways of life in eighteenth-century Kamchatka and Alaska had not been so very different. As Boas pointed out, the implications for American history could be huge. Although his theory proved impossible to substantiate at the time – evidence discovered by archaeologists in 2019 suggests there may indeed have once been a land bridge between the two continents – Boas's project yielded a cache of cylinder recordings which now remain key evidence of a lost culture.

This was a time when most anthropologists on musical quests needed musicologists to transcribe and analyse: Boas was one of the few who could dispense with such help. On this trip he also collected instruments, and insisted that his fieldworkers study their use. Rattles should be 'fully explained', he told one assistant:

> Please inquire particularly in regard to the significance of the raven rattle with hawk face on its lower side and lying figure on its back. What is the legend of the origin? How are they used and how are they held in dances? What is the difference between these rattles and the round rattles, most of which represent birds or heads? What is the use of the rattle set with puffin-beaks?

On the Asian side the musicological pickings were slimmer, thanks to native wariness of recording technology. Some singers in Kamchatka and on Sakhalin Island believed there was a little creature inside the phonograph with an amazing ability to learn songs, while older people tried to dissuade the young from risking the theft of their voices; some feared that spirits would fly into the recording horn and be trapped there forever.

* * *

Boas was the first ethnologist to study the performance aspects of song, subjecting prayers, love songs, children's songs, and war songs to analytical scrutiny. With the Thompson Indians he noted the singers' gestures as they became ecstatic:

> One of them sang a prayer. While singing he danced and reached out to the sun with both arms while looking upward. Then he brought them down slowly, looking to the ground. Before that he had crossed his hands in front of his chest with the palms outward, moving them to the left and to the right as if he wanted to embrace the celestial body.

Then an old woman sang 'the song which serves to cleanse women who had borne twins. She took bundles of fir branches and hit her shoulders and breast with them while she danced.' When film entered the ethnomusicological armoury, Boas seized on it.

Meanwhile, music had become the model for his idiosyncratic theory of primitive art. He suggested that all decorative patterns were derived from the rhythmic actions necessary to produce them, and he adduced music as a prime example of this. In his book *Primitive Art*, published in 1927, he described music's place in nomad societies with a poetic flourish:

Decorative art requires rest and quiet, a stationary abode … The life of hunters is not favourable to the prosecution of such work … He is not all the time following strenuously the tracks of the game, but often he resorts to trapping, or he sits still, waiting for the game to appear. During such time his fancy is free to wander, and many of his songs take shape during these moments.

For Boas, music was the key to culture in all its forms, even with the simplest of percussion instruments:

The rattle … is not merely the outcome of the idea of making a noise … It is, besides this, the outcome of religious conceptions, as any noise may be applied to invoke or drive away spirits; or it may be the outcome of the pleasure children have in noise of any kind; and its form may be characteristic of the art of the people. Thus the same implement belongs to very different departments of a psychological museum.

In other words, context and purpose were paramount. And for him, the purpose of music itself was to underpin his vision of anthropology as a tool for promoting cultural equality, particularly in a country where blacks and Native Americans were suffering cruel discrimination.

As professor of anthropology at Columbia University from 1899 to 1936, Boas was hugely influential, leaving his mark on many generations of students. Some of those, like Margaret Mead and George Herzog, went on to become gurus themselves. Mead's Polynesian findings underpinned the Sixties' child-rearing debate, and Herzog tutored musicological eminences including Alan Merriam and Bruno Nettl, who built substantially on Boas's work among the Amerindians. Alan Lomax, ploughing his furrow in the blues, frequently sought Boas's advice.

It was Margaret Mead who pinpointed what made Boas unique. First, the purity of his intentions: 'As he was not working for personal power but for the good of mankind, he had the moral freedom that goes with self-elected, complete dedication.' And then there was his open mind: 'There are no methods named after Boas, just as there is no Boas school.' But Boas was instrumental in establishing ethnomusicology as an academic discipline, and in linking it with linguistics, poetry, folk tales, myth, and dance. Under his guidance the American Museum became the first in the world to collect sound recordings, using the cylinders he and his colleagues had brought back from the Jesup North Pacific Expedition as a foundation. He thus set a trend which was followed by the Smithsonian's Bureau of American Ethnology, and by the soon-to-be-massive Phonogramm-Archiv in Berlin. Meanwhile the Amerindian music which he and his colleagues had recorded helped inspire composers who were at that time striving, with the enthusiastic backing of Dvořák, to create a genuinely 'American' music.

By the force of his intellect, his idealism, and his crazy courage, Franz Boas shaped the course of musicology to a degree no other scholar had done before, or has done since.

Sources

Douglas Cole's biographical study of Boas's first forty-eight years is richly detailed on the development of his ideas, his personal life, and his academic career, but has little on his fieldwork. For the latter, Ira Jacknis's paper in *Franz Boas and the Music of the Northwest Coast Indians* fills the gap, while Sean O'Neill's paper 'The Boasian Legacy in Ethnomusicology' assesses Boas's academic impact, and his continuing influence through his disciples, and in turn through theirs. Margaret Mead's essay, 'The Anthropology of Franz Boas', gives a flavour of his tutorial method.

Bibliography

Cole, Douglas, *Franz Boas: The Early Years, 1858–1906* (Seattle: University of Washington Press, 1999)

Jacknis, Ira, 'Beyond Boas? Re-assessing the Contribution of "Informant" and "Research Assistant"', in *Franz Boas and the Music of the Northwest Coast Indians, From Constructing Cultures Then and Now* (Washington, DC: Arctic Studies Center, Smithsonian Institution, 2003)

Mead, Margaret, 'The Anthropology of Franz Boas', *American Anthropologist*, vol. 61, no. 5, part 2 (1959)

Müller-Wille, Ludger, ed., *Franz Boas: Among the Inuit of Baffin Island, 1883–84* (Toronto: University of Toronto Press, 2016)

Nettl, Bruno and Victoria Lindsay Levine, 'Amerindian Music', *New Grove Dictionary of Music and Musicians* (London: Macmillan, 2001)

O'Neill, Sean, 'The Boasian Legacy in Ethnomusicology: Cultural Relativism, Narrative Texts, Linguistic Structures, and the Role of Comparison', in Regna Darnell, Michelle Hamilton, Robert L. A. Hancock, and Joshua Smith, eds, *The Franz Boas Papers*, vol. 1 (Lincoln, NE, and London: University of Nebraska Press, 2015), 129–60

11 Komitas Vardapet, in a photo from c. 1900; in 1912 he sent it as a gift to his friend, the singer and pianist Margarit Babayan.

6

Voice of Armenia

The tragedy of Komitas

SOGHOMON SOGHOMONIAN WAS born in 1869 in Kütahya, an Armenian Christian enclave whose inhabitants suffered systematic oppression under the Ottoman yoke. Even those Armenians who could speak their ancestral tongue were forbidden to do so outside church. Soghomon's father, a cobbler, sang and played the lute; his talented but melancholic mother – sixteen when she gave birth to him – wove carpets, composed songs, and wrote poetry. Soghomon was in his infancy when she died; his father turned to drink and also died prematurely. School friends remembered Soghomon as a waif wandering the streets; one recalled 'a thin, malnourished, serious, kind little boy' who in winter would come to school hungry, and frozen blue.

He had one great asset – a strikingly beautiful voice, spotted when he was eleven by an emissary charged with finding orphan singers for the choir at Etchmiadzin Abbey, which was then, as it still is, the spiritual centre of Armenian culture. There he quickly shone as a singer of both church music and Turkish folk songs; he became the seminary's comedian, specialising in mimicking the songs and dances of different regions. And with a succession of brilliant teachers he began his lifetime quest to document the folk music which had permeated his childhood.

He went out into the fields, and listened to the songs of the pilgrims who came to Etchmiadzin; at that time the Armenian language encompassed dozens of dialects, with a corresponding number of musical styles. Despite having no knowledge of music theory he began harmonising these songs for a student choir; when he was seventeen he enlisted his fellow-students as co-researchers. He also embarked on a parallel quest to crack the code governing the *khaz* notation system of the early Armenian Church. Success in this would allow its canticles to be performed as they had been before their exposure to Persian, Turkish, and Kurdish influences: his goal was to distil the essence of the Armenian sacred tradition.

Like all victims of broken homes, he needed a support framework: he made Etchmiadzin his home, and took orders as a *vartabed*, celibate priest. It was traditional that ordinands should be given a new name, and the one he took,

Komitas, was to honour Komitas Aghayetsi, a composer-priest of the seventh century. And it was as Komitas Vartabed – or Notaji Vartabed, the 'note-crazy priest' to the villagers whose songs he hoovered up – that he was henceforth known to the world. At twenty-six he published his first collection of transcribed folk music, *The Songs of Agn*: wedding songs and love songs, lullabies and dances.

This caused ructions in the seminary, whose conservative members found it shocking that a celibate priest should sing and teach such things. He transferred to an outpost of the Armenian Church in more cosmopolitan Tbilisi, then went to study in Berlin, emerging after three years as a formidable scholar and an inspiring choral conductor. When the Berlin branch of the International Musical Society was formed he was invited to speak at its inaugural meeting, arguing that the Armenian *khaz* could serve as a model for the study of the ancient Roman, Greek, and Assyrian traditions.

Returning in 1899 to Etchmiadzin, he created a polyphonic choir and began writing the papers which would put him in the history books. He was now conducting his research on an industrial scale, giving his students paper and instructing them to write down the songs they heard when they went back to their villages; he spent his summers in the countryside, observing how songs were interwoven with life-cycle rituals. Texts thus caught on the wing were spelled out in all their improvised specificity; melodies were given with lists of tiny variations in pitch and rhythm; dances were broken down into prescribed movements for every part of the body. Ask a villager who was the composer of a song, he said, and you'd be given the name of the village star; ask that star, and he'd either give you another name, or shrug his shoulders. 'All peasants know in some degree how to compose,' he declared. 'Nature is their infallible school.' He writes of joining a village festival at midnight and watching as a round-dance song is constructed. It begins with a soloist giving a line repeated by the chorus, which is then answered by another line. As the dance gets animated the melody is modified again and again, and he notes down all the variants. Another soloist takes it up in pitch, after which yet another soloist takes over; finally the best singer in the village – bashfully protesting, yet burning to perform – gives the song its final shape. When it's all over, he asks if they could sing the song in one of its intermediate forms, but they won't – 'because it wasn't good'. He concludes: 'A song, you sing it, and that's all; why bother to ask who created it, where, when, and how? That day I noted thirty-four new songs.'

* * *

In contrast to the emerging German school of ethnomusicology – which focused on technicalities of tuning and rhythm – Komitas took an anthropological view. And he brought to his researches an instinctive empathy, as in his account of an orphaned girl whom he spotted sitting on a roof making dung cakes for fuel. First he gives the melody, a complex vocal line involving oblique shifts in tonality, and its text with the refrain 'Dear mother, you left me homeless, what shall I do?'. A second girl interrupts her and they start chatting, and when she leaves the first girl develops her song with even more artful figurations, until an old woman angrily tells her to stop and come down. 'Over time,' he comments, 'this song will be forgotten, or be at best a vague memory, for the creation of songs for the peasant is as ordinary and natural as daily conversation is for us. If we don't note down what is sung today, we won't remember it later.'

Armenian peasants had no concept of art song, music for its own sake: Komitas was acutely aware that as old customs died out, so would the songs associated with them. One of his most striking commentaries is on a ploughing song from a mountain village in the Lori province, where work begins at nightfall, and where the plough is a medieval leviathan requiring twelve yoked oxen and the menfolk from several families.

The ploughing and the song begin with an invocation to God, and an exhortation to the animals and the boys who will ride on their yokes. The key lines and refrains combine religiosity with practicality, but into these the singers weave comments on everything they see, whether it's slackers (human or animal) or people they see passing by – a woman lighting her lamp, another fetching water from a well. The meticulous thoroughness of Komitas's musical analysis in terms of scale, rhythm, and word-setting would meet the most stringent demands of present-day ethnomusicology, and his conclusion has a lovely symmetry. As he triumphantly shows, everything is based on the number five, whether it's the pentasyllabic poetry, the number of lines in the melody, the phrases in each line, or the beats in a bar.

He sums it all up with a gloriously poetic justification for these quasi-scientific exertions:

> The day has rested and the night is ready for work. Two seas have served each other – the bright blue of the sky and the vigilant black of the earth. The moon has risen above the stars to plough the rows of clouds. Above is life that moves the mind and heart, below is a world of effort. The peasant awakes, the plough takes heart and encourages him, tearing the field, piling up waves of soil to right and left. The whole team is breathing heavily, the oxen are murmuring, the men are shouting, the breeze is whistling, the flowers are whispering, the brook is plashing. Meanwhile the plough-wheel creaks and whimpers ... The dark and light of the peasant's life, his labour and his hopes, give birth to our beautiful song.

The first few years of the twentieth century saw Komitas's fame dramatically spreading. His magnetic power as a conductor and his lectures in Berlin, Venice, and Paris (where he founded other choirs) bolstered his reputation as the voice of Armenian music: he invoked Wagner's example as the man who 'gave a national music to Germany', though he took care not to draw any musical parallels. One of his biggest fans in Paris was Debussy, who declared that one song arrangement alone (an exile's lament entitled 'Antuni') would have been sufficient to earn him a place in the pantheon of composers.

All the photographs of Komitas at this time show a dapper gent with neatly chiselled features, burning dark eyes, and a shy demeanour, forming the still centre of group after group of students and choristers. He lived ascetically, sleeping on the floor without mattress or pillow, and he preserved a striking humility, signing his choral arrangements 'harmonised by Komitas Vartabed', rather than the 'composed' which would have been more accurate. Yet he spent his thirties at war on two fronts. One of these was the simmering conflict with his conservative superiors, who did all they could (including drastically cutting his salary) to stymy his efforts to promote his beloved folk music, and to realise his dream of founding an Armenian music conservatory. The other war was private: an agonising struggle with his celibate conscience over a passionate affair with the charismatic Armenian singer Marguerite Babayan.

Komitas was so desperate to escape the claustrophobia of Etchmiadzin that in 1910 he accepted an invitation to create an Armenian choir in Constantinople, which had not yet had its name changed to Istanbul, and where there was a big Armenian community and a Westernised intelligentsia. He did this with justifiable anxiety, knowing he was moving to the heart of an empire which had permitted the massacre of thousands of Armenians in the multi-ethnic Turkish town of Adana just one year previously; he left most of his belongings behind, to be forwarded only if he decided to settle. In Constantinople he created a 300-voice mixed choir, and began rallying the city's Armenian intellectuals, but the old problem resurfaced, with conservative Armenian clerics trying once again to halt his performances, and denouncing him to the Turkish secret police as a political subversive. Defiantly he went on performing, and counter-attacked by accusing the local Armenian clergy of singing the austere Armenian canticles as though they were Turkish party songs. In 1911 he made a triumphant tour of Egypt, where he sang and clowned to the delight of expat Armenians, and where he created yet another local Armenian choir.

* * *

Politics, however, were now closing in. The Ottoman ban on the Armenian language had reflected the Turks' hope that the Armenians would become assimilated. But the Armenian activists' push for a homeland within the Ottoman Empire, plus their cultural renaissance – exemplified by their triumphant celebration of the fifteen-hundredth anniversary of their alphabet in 1913, for which Komitas composed a song – put paid to that idea. Komitas was now so fashionable a figure in Constantinople that he was even invited to participate in a fundraising concert for the Turkish military.

But the noose was tightening: the Young Turks, whose goals were sharia law and Turkic racial purity – some things don't change – were now viciously in the ascendant. With the outbreak of the First World War, in which Turkey was soon encircled by Allied forces, a state of emergency was declared, and the 'Armenian question' was tackled, as the Young Turks thought, once and for all: all Ottoman Armenians were ordered to surrender their 'weapons', kitchen knives included, while popular anti-Armenian sentiment was stoked up on the streets.

Watching hostile demonstrations from his window, Komitas took refuge in work. Believing he had found the key to the ancient Armenian notation system, he arranged the entire Divine Liturgy for male chorus, and during an extraordinary burst of productivity in 1913–14 published suites of wedding and fortune-telling songs, plus six suites of peasant songs, and created yet another choir; he also made sketches for what would have been the first Armenian opera. Now universally acknowledged as the de facto ambassador for Armenian musical culture, he went back to Paris to deliver three lectures containing the summation of his research into both the sacred and secular traditions. Meanwhile his presence at official gatherings in Constantinople was still being used as a fig-leaf for the Turkish government's pretension to cultural pluralism.

On April 24 in 1915 the genocide was triggered, with the arrest of 2,345 prominent Armenians suspected of having 'nationalist sentiments': parliamentary deputies and lawyers, doctors and journalists, scholars, and musicians including Komitas himself. It seems he meekly accepted his arrest as though he had long expected it, like the protagonist of Kafka's *The Trial*. The victims were initially treated so politely that many assumed their trouble would blow over, but, as with the Nazi round-up of Jews in Paris in 1942, the deportees' treatment soon turned brutal: they were bundled into bullock carts, and driven without food or water to prisons in the remote countryside. Of the 291 men incarcerated in Komitas's group, only forty survived: the rest were either clandestinely executed, or murdered by bandits, or died from starvation and disease. He himself was one of eight to be spared thanks to a mysterious telegram from the Ministry of the Interior (thought to have been inspired by the American ambassador, Henry Morgenthau, who was one of his fans); Komitas learned of his release as he was celebrating mass for his imprisoned co-religionists.

He returned to Constantinople to find his house ransacked and his archive destroyed. He tried to salvage what he could of his work, but never recovered from the shock of his incarceration, and of what he had witnessed: post-traumatic stress disorder turned his brain and rendered him mute. Friends tried many ruses to help him recover, but his response was psychotic; after a spell in a Turkish asylum he was sent to a succession of psychiatric hospitals in Paris, where, after seventeen years of intensifying paranoia, he died. The genocide may not have killed him, but it killed his creative spirit, and it obliterated much of the Armenian, Turkish, and Kurdish music he had so devotedly collected.

* * *

What was the impulse which drove his musical quest? His biographer, the Canadian-Armenian psychiatrist Rita Soulahian Kuyumjian, contends that his drive to uncover the roots of his musical heritage was essentially a private matter. It represented, says Kuyumjian, a sublimated attempt at mourning – and even symbolically resurrecting – the parents he had lost in childhood, with the remedy he applied to his own wounds helping to heal the wounds inflicted by history on the Armenian people as a whole.

This might help explain why his music has become the rallying point for the Holocaust Day observances which are faithfully marked by Armenians every year, all over the world. A glowing tribute from Aram Khachaturian – often erroneously thought to be the founding father of Armenia's classical tradition – makes clear on whose brow that laurel should be placed: 'Komitas's music is of such stylistic purity, its language so sublime, that it is impossible to pass it by, impossible not to feel its closeness, or refuse its influence.'

'It is difficult to make clear the uniqueness of Armenian folk music to foreigners, particularly Europeans,' Komitas wrote. 'Our folk songs and dance songs … portray an altogether different fervour, different sentiment, and different meaning from those of other Eastern traditions.' He organised his findings with precision, distinguishing them geographically and according to social function; he recovered songs of the medieval *gusan* minstrels and *ashug* folk-poets with their Middle Eastern modes, and he was the first to transcribe Kurdish melodies. Like Bartók he didn't collect in the cities, because in his view the true Armenian tradition could only be found among the peasantry.

Thanks to YouTube we can listen to him singing some of his finds with piano and violin accompaniment. His voice has a restrained but expressive vibrato, long-held notes rounded off with delicate ornamentation. To listen to the three-part choral versions which he made of these monophonic songs is to understand why Debussy was so admiring. With their intricate polyphony they are miniature masterpieces, packed with drama incorporating shouts, laughter, and all the sounds of village life, as well as the hope and sadness of a community under the perennial threat of violent obliteration. His arrangement of the Lori ploughing song, with its melodic leaps and falls, its surges of power and sudden *pianissimi*, can make the spine tingle. Like Musorgsky, Komitas stipulated that the performance of his settings should remain faithful to the rhythms of speech.

The tragedy of Komitas's life has a perennial attraction for Armenian film-makers and novelists, while droves of Armenian musicians have made their own arrangements of the melodies which he collected. These include the seven short dances, each from a different region of the country, out of which he created the little suite which is his only solo piano composition. The style of these miniatures is austere yet suggestive, evoking the instruments on which the dances would originally have been performed: the *pogh* flute (with which Komitas illustrated points in his lectures), the *dhol* and *dap* drums, the double-reed *zurna*, and the apricot-wood *duduk* oboe, whose mournful beauty is regarded as the expression of the Armenian soul.

Sources

Komitas's essays and commentaries in *Armenian Sacred and Folk Music* are technical but accessibly clear. Rita Soulahian Kuyumjian's *Archaeology of Madness* is the only decent English-language biography of Komitas. Lusine Grigoryan's CD *Komitas: Seven Songs* includes all of the composer's piano music; the scores on her website lusinegrigoryan.com illustrate one of the many ways in which Komitas's music is being reworked today.

If the most bewitching arrangements to date are those orchestrated by Serouj Kradjian and sung by the soprano Isabel Bayrakdarian, the most intriguing are those by Levon Eskenian and the Gurdjieff Ensemble. For each of the dance arrangements for piano and voice, Eskenian's starting point was Komitas's indication of the folk instruments on which he had heard the music originally played. Eskenian has rearranged this music for those same instruments: here folk music is transformed into art music, then back again in the reverse direction.

Bibliography and recordings

Komitas, *Armenian Sacred and Folk Music*, translated by Edward Gulbekian, introduction by V. N. Nersessian (London: Curzon, 1998)

Kuyumjian, Rita Soulahian, *Archaeology of Madness: Komitas, Portrait of an Armenian Icon* (Princeton, NJ: Gomidas Institute, 2001)

Komitas: Seven Songs, Lusine Grigoryan, piano, ECM New Series 2514, 481 2556

12 Edwin Clay's mud-caked boots testify to Cecil Sharp's interruption of his singing at work: a photo taken at Brailes, Warwickshire, c. 1900.

7

Britain's folk-song revivals, and the contentious Cecil Sharp

IT WASN'T THE German musicologist Carl Engel who coined the mocking phrase *Das Land ohne Musik*. That was another German, Oskar Schmitz, but Engel did indicate a glaring gap in England's musical landscape during Victoria's heyday. 'It seems rather singular,' he wrote in 1879,

> that England should not possess any printed collections of its national songs with the airs as they are sung at the present day, while almost every other European nation possesses several comprehensive works of this kind … Surely there are English musicians who might achieve good results if they would spend their autumnal holidays in some rural districts of the country, associate with the villagers, and listen to their songs.

At that very time a resistance movement, chronicled by Steve Roud in his book *Folk Song in England*, was brewing among British composers who were sick of what they regarded as their countrymen's xenophilia for Mendelssohn and Wagner. The 'English Musical Renaissance' was the label pinned on this group which included Hubert Parry, Charles Villiers Stanford, and Alexander Mackenzie. And although they had no interest in folk music – their concerns were symphonic – they regarded folk music as so useful to their nationalist cause that all three became vice-presidents of the Folk-Song Society when it was founded in 1898.

The notion of an oral folk-song tradition in England had taken root during the nineteenth century. Thomas Hardy, writing down such snatches of old ballads as he could glean from aged singers, was one of many amateur collectors of songs from the countryside (songs from the cities would remain overlooked for several decades longer). But the first English folk-song collector in the modern sense of the term was John Broadwood, grandson of the founder of the piano-making firm, who published a book of sixteen songs in 1847 entitled *Old English Songs as now Sung by the Peasantry of the Weald of Surrey and Sussex*. According to his niece Lucy Broadwood, who was a pioneering collector and founder of the Folk-Song Society, John Broadwood 'had an extremely accurate musical ear … and was before his time in sympathising with the dialect, music, and customs of country-folk. Family tradition describes the polite boredom with which his traditional songs, sung exactly as the smocked labourers sang, were received by his friends and relations.' When his arranger for publication objected 'to the way the tunes appeared to be … Mr Broadwood, confirming his vocal intervals by vehement blasts on his flute, replied, "*Musically* it may be wrong, but I *will* have it exactly as my singers sang it."'

Lucy herself was an accomplished pianist and singer whose collecting was done under carefully controlled conditions, sometimes by post. Her approach was rigorously academic, but she made some notable discoveries in Sussex villages, and *English County Songs*, which she co-published with the *Times* critic J. Fuller Maitland in 1893, played a major part in putting folk song on the map. As editor-to-be of the Folk-Song Society's journal she established a network of collectors, the most influential of whom – until Cecil Sharp came along – was Sabine Baring-Gould, with whom she went on collecting expeditions in Cornwall.

Born in 1834, Baring-Gould came from a land-owning family and doubled as a magistrate and Anglican rector, but he was not typical of his breed. He was a historian and amateur archaeologist, as well as a prolific novelist and hymn-writer, 'Onward, Christian Soldiers' being his best-known product. He was also an eccentric rebel with a genuine care for his impoverished parishioners; before inheriting his family estate, he worked among the poor in Pimlico. He'd been interested in folklore from an early age, but it took a chance dinner-table conversation when he was in his fifties to spark his quest for Devonshire folk songs. He told his fellow-diners

> how, when I was a boy, I had ridden round Dartmoor and had put up at little taverns. In them I had seen men sitting and smoking, and had heard them sing ballads … My host said to me, 'Come, you are the man to undertake the job of collecting these songs and airs. It must be done at once, or it cannot be done at all, for in a few years they will be lost.'

Thus began, in 1888, a productive voyage of discovery. Lacking the ability to notate tunes on the hoof, he enlisted two musical friends to help. He started with farmers, but all they knew was popular published stuff: 'I speedily discovered that what I wanted was to be obtained mainly from such men as could neither read nor write.' Most of the 'song men' from whom he collected were old; many were sick or maimed from their work. 'Your honour,' one said sadly, 'I haven't sung these thirty years. Volks now don't care to hear my songs. Most of em have gone right out of my head.' Baring-Gould recalled his last meeting with his most fecund source, a crippled stone-breaker named Robert Hard, whom he had enticed into his vicarage drawing-room on a cold winter night: 'I had in old Hard. Then and there I obtained from him a further crop of ballads. That was the last reaping, for in the ensuing bitter frost the aged man was found dead, frozen on a heap of stones by the roadside.'

Things didn't always go to plan. Returning a second time to a locally celebrated singer who was dying, Baring-Gould was stopped at the door by his wife: 'What do you mean coming here and getting my husband to zing his old drashy songs, when he ought to be preparing to meet his saviour? No, you shan't zee him. He's in bed and shall remain there. I've took away his trousers and burnt em, so he must remain abed till he dies. I don't want nother you, nor nothing of yours here.' Baring-Gould's singers could also pose practical problems:

> She sings ancient ballads, walking about and pursuing her usual avocations whilst singing. She cannot be induced to sit down and sing – then her memory fails, but she will sing whilst engaged in kneading bread, washing, driving the geese out of the room, feeding the pig: naturally, this makes it a matter of difficulty to note her melodies. One has to run after her, from the kitchen to the pig-sty, or to the well-head and back, pencil and notebook in hand.

Baring-Gould's sympathetic curiosity about the lives of his sources was not allowed to impede his quest. Another of his stars was James Parsons, a hedger and thatcher nicknamed the Singing Machine on account of his ability to sing without repeating himself from sunset till dawn. 'After having pretty well exhausted his store of songs,' Baring-Gould reminisced,

> I learned that he had met with an accident. In making 'spears' for thatching, he had cut with the chopper into his kneecap, and the oil had run out. The local doctor told me that he feared he would hardly be able to pull the man through, so I said to Mr Bussell [his amanuensis], 'Come along with me, and we will see old Parsons in his bed, and will try to extract some more songs from him. It will never do to let him carry his treasure into the churchyard.'

What sort of 'treasure' was that? Baring-Gould applied serious scholarship to the songs he collected, tracing some of them back centuries to their putative origin, and registering those which were embroideries on broadside ballads. Researching in the British Museum, he sometimes encountered the composer Arthur Sullivan who was also researching ballads, but he noted with competitive satisfaction that Sullivan's research went no further back than the eighteenth century, while his took him back to the Stuarts.

As a historian, he felt it his duty to present the Plymouth City Library with manuscripts of his collection, including the original texts, alternative versions, and melodies. As a born populariser, however, he also wanted to spread the word, hence his publication in 1889 of *Songs of the West*, followed by *A Garland of Country Song* in 1895, sales of which collections he boosted with his own travelling song-group. But for this to happen, many songs had first to be cleaned up: sexually explicit lyrics had to be 'chastened' (his word), and verses which would have offended Victorian notions of propriety had to be replaced by inoffensive ones. He was entirely unapologetic about this, invoking the precedent of similar cleanings-up by Robert Burns of his Scottish songs, and by Walter Scott of the Border Ballads. 'The task had – and has – to be undertaken so as to rescue exquisite melodies from being killed by the words to which they are wedded,' he wrote. 'It is necessary for the editor to modify words, expressions, even statements of events recorded, so as to make the ballads and songs tolerable to men and women of culture.' That word 'culture' indicated the unbridgeable gulf between the world of the unlettered poor and that of the emerging bourgeoisie. But it was typical of the time that in male company Baring-Gould could thoroughly enjoy a ribald lyric: he was highly amused to see the embarrassment of a 'modest-minded' clergyman who had offered to write down a song man's offering. The ballad told of a girl's lust for a 'gay cavalier', and of her cross-dressing to get near him, and its denouement was 'what might have been anticipated'. The manuscript, noted Baring-Gould, 'was begun in a firm hand, but after a few verses the writing became shaky, and the final stanzas were quite illegible'. No lady could have been allowed to hear that. Baring-Gould's policy of systematic bowdlerisation was endorsed when, in 1906, he co-edited *English Folk-Songs for Schools* with Cecil Sharp – but here we must go back a pace, because from the moment Sharp joined the folk-song movement at the turn of the century until his death in 1924, he was its dominant force.

* * *

Born in 1859, Sharp was originally destined for a life in commerce, but his passion was music; he trained himself to play the piano and organ, and was a born conductor. On graduating in mathematics from Cambridge he went to Australia where he composed and became a small-time music impresario; a paralysing attack of typhoid brought him back to London, where he took the job of music teacher in the prep school for Eton, and was for nine years principal of the Hampstead Conservatoire. Declaring himself a Christian socialist, quoting Wagner's patriarchal views on love in a letter to his bride-to-be, and naming his first daughter Iseult and his son Tristan, he nailed his ideological and musical colours to the mast.

His discovery of his métier was romantic, as recounted by his biographers – A. H. Fox Strangways, another music critic of the *Times* (and a pioneering collector of North Indian music), and Maud Karpeles, who was first Sharp's amanuensis, then his collaborator, and finally the torch-bearer for his posthumous crusade. Looking out of the window on Boxing Day 1899 while staying in the Oxfordshire village of Headington, he saw a procession appear on the snow-covered drive: eight men dressed in white, decorated with ribbons and with bells strapped to their shins, and carrying coloured sticks and handkerchiefs; accompanying them was a concertina player and a man dressed as a Fool. The men formed into two lines, and when the concertina struck up they began jumping high in the air and waving the handkerchiefs while the bells marked the rhythm: this was the Morris dance 'Laudnum Bunches'. Each taking a stick, they then enacted the ritual of 'Bean Setting', followed by three other dances. Sharp was spellbound, and quizzed them at length; they apologised for being out at Christmas – Whitsun was the proper time – but work was slack and they saw no harm in earning an honest penny. With help from the concertina player, William Kimber, Sharp noted down all five tunes.

He claimed ever after that this incident was both the start of his career and the beginning of the English folk-music revival – he had no false modesty about his own importance. He was now turned on to rural music, but initially he sought it in printed collections, from which he compiled *A Book of British Song for Home and School*. Realising the difference between songs in their edited, published form, and songs caught on the wing, he then resolved to pursue the latter, initially with the help of his friend Charles Marson, vicar of the village of Hambridge in Somerset. Sitting in the vicarage garden he found himself watching a man mowing the lawn and singing quietly to himself. Sharp whipped out his notebook, and asked the mower – appropriately named John England – for the words: 'I sowed the seeds of love, And I sowed them in the morning ...' At a choral supper that evening, Sharp accompanied that song in his own setting for soprano and piano, one member of the audience declaring that it was the first time the song 'had been put into evening dress'. Over the following days, Sharp and Marson (who noted the words) collected a hundred more songs in Hambridge and neighbouring villages. This part of Somerset was fruitful terrain, since shirt-making and glove-sewing were the local cottage industries, and workers used to gather in one room to brighten their labour with song.

Some of Sharp's singers were shy, others could hardly remember the songs of their youth: 'Forty years agone,' said one, 'I'd a-zung un out o' sight.' 'When you come to me all at once, I can't come at it,' said another, asking for time to 'bide and stud'. Others were well aware of the treasure they carried in their heads. 'One old woman once sang to me out in the open fields where she was [gathering stones], and between the verses of her song ['The lark in the morn'] she seized the lapel of my coat, and looked up into my face with glistening eyes to say "Isn't it lovely!"'

Two sisters who between them gave him a hundred songs would have given him three times that number if he'd also included composed songs. One singer wrote to him: 'I sometimes get an old line or refrain come into my head, and I think that's one of Granny's old songs, I wonder if Mr Sharp has that; but it goes so quickly, and I have no one now to jot it down, I forget the dear old ditties.' Sharp's success as a collector owed much to the friendship he established with his singers, to whom he would give instruments and presents – tobacco for the men, blouses for the women – as well as money. All this was financed from his earnings as a teacher (better-paid work as a lecturer only came later); he did all his travelling by bike. Sitting on an upturned tub in a wash-house, and noting down a song by a woman at the copper, he was disconcerted when another woman asked: 'You be going to make a deal o' money out of this, sir?' He was relieved when the singer came to his defence, saying 'Oh, it's only his hobby', whereupon the other woman commented, 'Ah well, we do all 'ave our vailins.'

Mistrusting the phonograph, which he thought made singers too self-conscious, he took down melodies in staff notation, and waited patiently for gems to surface. His singers would first give him the songs they thought he would most like, but these would usually not be folk songs; he got to the latter by asking for 'songs that have no music to them'. He had to be tenacious in his pursuit of Gypsy songs, but he was often successful, on one occasion deflecting threatened violence from a jealous husband with the words: 'A happy Christmas to you. Stop a moment and listen. I've got your wife's voice in a box.' Jealousy was instantly dissolved in wonderment, Sharp reported triumphantly. He once took down two songs from a 'bird-starver' whose job was to hammer a tea-tray to scare birds from a patch of mangold seeds: 'He was quite prepared to sing, but his conscience would not allow him to neglect his duty. So we arranged that he should hammer his tray between each verse of his songs, and thus combine business with pleasure.'

* * *

In the preface to the first volume of *Folk-Songs from Somerset* in 1904, Sharp and his co-editor Charles Marson stressed that their collection was 'presented as nearly as possible as it was taken down from the lips of the singers; in the tunes with exact fidelity. Anything like a peculiar use, archaisms, and rare words, we have carefully kept.' On the other hand Sharp was, like Baring-Gould, always ready to bowdlerise a text if its bucolic forthrightness offended Edwardian sexual propriety (the sex in 'The foggy, foggy dew', for example, had to be chastely sublimated). This was because although his primary purpose was discovery, his ancillary one was to embellish his discoveries for further use (and he did at least preserve his original notebooks for specialist study).

One of his collaborators, the Reverend Francis Etherington, left an admiring portrait of the master at work in the evening after his labours in the field: 'From his pencilled notes he played the tune over slowly and very softly, then there was a swift sort of disentangling and a bold un-harmonised statement emerged. Then came the accompaniment. It was like watching an Indian craftsman doing that delicate beating of filigree silver work ... the setting of a jewel.' As he played, Sharp would smile. 'That was the man at his most complete: the reverent artist, finding fulfilment in putting a beautiful thing in its right setting, so that it would catch the light and give reflections of its own fires.' As Sharp explained: 'I get right inside these beautiful melodies when I try to translate them into harmony, and the further you dive into them, the more seductive and glorious they appear.' Ralph Vaughan Williams, who collected songs in East Anglia, much admired the sensitivity of Sharp's settings.

Since almost all English folk song was conceived as a melodic entity not needing harmonic support, Sharp may seem to contemporary ethnomusicologists to have been taking shocking liberties, but until his emergence most song collectors had no agreed communal purpose, beyond quietly publishing their finds in the *Journal of the Folk-Song Society*. Karpeles writes with disdain of the 'antiquarians' who wanted to preserve their precious songs from vulgarisation. Cecil Sharp was in the populist camp: his aim was to revive folk song, and bring it back into everyday life. He began giving lectures, playing the piano for sung illustrations; he appealed (unsuccessfully) for public funds to assist collectors, and suggested that their researches should be systematised, though as Karpeles points out, this latter proposal was unnecessary because British collectors took scrupulous care not to trespass on each other's territory. On the question of copyright, Sharp's view was clear: 'The law protects the product of the man's brain, not the thing on which he exercises his wits ... A collector who takes down a song from a folk-singer has an exclusive right to his *copy* of that song... It is always open to someone else to go... to the same source, exercise the same skill and so obtain a right to *his* copy.'

And for Sharp the campaign had to start in school. When the government published a blue-book on the teaching of singing – complete with a list of approved 'national or folk songs' – he saw his chance to open a public argument with himself centre-stage (which was where he always liked to be), and he launched into print in the influential *Morning Post*. 'The precept of the Board of Education ... was admirable, its practice was deplorable,' he wrote, pointing out that there were hardly any genuine folk songs on the list; he followed this up with a withering blast in the *Daily Chronicle*.

The Irish composer Charles Villiers Stanford, who as professor of composition at the Royal College of Music was a leading member of the musical establishment, defended the book. 'Archaeologists who have personally dug up an antique are apt to glorify it at the expense of those which have been dug up by their predecessors,' he sneered. 'If [Sharp] will stick to his excavating, we may be the richer for some antiques, but he need not, in order to exhibit them, relegate the Elgin marbles to the hayloft.' Sharp's riposte was no less firm. He agreed that the sailor's song 'Tom Bowling' – composed by the prolific Charles Dibdin and one of the titles on the list – had become a 'people's song', 'but I deny that it is a song made by the people, as well as sung by them ... The one [genre] is individual, the other communal and racial' (in 1906 'racial' did not carry the overtones it would acquire twenty years later). Pursuing the correspondence, and thus aligning himself with Kodály, Bartók, and other song collectors across Europe, Sharp went on to argue that the country's neglect of its folk music was one reason why it had 'no national school of music'. The way folk song was beginning to permeate the compositions of Vaughan Williams, George Butterworth, and Gustav Holst – who based his *Somerset Rhapsody* on tunes collected by Sharp – reflected the relevance of this assertion.

The following year Sharp published *English Folk-Song: Some Conclusions*, written in a fizz of zeal while he suffered from intermittent blindness: 'I felt the book *must* be written, and I went straight home from the meeting of the Folk-Song Society and wore out three fountain pens.' His chapter on tonality was a manifesto:

> If [the modern musician] were to go down to the country, seek out the old peasant singers, and hear modal tunes sung by those to whom the modes are the natural scales, he would understand what is meant by the specific musical qualities of the various modes. He would get rid, once and for all, of the idea that modal music has no message for the modern ear; that the modes are merely archaic survivals, of no present value whatever, except for manufacturing what are commonly known as Wardour Street effects. He would, on the contrary, derive from the modal folk-tune a definite musical impression, fundamentally different from any that he had hitherto experienced. He would, assuredly, yield to its fascination and realise that the modes really offered a new channel of musical expression, and an escape from the present restricted tonality. There is a world of difference between a dead language and a living one.

Sharp's theory of folk song was Darwinian, with its evolution obeying three principles: persistence, variation, and selection. As Fox Strangways put it:

> The folk-singer's well-known and remarkable memory makes for persistence, his fancy for variation, and the community selects ... The process may

be compared to the behaviour of a flight of starlings. The flock 'persists' in its unanimous course, individuals dart out from that and 'vary' it, and the flock 'selects' which, if any, individual it will follow. The flock of starlings is looking for a suitable place to roost in; the singing community is looking for a song which shall satisfy its understanding and its sense of beauty.

The critical response was mixed. While the *Guardian* welcomed it as 'a bombshell amongst musicians', the *Times Literary Supplement* was patronising: 'As a collector Mr Sharp deserves both praise and support, but he might well leave to others the work of analysing the treasures he has found.' It was significant that Sharp's name did not appear in the folk-song section of the 1910 edition of *Grove's Dictionary of Music and Musicians*; his entry in the current edition is still minimal.

Meanwhile, from its germination in Headington, Sharp turned the Morris-dance side of his activities into the foundation for a national folk-dance revival, in which the original concertina player William Kimber – 'a bricklayer by trade but a dancer by profession' as one admirer put it – played a key role; a network of clubs was set up, the music was published, and official blessing came from the Board of Education. Sharp also collected sword dances from Sheffield miners, and drew on manuscripts in the British Museum to revive the country dances which John Playford had collected in the seventeenth century. And just as Sharp had polarised the musical world, so did he the world of dance. Some accused him of pedantry, with controversy raging over 'fake' and 'corrupt' dances, and over the precise nature of the 'Morris step'. But the English Folk Dance Society, of which he became director, was another fruit of his labours. It came as a terrible blow to Sharp when four of his closest colleagues in the dance revival – including the composer George Butterworth – were killed on the Somme in 1916; these talented and idealistic young men were the people on whom he had been relying to carry the torch when he was gone.

Sharp may have switched his focus to dance, but he continued his song collecting, notably with a singer of sea shanties named John Short in Watchet on the Bristol Channel. After fifty years at sea, Short held the office of town crier; Sharp fell in love with his voice which, though resonant and powerful, was 'yet so flexible that he can execute trills, turns, and graces with a delicacy and finish that would excite the envy of many a professional artist'. Since Short needed to be by the sea to get properly inspired, the pair, said Karpeles, 'would sit side by side on the quay, and John Short would sing happily through the noise of wind and waves, while Cecil Sharp smoked his pipe and jotted down the tunes'.

* * *

13 Sharp with Winster Morris Dancers in Derbyshire in 1908.

What Sharp described as the coping-stone to his English research was put in place when he and Karpeles made three trips to the Appalachian Mountains in 1916–18. On arduous and hazardous forays to remote villages – with Sharp in frail health – they gathered five hundred songs and ballads from 281 singers, with Sharp's personal charm (plus presents) conquering both reluctant performers and the commonly held suspicion that they were German spies. In this region, at this time, folk music was almost the only music people knew, so Sharp and Karpeles didn't have to dig to find gold. But since song was intertwined with everyday life, rather than being matter for performance, they sometimes had to wait. 'There now,' said a woman who had temporarily forgotten a song, 'if only I were driving the cows home, I should remember it at once.' When interest flagged, Sharp and Karpeles would trade English songs for Appalachian ones. 'The singers are just English peasants in appearance, speech, and manner,' Sharp said of the inhabitants at White Rock, and practically all their songs could be traced to English or Lowland Scottish sources. He regarded the Presbyterian missionaries' efforts to educate the Appalachians as musically harmful: 'I don't think any of them realise that the people they are here to improve are in many respects far more cultivated than their

14 Cecil Sharp in the Appalachian Mountains, where this photo of him was taken at work with his assistant Maud Karpeles.

would-be instructors, even if they cannot read or write … The hymns that these missionaries teach them are musical and literary garbage.'

Three decades later Maud Karpeles retraced their steps alone to Appalachia, but found that the region was 'no longer the folk-song collector's paradise, for the serpent, in the form of the radio, has crept in'. But she did find forty of their original singers – or at least their children – and had the pleasure of presenting some with the book in which their songs had been published. And as she pointed out, the story was indeed a romantic one: 'They originate in England; are carried to America where they live for a couple of hundred years by oral tradition; they are then written down by Cecil Sharp who brings them back to England; some thirty years later they are carried back in printed form to America, the country of their adoption, where they again take on a new lease of life.'

Sharp spent his last years supervising the rapid growth of the English Folk Dance Society, and the integration of that dance into the school curriculum; he was still collecting and lecturing in his final weeks. He may have been egotistic and arrogant, but even his opponents were agreed on his generosity of spirit. What he achieved in the space of twenty-one years was extraordinary – collecting five thousand songs (winnowed down to five hundred for publication) was only a part of it – and he came just in time to catch songs whose oral transmission had virtually ceased. He had huge blind spots, totally ignoring the broadside tradition, and blanking out all songs from the industrialised cities; he was also unaware that many of the songs he collected had been written by professionals. And his image of 'the peasant' was patronising in the extreme. 'The peasant is the sole survivor of a homogeneous society with few class distinctions,' he declared in a lecture. 'He is gentle, unobtrusive, unassertive.'

'Thirty or forty years ago,' he wrote in 1907, 'every country village in England was a nest of singing birds.' A slight exaggeration, no doubt, but his magic touch did induce some people to live up to that image. And as he described it, his self-appointed mission drew strength from its persuasive simplicity: to give back the songs and dances – which he regarded as different emanations of the same spirit – to the people whose heritage they were.

* * *

Cecil Sharp cast a long shadow. A few voices were raised against the consensus he had imposed – Lucy Broadwood vigorously challenged his paternalist idealisation of the 'peasant' community – but by and large it held sway until the advent of the new British folk-song revival in the Sixties. This was powered by the arrival of jazz and blues from America (and their torch-bearer Alan

Lomax), by the awakening of folk culture in England's industrial north, and by a Marxist revision of the first revival's rural romanticism.

The revisionists were led by the historian Dave Harker with an incendiary article in the *Folk Music Journal* in 1972, which he amplified twelve years later in his book *Fakesong: The Manufacture of British 'Folksong', 1700 to the Present Day*. Harker's specialism was printed broadsides, which he regarded as the source of most of what is covered by the words 'English folk song'; he drew on the work of cultural historians like Raymond Williams and E. P. Thompson, and he wrote from a rigid Marxist standpoint. In Harker's view Sharp was – like almost all the other song collectors of his time – 'a product of metropolitan-oriented English bourgeois culture' who knew nothing about the true history of popular music, or about the literary and musical sophistication of its exponents. Harker argued that Sharp's song collecting was arbitrarily selective and geographically skewed, and that he tampered with texts; that he was blinded by his nostalgia for an imaginary rural golden age, and that he took no account of the singing that would have gone on in the 'fairs, merry-makings, markets, weddings, races, and dances in Somerset towns and villages in the middle decades of the nineteenth century' where broadsides were sold, and where words and tunes were 'spread like seed-corn in the countryside'.

There is no denying that these points have considerable validity, but when Harker wound up his catalogue of Sharp's crimes he went over the top:

> No matter what working men and women sang, loved, or treasured, now that the products of their culture had been traded for a mug of cider, a quid of tobacco, a few pounds or some other trinket, they were Sharp's property, to do with as he thought fit. ... What Scott and Burns had done for bourgeois poetry, a hundred years before, Sharp wished to do for bourgeois music.

In other words, to bowdlerise and plunder on bourgeois society's behalf. A graceful riposte to this indictment came from another broadsides specialist, Leslie Shepard: 'If there is some mythology involved in the vanishing rural ethos, at least one cannot deny its beauty, emotional maturity, good manners, and tolerance, to which writers like Marson, Sharp, and others attested.'

For twenty years Harker and his friends imposed a counter-orthodoxy. But then Mike Yates – the editor who had published Harker's original article in the *Folk Music Journal* – decided to retrace Sharp's steps in the Appalachians, to check out his findings. Yates had agreed with some of Harker's strictures on Sharp's English collecting, but he was forced to give Sharp's American research a clean bill of health. More recently, in a neat piece of poetic justice, the historian C. J. Bearman published two papers in 2002 which demolished Harker's methodology *de haut en bas*. Live by the sword, die by the sword.

Folk music's new impetus in the north was fuelled by the singer/impresario A. L. Lloyd's song collection *Come All Ye Bold Miners*; this was the offshoot of a competition he ran as part of the North's contribution to the Festival of Britain in 1951. He invited miners to submit songs about life in the pits, and a longer-term result was a series of LPs from the industrial north, their high point being Lloyd's own compilation *The Iron Muse*, which included an excoriating rendition of the 'Blackleg Miner'. These records came out on the Topic label, which was backed by the Workers' Music Association, which was backed in turn by the Communist Party of Great Britain.

Lloyd was also co-editor with Ralph Vaughan Williams of *The Penguin Book of English Folk Songs*, and in 1967 he published his genially provocative book *Folk Song in England*. This is a wonderful amalgam of passion and global erudition, and it became the folkies' Bible, laying out a credo founded on two assumptions. First, that in the twentieth century the energy of English folk song had migrated from the countryside to the industrial cities. And second, that the new folk revival had emerged from the grass roots, rather than being imposed from above as the first revival had been, with its echoes of literary Romanticism and its middle-class high priests, many of whom did indeed wear dog-collars.

'Though the performance of folk-song lingered on in the countryside, the composition of new stuff had to all intents ceased in the villages by the mid-19th century,' Lloyd wrote in his sleeve note to *The Iron Muse*. 'But among industrial workers the creation of new songs celebrating strikes, pit disasters, workshop incidents etc persisted, and seems lately to have taken on a fresh lease of life.' More songs were generated in the mining, spinning, and weaving industries than in steel and the railways, he observed, 'though surprises may be in store for the searcher. As yet the industrial community is only dimly aware of its own self-made cultural heritage.'

Thanks to a handful of dedicated left-leaning souls led by the song collector Peter Kennedy, BBC radio began to celebrate that cultural heritage. Lloyd, Lomax, and the charismatic folk-singer Ewan MacColl (aka Jimmy Miller) all made programmes, with Charles Parker's 'Radio Ballads' placing the songs of work in the context of the actual sounds of that work. The most celebrated of those programmes were *Song of a Road* in 1959 (about the building of the M1 motorway) and *Singing the Fishing* (made among the herring fleets of East Anglia). Studio narration was replaced by a musical narrative which was recorded on location and sung by MacColl and Peggy Seeger, the American folk-singer whom MacColl later married. Bob Copper was one of many singers who were encouraged to ransack their memories – and those of their friends – for songs which had got lost in the mists of history. In the Seventies, folk clubs proliferated in what amounted to another revival, which chimed happily with the optimistically socialist temper of the times.

Sources

Sabine Baring-Gould's autobiographical books, of which *Further Reminiscences* is the best, vividly evoke his work and his world. For the full sweep of Cecil Sharp's life, the biographies by Fox Strangways and Maud Karpeles should be read in sequence; Harker's *Fakesong* presents the case for the prosecution, and Steve Roud's definitive history *Folk Song in England* puts Sharp's achievement into a balanced perspective. Roud and Bishop's *The New Penguin Book of English Folk Songs* gives copious historical background notes as well as notations. A. L. Lloyd's *Folk Song in England* is a campaigning history which also draws on his work in Australia and the Balkans. Carl Engel's *The Literature of National Music* is a series of essays first published in the *Musical Times*. Michael Brocken's *The British Folk Revival* offers an account of that movement.

Bibliography

Baring-Gould, S., *Further Reminiscences: 1864–1894* (London: John Lane The Bodley Head Ltd, 1925)

Brocken, Michael, *The British Folk Revival* (London: Ashgate, 2003)

Fox Strangways, A. H., *Cecil Sharp* (London: Oxford University Press, 1933)

Engel, Carl, *The Literature of National Music* (London: Novello, 1879)

Harker, Dave, *Fakesong: The Manufacture of British 'Folksong', 1700 to the Present Day* (Milton Keynes: Open University Press, 1985)

Lloyd, A. L., *Folk Song in England* (London: Paladin, 1967)

Roud, Steve, *Folk Song in England* (London: Faber, 2017)

Roud, Steve and Julia Bishop, *The New Penguin Book of English Folk Songs* (London: Penguin, 2012)

15 Percy Grainger (1882–1961): 'I live for my lusts & I don't care if they kill me or others'.

8

'I in seventh heaven – Perks'

The ineffable Percy Grainger

PERCY GRAINGER MAY have been one of the first song collectors to make live recordings, but that wasn't the reason for his worldwide fame, nor is it the principal reason why he is remembered today. His virtuoso pianism, admired by Ferruccio Busoni and Leopold Stokowski, made him a celebrity on both sides of the Atlantic; his wild onstage behaviour – vaulting over the piano, running round the auditorium during the orchestral sections of a concerto – simply added to his allure. Meanwhile the scintillating arrangements of folk song which he 'dished up' (his phrase) for solo piano, or for any ensemble to hand, would have made him rich, had he not given so much money to charity and needy friends; his arrangement of 'Country Gardens', which he and Cecil Sharp collected in 1908, became a show-stopper which is still often played as an encore.

Despite the exuberant colour of his orchestral works, he wasn't a major composer. But he was a major musical revolutionary, born out of his time: his belief in music as a democratic force transcending nationality and culture, and his championing of a 'free music' which could burst asunder restraining conventions, would have earned him an honoured place among the avant-garde today. But his sexual proclivities, combined with his startlingly un-PC views about race, won him notoriety. The straitlaced view among ethnomusicologists is that those proclivities had a disastrous effect on his work. But it could equally well be argued that they helped fuel his eccentric and original artistic crusade.

Born in Melbourne in 1882, he had an upbringing which marked him – literally – for life. His sweet-natured and cultivated father was given to drunken philandering. This led to the syphilis which he passed on to his wife Rose, who vainly tried to keep him in order with a horsewhip. As a result the bond between the mother and her only child became pathologically close – 'us two against the World', as Grainger put it. This was the big love affair of his life, and it lasted until he was thirty-nine, when a deranged Rose jumped out of a window of the Aeolian building in New York.

But Percy's infant transgressions had also been rewarded with the whip, and that treatment, which continued into his teens, seemed to him both just and appropriate; one might almost say he felt comfortable with it. Thus was set a pattern from which he never deviated, and which fed into his inbred psychological tendencies. He had devoured Dickens and the Icelandic sagas as a young child, savouring their evocations of violence which caused him, he wrote excitedly, to 'shake with delight'. Each person, he added, 'must have some subject that fires him to madness', and extreme physical violence was his subject. He had admired from an early age the blond and blue-eyed Nordic image of masculinity. And onto that image he projected flesh-mortifying fantasies which, as a student in Frankfurt, he did his best to emulate in real life: carrying huge loads on route-marches, dicing with death by climbing high buildings, stripping naked and standing like a statue in the snow.

In his case sex meant flagellation, both given and received, which for him was the purest expression of love. He eagerly photographed weals, and was a connoisseur of whips; his female partners in this game – some chosen by his mother – seem to have put up with it cheerfully, as a price worth paying for his charismatic company: he was effeminately pretty, and tough as nails. For his second wife, a Swedish society beauty, bloody flagellation was just one facet of a relationship in which she loyally supported his musical and social endeavours for three decades.

In a letter in 1930 to the English composer Roger Quilter, he declared: 'I live for my lusts & I don't care if they kill me or others ... I feel that a hot parched wind from the Australian desert has entered my soul & with a fury of heat I must go thru ... no sadist can call life poor or disappointing who can realise his cruellest, wildest dreams ... I would not exchange with the angels.' And this jaunty defiance transferred itself to his music: 'A man cannot be a full artist unless he is manly, & a man cannot be manly unless his sex life is selfish, brutal, wilful, unbridled.' In an essay entitled 'Notes on Whip-Lust', written in his sixties, he made the same connection more explicitly. After describing one of his teenage fantasies – of a woman's body suspended by fish-hooks inserted into her breasts – he goes on to argue that such fantasies are just part of that 'life-wildness' which leads young men to do foolhardy things, nations to go to war, crowds to lynch, and he likens the resultant 'stir' of excitement to the one 'that crams a whole rebirth into a crowded all-within-a-fifth-y chord in Tchaikovsky' – quoting a phrase from the 'Pathétique' Symphony. Yet he was at the same time a vegetarian and a pacifist.

He adduced Kipling's poetry as a prime influence on his becoming 'a composer whose musical output is based on patriotism and racial consciousness'. But his aesthetic inclinations, as well as his blue-eyed obsession (he compiled a 'blue-eyed dictionary' full of his cumbersome Anglo-Saxon coinages), drove him to champion the music of his friends Grieg and Delius against what he saw as the tyranny of the tradition represented by Haydn, Mozart, and Beethoven. The music of the latter was architecture in sound: he wanted music which flowed like a stream, and he developed a doctrine for this which he dubbed Free Music. As he proclaimed in a series of lectures broadcast from Melbourne in 1934: 'Free Music (towards which all musical progress clearly points) will be the full musical expression of the scientific nature-worship; begun by the Greeks and carried forward by the Nordic races. It will be the musical counterpart of Nordic pioneering, athleticism, and nudism.' If that has a queasily pre-Nazi ring, other declarations from those lectures paint a more seductive picture of this idealised form of music: regular rhythms were 'slave-driving, soul-stultifying', while 'subtle, irregular, unrepetitious rhythms hold fine influences toward freedom and rapture ... We can imagine the music of the future consisting of free and unpredetermined melodic lines of sound – swooping through tonal space in gradual curves as a bird sails through the air, untrammelled by those arbitrary divisions of tone called scales.' The theremin was his preferred instrument for this music, which he conceived as a parallel exercise to Schoenberg's harmonic emancipation, and which he believed could be better realised with the aid of machines than with human performers.

* * *

So what is Percy Grainger doing in this book? The answer is that the best of him lay in his visionary musical globalism: in his appreciation of the musics from India, Indonesia, and Madagascar which he devotedly transcribed and arranged, and in his drive to undermine the then-widespread assumption that musical progress in both Western and 'primitive' cultures necessarily implied a movement from simplicity to complexity. And in song collecting, which he described as 'the deepest duty I know', he broke new ground.

As a child he had been fascinated by the music of the Chinese people who had settled in Melbourne after the Australian gold rush, and after establishing himself in London in 1901 to set up shop as a society pianist, he came into the orbit of Lucy Broadwood, editor of the *Journal of the Folk-Song Society*. The world's loveliest melodies, he asserted, 'are found in folk-song, or in music (like the Javanese) that lies mid-way between folk-music and art-music'. These melodies were in almost all cases unaccompanied, he added, with the singer 'able to concentrate all his creative powers upon expression in a single line'.

He had already collected songs in Scotland, but his first serious involvement came when he proposed a special competition at the annual folk-song festival at Brigg in north Lincolnshire. A prize of ten shillings and sixpence would go to whoever could 'supply the best unpublished old Lincolnshire folk song or plough song ... to be sung or whistled by the competitor, but marks will be allotted for the excellence rather of the song than of its actual performance'. Old people were particularly encouraged to bring 'the best old song they know'. The winner, with a song called 'Creeping Jane', was a 72-year-old farm bailiff called Joseph Taylor whose effortless high notes and complicated 'twiddles' and 'bleatings' greatly impressed Grainger. The runner-up was an 85-year-old whose song, 'Come all you merry ploughboys', seemed interminable, and whose deafness prevented his hearing the chairman's pleas to stop.

Returning to Lincolnshire for a 'folk fishing cruise' on his 'byke', Grainger collected more songs from farm-workers – he simply got them to put down their tools and sing – and he collected more from Taylor, including the graceful 'Brigg Fair' which became one of his most celebrated discoveries. (Delius was entranced by Grainger's choral arrangement of it, and made it the basis for some orchestral variations.) One singer was so keen to ensure that Grainger got all his words that he wrote them on a wall and tore off a seven-foot strip of wallpaper for him to take home. He had to resort to trickery to extract rare songs from a reluctant old lady, getting her granddaughter to smuggle him into her front room and hide him under the bed with his pencil and manuscript paper, while she coaxed the old lady to sing.

The Brigg workhouse was his most fruitful source of songs, and it was there that he made his first attempt to collect the sailor's song 'Lisbon Bay' which Cecil Sharp had collected a year earlier in Somerset. But Grainger's exponent of it – Mr Deene of Hibaldstow, who had a weak heart – broke down in tears in the second verse, so affected was he by the memories it called up, and the matron wouldn't let him finish. On a return visit the following year, and now armed with an Edison Bell wax cylinder phonograph, Grainger got an initially reluctant Deene – who had fallen and gashed his head – to deliver the entire song, justifying it on the grounds that 'I thought he might as well die singing it, as die without singing it'.

'Heartoutbursts', which was Grainger's blue-eyed dictionary term for such songs, seemed particularly appropriate, and he was very sensitive to the circumstances of his singers. When, twenty years later, he published his wind-band collection *Lincolnshire Posy* he dedicated it 'to the singers who sang so sweetly to me', adding that he had penned his preface in rancour 'at the memories of the cruel treatment meted out to folksingers as human beings (most of them died in poor-houses or in other downheartening surroundings) and at the thought of how their high gifts oftenest were allowed to perish unheard, unrecorded, and unhonoured'. In 1907–9 Grainger collected songs in Gloucestershire, where the painter John Singer Sargent and the writer H.

G. Wells accompanied him – he was socially well-connected – on trips to workhouses to 'dredge' for material. Noting that Grainger also jotted down the banter and mannerisms of his singers, Wells remarked: 'You are trying to do a more difficult thing than record folk-song – you are trying to record life.' Grainger also noted down the street-cries of milk and muffin vendors in London, and in Dartmouth sea shanties. His telegram to Rose, after collecting some songs from a 'deep-sea sailor' called John Perring, was ecstatic: 'Found Genius Sea Chanty singing man – I in Seventh Heaven. Perks.'

Grainger was the first folk-song collector in Britain to make live recordings with the Standard Edison-Bell Phonograph. And the new technology allowed him to transcribe ornamentation with greatly increased fidelity by playing the songs at reduced speed, and by prefacing each recording with a note on a pitch-pipe. His star Joseph Taylor, whose singing he persuaded the Gramophone Company to record and release on disc, likened the process to 'singing with a muzzle on', but singers in Gloucestershire were impressed. On hearing a playback, one remarked 'he's learned quicker nor I', while another commented 'it do follow up we wonderful'. Grainger wrote to Sharp that he wanted the tunes he collected to be presented to the public 'in as *merely scientific* a form as possible, for the time being. I don't wish to come forward as an arranger yet awhile'. And he stayed true to this aim for the rest of his life, as the Grainger Museum which he established in Melbourne demonstrates. This was designed as both a warts-and-all mausoleum – he wanted his skeleton to be on display, a wish not granted – and also as a monument to his musicological scrupulousness, viz. his tireless pursuit of every nuance in every recording, and every detail about his singers which might be relevant.

That scrupulousness led to a parting of the ways for him and the English folk-song community. In 1908 Grainger published a selection of his folk songs in the *Journal of the Folk-Song Society*, and he prefaced it with an essay on 'collecting with the phonograph' which reads both as a list of technical dos and don'ts, and as an aesthetic manifesto which still has resonance today. It was a crime, he suggested, to collect a narrative song consisting of several verses, and to distil from them a tune which was expected to hold good throughout the song.

> As a composer will differently harmonise and score repetitions of the same theme to satisfy his craving for contrast and variety, so will the same instincts … lead the creatively-gifted folk singer or chantyman to evolve more or less profuse melodic, rhythmic, and dynamic variants out of his 'normal tune' to meet the emotional needs of different verses, and match their changing word-rhythms … It is into these small details that he puts the intimate flavour of his personality.

83

Commenting on this essay, Cecil Sharp began by congratulating Grainger, but went on to express serious reservations about reliance on the phonograph. 'In transcribing a song,' he wrote,

> our aim should be to record its artistic effect, not necessarily the exact means by which that effect was produced ... it is not an exact, scientifically accurate memorandum which is wanted, so much as a faithful artistic record of what is actually heard by the ordinary auditor ... No doubt it is much easier to note down the 'great or slight rhythmical irregularities ever present in traditional solo-singing' from a phonograph than from a singer. The question is, is it worth doing at all?

What Sharp and his colleagues were after was the Ur-version of any song, shorn of variations and 'inconsistencies' in its performance. In the face of what must have seemed like lordly amateurism, Grainger began to look for kindred spirits further afield.

* * *

During a concert tour to the Antipodes in 1909, Grainger peeled off to investigate the music of the Maoris on New Zealand's North Island, and, meeting a collector named A. J. Knocks who'd gone native in Otaki, he struck gold. Knocks insisted that he listen to his Rarotongan recordings from the South Sea Islands, 'and I straightway noted them down in his cobwebby, dirty, manuscriptbelittled, brokenwindowed, queersmelling house ...' The songs' improvised polyphony, he wrote, 'had tons of rhythmic delights. Sometimes their spirit is very sweet, rocking & kittenish, & at times fierce & rending like tiger claws.' He likened its 'subtle complex texture' to that which he found in the music of William Lawes and J. S. Bach. On this trip he also recorded Maori songs, 'not sung in harmony ever as far as I can make out, but queer interesting intervals they use, & they sing and recite like heroes; such wantonness, laziness, energy, unselfbeknownst attack, & strong coaxing throbbing voices'.

The other region which Grainger repeatedly visited was the Danish peninsula of Jutland, where Faroe-island folk music was still to be heard. His local informant was the Danish folklorist Evald Tang Kristensen, who had been collecting songs since the 1860s and whose work Grainger revered: he too had fallen foul of a folklorist community which contemptuously regarded his fidelity to nuance as eccentricity. Tang Kristensen, who founded the Danish Folklore Society and amassed a huge collection of artefacts as well as songs, encouraged Grainger to master local Jutland dialects, and although their first projected collecting trip was prevented by the outbreak of war in 1914, they reconvened in the Twenties, gathering and analysing eighty songs, many of

Lindebo - Herning d. 26/8 1922.

16 Grainger recording in Jutland with the Danish folklorist Evald Tang Kristensen.

which proved little-changed since the Danish researcher had collected them fifty years before.

It was the British folk-song collector A. L. Lloyd who most accurately pinpointed the importance of Grainger's research:

> To vary the psychological climate [the folk singer] would not as a rule put drama and pathos into his voice ... more likely he would convey the mood of the song by a small alteration of pace, a slight change of vocal timbre, an almost imperceptible pressing or lightening of rhythm, and by nuances of ornament that our folklorists, with the exception of Percy Grainger, have consistently neglected in their transcriptions; more's the pity.

In an influential essay in 1915 entitled *The Impress of Personality in Unwritten Music*, Grainger penned some prophetic words:

> We see on all hands the victorious on-march of our ruthless Western civilization (so destructively intolerant in its colonial phase) and the distressing spectacle of the gentle but complex native arts wilting before its irresistible simplicity ... Soon, or comparatively soon, folk-music on Southern plantations, or in Scandinavia, Great Britain, Russia and Spain, will be as dead as it already is in Holland and Germany. Against that day – which, however, we may confidently expect to find compensatingly more gloriously rich in

art-music than any previous age – let us make noble efforts to preserve, for the affectionate gaze of future eclectics, above all adequate printed records of what still now remains of a phase of music which, in the nature of things, can never be reborn again, and which comes down to us so fragrant with the sweet impress of the personality of many millions of unknown departed artists, men and women.

Sources

John Bird's masterly biography remains the best account of both the life and the work of Grainger, while the Gillies *Self-Portrait* adds much fascinating information, as does Thwaites's *Companion*. Grainger was a prolific writer, and his manifesto in the *Musical Quarterly* is a key document.

Bibliography

Bird, John, *Percy Grainger* (London: Paul Elek, 1976)

Gillies, Malcolm, David Pear, and Mark Carroll, eds, *Self-Portrait of Percy Grainger* (Oxford: Oxford University Press, 2006)

Grainger, Percy, 'The Impress of Personality in Unwritten Music', *Musical Quarterly*, vol. 1, no. 3 (July 1915), 416–35

Thwaites, Penelope, ed., *The New Percy Grainger Companion* (Woodbridge: Boydell, 2010)

Carrying the torch

Collectors in Northern and Eastern Europe

IT WAS MILY Balakirev who collected 'The Song of the Volga Boatmen' in Nizhny Novgorod in 1860; he was one of several Russian composers who went on collecting trips down that river, and further south to the Caucasus. They were impelled by the Slavophile romanticism that was then the fashion among Russian intellectuals, but with the exception of Musorgsky they all treated what they found as raw material for conventional salon music.

The folklorist on whose discoveries Stravinsky drew for the wedding songs in *Les noces* was the real thing. Pyotr Vasilyevich Kireyevsky (1808–1856) was Russia's leading collector in the 1830s and 40s, and both Pushkin and Gogol sent him song texts they had come across. He faithfully reproduced what his informants sent, keeping local dialects and regional variants intact, and including descriptions of performance. The result, says historian Richard Taruskin, was 'a panorama of wedding customs throughout the length and breadth of Russia that may appear indiscriminate and redundant, but that in fact provides an unprecedentedly rich assemblage of the artefacts of Russian *bït*, life-as-lived'. Kireyevsky began to publish his songs in the 1840s, then after an unexplained change of mind stopped completely; a selection of his songs was published in 1911, and that was Stravinsky's source. Thousands more Kireyevsky songs still await publication today.

Spurred by an awareness that industrialisation and urbanisation were ringing the death knell for folk music, song collectors proliferated during the latter years of the nineteenth century and the beginning of the twentieth, most of them operating without the luxury of recording equipment. The Czech poet Karel Jaromír Erben (1811–1870) published 2200 texts and 811 melodies of Bohemian folk song; Leoš Janáček (1854–1928) did the same for Moravian music.

Topping the league for sheer productivity was Vasil Stoin (1880–1938), a Bulgarian violinist-musicologist who with his assistants gathered – without recording technology – many thousands of folk songs from every part of Bulgaria between 1926 and 1937. His method was go out into the fields and vineyards, catch the music on the wing, and whistle what he had noted down, letting the singers verify its accuracy. His classifications, by metre, rhythm, scale, and function, were as scientific as those of Bartók, who drew on his work for his own purposes.

Like Bartók, Stoin was a patriot: his country had been liberated from the Turkish yoke two years before his birth, and refugee groups were in constant movement, taking their musics with them. Stoin's aim was to provide future generations with the songs of their country, complete with their asymmetric rhythms and characteristic dissonances. He caught this music in the nick of time, in its pre-industrial state.

Iceland's rugged folk music was first subjected to systematic scrutiny by the pastor Bjarni Thorsteinsson (1861–1938), another researcher armed with only pencil and paper. Published in 1906–9, his *Íslensk þjóðlög* (Icelandic Folk Songs) contained over 500 songs transcribed by Thorsteinsson plus contributors from various parts of the country. But as the musicologist Árni Heimir Ingólfsson points out, since folk material was seen as an embarrassment by a country wishing to make its mark in a new century, he had trouble getting the work published; it was rejected by the Icelandic Literary Society, at the time virtually the sole publisher of scholarly books in Icelandic, and it was only through a substantial grant from the Danish Carlsberg foundation – established by the founder of the eponymous brewery – that the book saw the light of day.

The song-collecting career of the Icelandic composer Jón Leifs (1899–1968) is another illustration of how thankless the work could be. Leifs had decided to make folk songs the basis of a new 'Icelandic' style, and had been 'trying to answer the question whether we in Iceland had some material like other countries, which might be reworked into a new music – some spark that might ignite that big flame'. And when, in 1921, he chanced to find Thorsteinsson's work sitting on his parents' bookshelf, he had that spark.

In 1925 Leifs and his wife made a song-collecting trip through north-west Iceland, travelling on horseback between farms and writing down 200 songs; his piano arrangements in *25 Icelandic Folk Songs* were the result. Realising that pencil and paper weren't ideally suited to rendering the songs' microtonalism and rapid ornamentation, he borrowed a phonograph plus a supply of cylinders from Erich von Hornbostel at the Berlin Phonogramm-Archiv, and set off on another expedition: he would deposit the cylinders in the Berlin collection, and would have the use of them for his compositional purposes. When the Icelandic parliament declined to fund the project, Leifs set up shop in Reykjavik, and advertised for his singers in local newspapers.

As Leifs's biographer Ingólfsson observes, his later forays were disappointing. Locals in one village on which he had pinned his hopes insisted that they knew no folk songs at all, and when he tried to record two celebrated septuagenarian *tvísöngur* (duettists), they had such trouble remembering the tunes that they were forced humiliatingly to consult Thorsteinsson's tome. Moreover, when Leifs visited the 66-year-old guru he got a frosty welcome:

Thorsteinsson declared that since Icelandic folk song was dying, collecting it was a waste of time; he even refused to give Leifs the names of local singers.

But the story didn't end there. The torch was picked up by the American composer Henry Cowell, who discovered Leifs's cylinders in the Berlin collection, and found a 'weird fascination' in their music 'which should be more known and heard, both for its bleak loveliness and for its historical scientific value'. He endorsed the view of Leifs and Hornbostel that *organum* in fifths had originated in Iceland, and had thence spread to Europe via churches. Events came full circle when Cowell began recording Icelandic expatriates in San Francisco, and composed a symphony 'in the spirit of national Icelandic music'.

If Leifs was one of many song-collecting enthusiasts working on the fringes of academic musicology, Constantin Brăiloiu (1893–1958) was the quintessential insider. Born in Bucharest, he studied in Vienna and Paris, founded the Society of Romanian Composers in 1920, and in 1928 founded and organised its folklore archive which became one of the largest in the world; he later co-founded the Archives Internationales de Musique Populaire in Geneva, and became a member of the elite Centre National de la Recherche Scientifique in Paris.

Brăiloiu was primarily a theorist whose rigorous approach to research – armed with an Edison phonograph and a cine camera – was summarised in his questionnaires: 'Que chante-t-on? Quand et où chante-t-on? Comment chante-t-on? Pourquoi chante-t-on comme on chante? D'ou viennent les chansons? Comment naissent les chansons?' He published numerous recordings of music from around the world, and made forty records for UNESCO, but at the same time he was a voracious collector in his own right, specialising in Romanian folk songs for funerals, weddings, and Christmas; his in-depth studies of children's songs, and of the limping *aksak* rhythm, are models of their kind. His influential essay 'Sur une mélodie russe', which focused on the austere structure of an old wedding song, moved its anonymous reviewer in the *Journal of the International Folk Music Council* to ringing eloquence: 'Amazement is the mother of perception … Presumably [these forms] sprang into existence from primordial ideas of pure forms in the world of sound, in the way that the geometrical style of the Neolithic Age delineated the pure forms of the visual world.'

And it was Bartók who took Brăiloiu's key observation on folk music as a motto for his own study: 'A folk tune really exists only at the moment when it is sung or played, and it only lives by the will of its performer, and in the manner that he wants. Creation and performance are intermingled here to an extent unknown in musical practice based on writing or print.'

Sources

Árni Heimir Ingólfsson's biography of Jón Leifs, *Jón Leifs and the Musical Invention of Iceland*, sets this composer's work in its folk-music context, and shows how that is central to Iceland's musical culture. Barbara Krader's essay in the yearbook of the IFMC, 'Vasil Stoin, Bulgarian Folk Song Collector', is a definitive assessment of Stoin's work. Richard Taruskin's *Stravinsky and the Russian Traditions* sets the work of Kireyevsky in its historical context.

Bibliography

Ingólfsson, Árni Heimir, *Jón Leifs and the Musical Invention of Iceland* (Bloomington: Indiana University Press, 2019)

Krader, Barbara, 'Vasil Stoin, Bulgarian Folk Song Collector', *Yearbook of the International Folk Music Council*, vol. 12 (1980), 27–42

Taruskin, Richard, *Stravinsky and the Russian Traditions*, vol. 2 (Oxford: Oxford University Press, 1996)

9

'And what does the gentleman want'

Béla Bartók as song detective

THE BIRTH OF mechanical song collecting is often symbolised by the photo-graph of Béla Bartók recording in the Slovak village of Dražovce. That was in 1907, eleven years after his compatriot Béla Vikár had begun recording bagpipers in the field, but the image still has archetypal force. Under Bartók's supervision, a woman sings into the horn of a phonograph. Standing to atten-tion is a line of other women, young girls, and middle-aged men – all in their Sunday best, awaiting their turn to sing. The importance of this communal moment is reflected in their unsmilingly serious faces: a new kind of history is being made.

17 Béla Bartók using a gramophone to collect songs from Slovak peasants in the village of Dražovce in 1907.

None of those present left an account of the experience, but a girl named Susana Cirt described a similar one ten years later, as Bartók and his friend the Italian conductor Egisto Tango came to record in the Romanian village of Torjas:

> It happened one Sunday ... The professors were well-built men, young and handsome! They asked my mother to agree to my singing into the gramophone for them ... I sang one nice verse, and then another one. It came back sounding so beautiful. The whole village gathered around us. *The whole village.* Everyone was wanting to sing. The professors asked me not to sing songs we'd learnt from soldiers, but only those from the mountain region here.

In the same year, seventeen-year-old Róza Ökrös, who was to become one of Bartók's most celebrated singers, was accosted by him while working in the fields, and asked if she would sing. 'In the evening he came to our quarters and sat down on a worker's case, with a night-light beside him,' she recalled sixty years later.

> I sat opposite him and sang. He noted it down. I was undoubtedly awe-struck, for no more songs came to my mind at that time. He was such a modest man, and did not press me to sing any further. There were many workers in the barn, and in the evening everyone retired to rest. Only I sang. I well remember how careful he was that my singing and his work did not disturb the others.

Bartók was in his mid-twenties when he realised that his vocation was to collect, collate, and conserve Hungarian folk music; circumstances had conspired to turn him into a Magyar patriot. Born in 1881, he was brought up initially in bourgeois comfort; his father and grandfather were headmasters, his mother a piano teacher. After the death of his father when he was seven, his mother's pursuit of employment meant the family had to move from town to town, through a country in which ethnic Hungarians were outnumbered by Slovaks, Romanians, Germans, Serbs, and Ukrainians. The Hungarians regarded themselves as the elect, but demographics were against them.

The abortive 1848 revolution, in which Lajos Kossuth led a Hungarian uprising against the Austrian yoke, had after much bloodshed resolved itself through Hungary becoming ruled in parallel with Austria by a dual monarchy. Music became the focus for a resurgent nationalism which the Hungarian gentry celebrated by sponsoring the *verbunkos* music of the Gypsies; this eighteenth-century army recruiting-dance had mutated into a seductive blend of languid and frenzied rhythms with florid ornamentation, and it was regarded as the quintessential expression of the Hungarian soul.

By the turn of the century a newly mutinous mood had arisen among the younger Hungarian intelligentsia; the Austro-Hungarian Empire's refusal to allow official recognition of the Hungarian language in the army, and the Austrians' insistence on their national anthem being played at all public events, drove Bartók and his friends to demand political autonomy. He insisted that his sister wear Hungarian national costume at his piano recitals, and in a letter to his mother he laid down the law about loyalty. Regretting that 'individual members of the Hungarian nation ... were so distressingly indifferent to everything Hungarian', he declared 'all my life, in every sphere, always and in every way, I shall have one objective: the good of Hungary and the Hungarian nation.' His mother's first language was German, but he begged her not to let the side down by speaking it in public; he himself made a point of replying in Hungarian when people in shops addressed him in German. Meanwhile his compositions had become permeated with verbunkos musical codes and 'Gypsy' scales; his early symphonic poem *Kossuth*, a fashionable success which included a parody of the Austrian anthem, was a hymn to the Hungarians' late leader.

For Bartók the *coup de foudre* came in 1904, while he was staying at a Slovakian resort and preparing a new work for performance. A Budapest family was staying in the same guest-house, and with them was their eighteen-year-old nursemaid Lidi Dósa, a Hungarian from Transylvania. As Dósa recalled seven decades later:

> I heard Bartók practising all the time ... and then, on one occasion, he heard me singing, I was singing to the child ... The song pleased Bartók, and he asked me to sing it again because he wanted to write it down. When he had taken it down, he went to the piano and played it. He then called me and asked if he was playing it properly. Well, it was exactly as I had sung it ... I had to sing continually, but he only wanted to hear the ancient village tunes. He only liked those I had learned from my grandmother.

Bartók's own account of this event concurred, despite being couched in the dry tones of a scientist: 'Making use of a chance opportunity ... I listened by way of experiment to a Szekely village girl, Lidi Dosa, and wrote down some 5–6 songs as she sang them, all entirely unknown melodies which were completely different from the known urban Hungarian popular song types. This first experiment pointed the way to unlimited possibilities: I decided I would follow this path, after suitable preparation.' And in a letter to his sister Elza in December 1904 he announced his change of direction: 'Now I have a new plan: to collect the finest Hungarian folk songs and to raise them, adding the best possible piano accompaniments, to the level of art song.' As Sándor Kovács points out, it was at that time the artist in Bartók, rather than the scientist lurking in the wings, who was leading the chase.

Dósa's song was entitled 'Piros alma' – 'The red apple' – and Bartók published a transcription of it in the music journal *Magyar Lant* (Hungarian Lyra). Its text went to the heart of European folk tradition, in which the red apple stands for virginity and fecundity; in some villages, after the blood-stained nuptial sheets had been displayed, the groom's parents would present the bride's with a bowl of red apples. 'The red apple fell into the mud/ Who picks it up will not go unrewarded/ I pick it up and wash off the mud/ And say farewell to my old sweetheart.' As Bartók's biographer David Cooper observes, the song's tonality was modal – a blend of Dorian and Aeolian – and pointed to a much earlier tradition than verbunkos.

* * *

This event marked the beginning of Bartók's transfer of allegiance from Hungarian 'national' music, as played by urban Gypsy bands, to the music of remote villages, but the next stage of his conversion came when he met a fellow-student named Zoltán Kodály at the Budapest Academy of Music; the pair became co-campaigners, and lifelong friends. Kodály, who was initially Bartók's mentor, had already done a collecting trip to the Slovak region of Galanta, and Bartók now followed suit; their aim was to jointly publish a book of folk-song arrangements for voice and piano. They issued an 'Appeal to the Hungarian People' soliciting support in creating a 'scientifically precise and complete collection of folk songs', and in their book's introduction they declared their two purposes: to support scholarly study, and to present the general public with the best examples. This latter aim had to be pursued with care: 'If brought in from the fields into the towns,' they wrote, 'folk songs have to be dressed up. However, attired in their new habit, they might seem shy and out of place. One must take care to cut their new clothes so as not to cramp their fresh country style.' (By a nice coincidence, precisely this sentiment was being expressed in the same year in Somerset, with the performance of Cecil Sharp's soprano-and-piano setting of his discovery 'The seeds of love' being described as the first time it 'had been put into evening dress'.) The book of twenty songs, with accompaniments written ten each by the composers, did not sell well.

Bartók's collecting strategy was to stay with family and friends and draw on their connections, and he went straight into top gear. In Tura, west of Budapest, he collected seventy-five songs in three days; with the aid of a new phonograph he went back and collected as many more. In the village of Doboz he recorded swineherds, shepherds, and domestic servants, sometimes over supper to get them properly oiled; trips to collect Slovak, Romanian, Ruthenian, Serbian, and Bulgarian melodies all contributed to a rich harvest. And patterns in that harvest began to emerge. From Transylvania, Kodály recalled, 'he came back with such a pile of pentatonic melodies that … the fundamental importance of this hitherto unnoticed scale suddenly became obvious.'

A letter to the violinist Stefi Geyer, with whom Bartók was for a while smitten, reflects the bumpy course his sessions could take, as his ruefully dramatised account made clear:

> Woman: And what does the gentleman want? (To her daughter) Bring a chair for the gentleman! Get the pigs in!
>
> Traveller: I've heard from your neighbour that you know all kinds of ancient folk-songs which you learnt from the old folks when you were a girl.
>
> W: Me? Old songs? You shouldn't make fun of me sir!
>
> T: Believe me, I'm not making fun of you. That's why I've made this long journey, especially to look for these very old songs which no one remembers except here … In 50 years no one will have heard of them if we don't write them down now.
>
> W: Oh, my singing days are past. I only know sacred songs now. [These were Bartók's pet aversion, the antithesis to what he was after. Conversational hide-and-seek continues with him getting ever more exasperated.]
>
> W: One has just come into my mind.
>
> Traveller: (brightening) Let's hear it!
>
> W: But what shall I do? Just say the words?
>
> T: No, sing the tune as it used to be sung.
>
> W: (sings to the end) 'I go around this wood …'
>
> T: I know, it's very nice. But don't you know anything older? Just think a little.
>
> W: Older than that? (She thinks … then suddenly to her daughter) For the love of God! Why did you let out the geese? (A painful pause) Now another has come into my mind.
>
> T: ?
>
> W: (sings) 'I was born in a rose bush …'
>
> T: (interrupting) That's no good, it's not even old, and it's sung by the gentry.
>
> [The tussle continues, with the woman insisting on singing more religious songs which Bartók doesn't want, and finally giving incomprehensible directions as to where he may – just possibly – find a singer with a better memory.]
>
> T: Thank you, God bless you! (departs downcast)

He signs off to Stefi in an explosion of frustration: 'And so *da capo al fine* from morning till night, Monday to Sunday! I can't bear it any longer. Impossible!'

18 One of Bartók's early collaborators was László Lajtha (1892–1963), a
noted song collector as well as a composer.

At other times, however, the chase went smoothly. At Christmas in 1910
he went to Transylvania and transcribed forty-five pieces in one thirteen-hour
shift, going on to record more until he ran out of cylinders. South Hungary, he
found, was 'a particular nest of ballads' where in one Romanian village an old
railwayman dictated seven long ones at a go, 'just as if he was reading them
out. I was notating for two and a half hours without a break; I could hardly
keep up.' His ideal way to collect was 'to go into a peasant home where there
is a gathering of good singers, friends, neighbours etc; first one person sings
a song, then another; phonographing too puts them in the right mood (for I
immediately have the song just recorded played back to them).' And his ideal
collecting-territory proved to be in Romania. Looking back in 1933, he wrote
that in Maramures and Bihar he'd been able, twenty years previously, to make
contact with

> pure, uncontaminated material … For miles on end in these parts there are
> villages with illiterate inhabitants, communities which are not linked by any
> railways or roads; here, most of the time the people can provide for their
> own daily wants, never leaving their native habitats except for such unavoid-
> able travel as arises from service in the army or an occasional appearance in

court. When one comes in to such a region, one has a feeling of a return to the Middle Ages.

All that was becoming history, however, even in the Thirties.

Bartók's collecting interests weren't confined to Europe: in 1913, he embarked with his wife Marta on a field trip to Algeria. He had made a thorough recce of the musical possibilities in Biskra, the inland town he'd chosen as their base, but was predictably hampered by local conventions regarding women singing for male strangers. Only when the local police department gave their blessing was the problem solved, and professional Berber dancer-prostitutes allowed to record at his hotel. The Bartóks then went over the mountains to record instrumentalists in Tolga; their journey took longer than expected because Bartók – ever the compulsive collector – insisted on looking for beetles for the insect collection he had been compiling, as his librettist Béla Balázs put it, 'with utmost pedantry and constant amazement'. He didn't delve into the complex Arab sound-world of *maqam*, but he did note the effect that varying accents in bars of equal length had in superimposing a second rhythmic pattern. As Kenneth Chalmers has observed, Bartók was thus hearing in the field the effect that Stravinsky was at the same time exploiting in the theatre with his scores for Diaghilev's Ballets Russes.

Perennially plagued by ill-health, Bartók was struck down on this trip by a fever so severe that his weight dropped to forty-seven kilos, but he fully intended to return to north Africa; he planned to fatten himself up in advance so that he could lose a quarter of a kilo each day without ill effects. He even went to the trouble of buying a Kabyl grammar, to be able to work with the Berbers: he loathed not knowing what songs were about, and made a point of learning the language of the singers wherever he went.

The outbreak of war in 1914 put paid to the idea of a return, or to any other collecting trips; the only significant research he did in the war period, in conjunction with Kodály and supported by officialdom, was of soldiers' songs collected in their barracks – a useful venue, in that their informants came from far and wide. The results of this were celebrated in a 'historical concert' at the Vienna Konzerthaus in January 1918, but to Bartók's annoyance his four-voice a cappella arrangements of Slovak soldiers' songs were performed in German. In his view the saving grace of this concert – packed to the rafters with Viennese high society – was that it did at least represent 'an opportunity for "real" Hungarian folk songs to be heard by those few Viennese musicians who accidentally dropped into that company of pluto-aristocrats'.

* * *

Revolution then thrust him into the limelight, where he was hopelessly ill at ease. When the Austro-Hungarian Empire fell apart, the moderate-socialist Károlyi government took power, and Bartók was lined up to be the director of a new folklore department of the Budapest Museum of Ethnography. After four months Károlyi resigned, and the Communist leader Béla Kun took over, appointing Bartók, Kodály, and Ernő Dohnányi as members of the Directorate of Music, and charging them with the organisation of concerts for the proletariat; Bartók was considered as a possible director of the Opera House. For a man so socially withdrawn, so resistant to compromise, and so obsessively breaking new ground in his own compositions, this was hardly sensible casting. Eighteen months later, red terror gave way to white terror as Kun's regime was supplanted by Admiral Miklós Horthy's reactionary anti-Semitic one, which would remain in power until the year before Bartók's death.

But unlike his colleagues on the musical directorate, Bartók was not punished by the new regime, perhaps because his fame was a sort of protection. And with characteristic belligerence he began to publish articles on the theme of 'Hungary in the throes of reaction' in European and American journals. Bartók's celebration of Romanian folk music led him to be denounced as unpatriotic by his employer Jenő Hubay, the director of the Liszt Academy; his defiantly lip-curling response was that since it had taken a Hungarian musicologist to do the job (there being as yet no Romanian capable of doing it), his work demonstrated Hungarian superiority.

Just as calamitous, from Bartók's point of view, was the carve-up of territory in the 1920 Treaty of Trianon, which shrank Hungary to one-third of its pre-war size. Three of the four towns where Bartók had grown up were incorporated into Romania, and the fourth into Czechoslovakia. Travel to them would now require a passport and a declaration of preferred nationality; Romania would be particularly hard for Bartók to enter, so he thus lost the greater part of his laboratory. Meanwhile the cost of recording cylinders had inflated twentyfold since before the war. In a letter in 1920 to the composer Philip Heseltine (aka Peter Warlock) who was one of his most ardent British supporters, Bartók remarked apropos his collecting activities that 'our political and economic situation has changed so much since this year that I must forever abandon this work, which is so dear and so important to me'.

In 1932 Bartók did go back to North Africa, this time as a guest at the Congress of Arab Music in Cairo, which represented an extraordinary milestone in music history. King Fu'ad had convened this event as part of his plan to bring Egypt up to par with the 'civilised' Western world; other guests included the composers Paul Hindemith and Alois Haba, Erich von Hornbostel (director of the Berlin Phonogramm-Archiv), the British Arabist

98

Henry George Farmer, and dozens of other musicologists from Europe and the Middle East. The congress was held under the auspices of Cairo's Academy of Oriental Music, which still stands today as a cultural counterpoint to the nearby Conservatoire, and the Academy's director spelt out the issues which the assembled specialists should address. These were to 'enhance the evolution' of Arab music; to establish a fixed musical scale; to adopt specific symbols for transcribing Arab tunes; to assess the appropriateness of specific musical instruments; to organise musical education; and to record indigenous songs. In a statement reflecting the national inferiority-complex to be found at that time in many conservatoires of the Middle and Far East, the conference would 'discuss all that was required to make the [Egyptian] music civilized, and to teach it and rebuild it on acknowledged scientific principles'. It's not difficult to imagine Bartók's response – or that of his romantically open-minded colleagues – to such a self-harming plan. As he wrote home, 'The Arabs want to modernise everything, and the Europeans (with a few exceptions) want to preserve the old.'

Each guest could choose which sub-committee they wanted to be part of, and for Bartók that choice was easy. 'There was only one section in question for me,' he wrote afterwards, 'that of the recordings, which I joined with great pleasure.' He would be advising the Oriental Institute on making recordings and setting up a phonogram shop, and he would be auditioning musicians from across the Arab and Turkic world. In the event he recorded, among other things, Mevlevi and Laythi *dhikr* performances, and a Coptic mass. And he carried on his perennial campaign on behalf of village versus city music, despite the fact that what excited him most was some wild exorcism music in Cairo.

One can hear Bartók's voice in the committee's decree that they should ignore 'music that does not adhere to Eastern melodies', and 'which emulates objectionable European music in its worst form, because recordings of such music are unfit to appear in an academy whose most important goal is education'. And one can hear it even more loudly in the committee's stress on folk music: 'Next to the refined music of the cities, there is another simpler one. It is the music of rural groups or nomadic tribes, songs by individuals who are not musicians, but whose music is connected with their work (songs of manual labour, sailors' songs, street vendors' songs commonly found in Cairo).' It was at Bartók's suggestion that two versions were made and pressed for each item recorded, in order to compare different versions of one piece by each performer; he also suggested that the records be sold without profit for educational purposes. As a result, 175 78rpm discs were recorded and sold on a special label by His Master's Voice.

Though Bartók was not part of the musical instruments sub-committee, he must have endorsed its majority view that most Western instruments would 'disfigure the beauty of Arab music'. The piano was at the centre of this argument: one side-effect of this congress was an effort on the part of piano manufacturers to produce an instrument which could register microtones. (Wandering through the corridors of Cairo Opera House in 1998, I chanced upon one of these rare objects, with a keyboard neatly subdivided into quarter-tones; electronic instruments now solve the problem with ease, if without the mellow suggestiveness of natural materials.)

Bartók's last collecting trip was in 1936 at the instigation of Paul Hindemith, who had been drafted in to help the Turkish government organise music education along European lines. Bartók's duties would be to advise on the collection of folk songs, and on 'how a Turkish national music should be developed from Turkish folk music'. In return he would be allowed to record Anatolian music for the Hungarian Academy of Science. Bartók was delighted to be able to explore what was for him virgin territory, and to pursue a question which had nagged him for years: 'whether there is some kind of link between the most ancient Hungarian folk music, undoubtedly of Asiatic origin, and Turkish folk music'.

He was profoundly unimpressed by the song collecting of his hosts in Istanbul. This was partly because they had simply snared any wandering musicians who happened to be in town: such people, he said, 'because of their wanderings, are never reliable sources of folk music, which is local'. Worse, he was shocked by the absence of any text notation. 'When I mentioned this lack to the Turks who were with me, they reassured me by saying, "Never mind, it is easy to make up for it any time: we are Turks and we understand the recorded texts." So he set them a test, which they failed ignominiously. '"You see," I said, what happens when a collector fails to note down the text directly from the performer."' He doubted grimly whether this schoolmasterly ticking-off would have any effect.

Based in the southern city of Adana and making forays into villages, he had more success with instrumentalists than with singers; his best find was a fifteen-year-old boy whose mystical terror of losing his voice into the phonogram had first to be allayed, but who then sang non-stop until midnight. Very few of the recordings were of women, thanks – as in Algeria – to the prohibition on female singers performing for male listeners. Back in schoolmaster mode, Bartók 'told the proper authorities that something ought to be done about this'. Either properly trained women should be sent out to collect the songs, or male collectors should be accompanied by their wives as chaperones. He concluded with a caustic jibe: 'It is very unfortunate that the cradle songs, for instance, should be recorded as sung by rasping male voices, when it is evident that the men never rock their children to sleep, either with or without a song.'

As for that nagging question of origins, he could report progress, thanks to his customary musicological detective work. Twenty per cent of the songs he collected in Turkey bore a clear similarity to old Hungarian music, he wrote, and

> it is evident that this is not a mere coincidence. No such tunes can be found among the Yugoslavs, the Slovaks of the West and North, or the Greeks, and even among the Bulgarians they are only occasional. If we take into account that such tunes can be found only among Hungarians, among the Transylvanian and Moldavian Rumanians, and the Cheremiss and Northern Turkish peoples, then it seems likely that this music is the remains of an antique, thousand-year-old Turkish musical style.

He signed off his account of this trip – which also took him to the Syrian cities of Aleppo and Raqqa – with some sadly prophetic words: 'I conclude by reporting that the Turks were not able to realise much of their fine plans; obviously the ever-increasing, menacing war clouds caused them to direct their energies in an entirely different direction – as has happened in so many other countries. *Inter arma silent Musae ...*'

Amid the clash of arms, the Muses fall silent.

* * *

For the intellectual underpinning to Bartók's work we have his seminal book *The Hungarian Folk Song*, published in 1924, plus his essays, polemics, and reviews, which can be bracingly pugilistic. A critic with the temerity to question the accuracy of Bartók's notations in his first book of Romanian folk music is dismissed as an ignorant dilettante, and has his arguments mercilessly torn to shreds. 'We categorically repudiate the charge hidden behind every line of the critic,' Bartók thunders, as well he might, given the fastidious precision of his notations, down to even the smallest grace-note melismas. He then offers to take part in a transcription competition – 'in any village whatever, accompanied by whoever' – and he theatrically promises to abandon all study of folk music if someone else can notate faster and more accurately than him.

That particular article also includes a blistering attack on 'Gypsy' music, a subject to which Bartók returned repeatedly: 'Gypsies pervert melodies, change their rhythm to "Gypsy" rhythm, introduce among the people melodies heard in other regions, and in the country seats of the gentry – in other words, they contaminate the style of genuine folk music.' Bartók did allow that 'real' Gypsy songs had charm, provided they were sung by 'non-musician [i.e. amateur] Gypsy musicians only': what he was gunning for, in his role as a musical patriot, was the music performed by the urban Gypsy bands, 'who belong to the ruling class'. Their crimes included peddling 'pseudo-folk melodies', and deforming *parlando-rubato* ones with excessive *rubato* and superimposed florid embellishments; Brahms and Liszt, he wrote, were their gullible collaborators. 'It is absolutely obvious that the melodies featured in Liszt's *Hungarian Rhapsodies* and Brahms's *Hungarian Dances* are not Gypsy products, but melodies by popular amateurs.'

But Bartók's invective cloaked a serious argument, relating to how it was that Gypsies could have come to usurp the local peasants' traditional role as village musicians. His tentative answer concerned economics and migration to the cities, but what fired his anger was the injustice done, in the process, to the country's ancient folk music. That, he said, was always tonal, possessed 'a truly perfect purity of style', was completely 'devoid of trashiness', and pertained to dances, weddings, funerals, and every kind of repetitive labour. He loved the 'full and impressive melancholy' of its melodies, its 'exquisite reserve', and its abstinence from vocal polyphony (which in Bartók's suspicious mind always conjured up ideas of ruling-class patronage); he eagerly speculated as to where this music might have come from. 'These melodies do not come from the folk music of our neighbours,' he wrote. 'We might rather suppose, because of their pentatonic scale system, that we are dealing here with remnants of an old folk music culture brought from Asia by the first Hungarians, a music which is perhaps in direct relation to the pentatonic music of the Cheremiss [from the Volga region], the Tatars, and the Kirghiz.' Subsequent musicological research has not shot down this intriguing hypothesis.

As to what folk music – or peasant music, as he preferred to call it – actually was, he supplied a definition in *The Hungarian Folk Song*: 'The term peasant music connotes, broadly speaking, all the tunes which endure among the peasant class of any nation, in a more or less wide area and for a more or less long period, and constitute a spontaneous expression of the musical feeling of that class.' It was, he said, 'impulsively created by a community of men who have had no schooling; it is as much a natural product as are the various forms of animal and vegetable life'.

Bartók's fieldwork took place over twelve years, during which time he collected and noted down almost ten thousand melodies. Thereafter he devoted himself to refining his classifications, to making ever-widening comparative studies of Polish, Ukrainian, Serbo-Croatian, and Bulgarian music, and to striving, not always successfully, to publish his results. Kodály continued collecting with the aid of young researchers, and with Bartók transcribing and analysing their work. But although the pair remained close collaborators for the rest of Bartók's life, there was the same gulf between their respective approaches to notation as there had been between those of Cecil Sharp and Percy Grainger in England two decades previously. Sharp was after the quintessential, Ur-version of a song, while Grainger wanted to catch all its minute variations: Kodály wanted to establish the 'typical' form, whereas Bartók strove to document all the 'mistakes', all the chance peculiarities of a performance. It's significant that Bartók hoped that through his friendship with Frederick Delius he might get to meet Grainger, but that meeting never happened.

There's an urgency running through all Bartók's writings, a fear, as he put it in 1940, that 'one day all folk music will have been swept away'. 'What do we need above all for detecting causalities and unravelling connections?' he asked. 'Data, data, and data – by the hundreds of thousands!' And his brain was teeming with possible connections: 'In 1912, I discovered among the Maramures Romanians a certain kind of highly ornamented, Orientally-coloured and improvisation-like melody. In 1913, in a village of Central Algeria bordering the Sahara desert, I heard a similar melodic style ... Who would have thought that the distance between the two phenomena – more than 2000 kilometres – could be bridged by a causal relationship?' Further research suggested to him that this was not a coincidence, but that there was indeed a causal link, though far back in time. And like many other exponents of comparative musicology, he had a distant vision: 'I suspect that when folk music materials and studies in sufficient number are at our disposal, all of the world's folk music will be traceable basically to a few primitive forms, primitive types, and kinds of primitive style.'

If Bartók were alive today, he might be running a global song-information exchange. His compulsive urge to catalogue, classify, and control his materials – combined with his incandescent intensity when performing - has led some commentators to diagnose autism. But as Cooper sensibly argues, those traits which might label him 'autistic' should rather be seen as connected with his father's untimely death, his dominating mother, his periods of debilitating illness, his constant financial insecurity, and with the political turbulence through which he lived. And in any case collectors are all, by definition, obsessives.

One of Bartók's most influential papers, published in 1936, was entitled 'Why and how do we collect folk music?', and it's full of dos and don'ts. Don't bother with pedlars or any other itinerants, because their magpie life-style means they can't be a reliable local source. Likewise avoid 'educated' informants, for the same reason. Don't collect songs learned at school or from the radio, because these will have been implanted in a peasant environment by external intervention. And as a rule women are more reliable informants than men: they travel less, their work is more conducive to song, and they have more appreciation for music: 'When a "living song collection" is sought, it will probably be [found] in the person of a woman.' Bartók quotes his friend Constantin Brăiloiu – the leading Romanian musicologist – with regard to the singers of mourning songs: 'Only women are permitted to lament: God beware that men should lament! They only weep.'

And in a paragraph which should give today's ethnomusicologists pause for thought, Bartók itemises the intellectual requirements for the job:

> The ideal folklorist possesses an erudition which is virtually encyclopaedic. Knowledge of linguistics and phonetics is necessary in order to perceive and record the most subtle dialectal pronunciation; he must be a choreographer to describe accurately the inter-connections of music and dance; only a general knowledge of folklore permits him to determine in minute detail the relationships between music and customs; without sociological preparation he would be incapable of checking the influence on folk music that is exerted as a result of changes which now and then disturb the collective life of the village. If he intends to draw inferences he must have a sound knowledge of history, above all the history of settlements; in order to compare the folk music material of hetero-linguistic peoples with that of his own country, he must learn foreign languages. And above all it is indispensable that he be an observant musician with a good ear.

In a postscript he doubts whether any such person has ever existed, or ever will.

* * *

The uses to which Bartók put his discoveries were often didactic: to alert Hungarians to their heritage, and to provide instrumentalists with ethnographically based and musically satisfying repertoire. His own oeuvre, meanwhile, is a magnificent testament to folk music's power to inform what we hear in the concert hall. In a 1920 essay entitled 'The Influence of Folk Music on the Art Music of Today' he laid out his credo with luminous clarity:

> Pure folk music can be considered as a natural phenomenon influencing higher art music, as bodily properties perceptible with the eye are for the fine arts, or the phenomena of life are for the poet. This influence is most effective for the musician if he acquaints himself with folk music in the form in which it lives, in unbridled strength, amidst the lower people, and not by means of inanimate collections of folk music, which anyway lack adequate diatonic symbols capable of restoring their minute nuances and throbbing life. If he surrenders himself to the impact of this living folk music, and to all the circumstances which are the condition of this life, and if he reflects in his works the effects of these impressions, then we might say of him that he has portrayed therein a part of life.

Yes, he might have been speaking about himself.

Sources

David Cooper's biography *Béla Bartók* is an excellent place to start, as it relates the song collecting to the composer's oeuvre at every stage of his career; Sándor Kovács's chapter in *The Bartók Companion* offers a lucid account of his ethnomusicological work and thought. The strength of Kenneth Chalmers's short biography *Béla Bartók* lies in its copious illustrations, which bring both composer and period vividly to life; Malcom Gillies's *Bartók Remembered* is an illuminating patchwork of testimonies. Ali Jihad Racy's account of the Cairo Congress in *Ethnomusicology and Modern Music History* is the most extended one in English; Kirsty Riggs's paper in the *Musical Quarterly* provides additional context. Benjamin Suchoff's edited volumes provide the intellectual hinterland: while *Béla Bartók Essays* cover the composer's whole literary output, *Béla Bartók: Studies in Ethnomusicology* fills in some gaps, and in *Bartók: Turkish Folk Music from Asia Minor* we see how minutely he studied the background of his informants, and how fastidiously he notated their songs. *Béla Bartók Letters* is an engagingly chatty selection.

Bibliography

Chalmers, Kenneth, *Béla Bartók* (London: Phaidon, 1995)

Cooper, David, *Béla Bartók* (London: Yale University Press, 2015)

Demény, János, ed., *Béla Bartók Letters* (London: Faber, 1971)

Gillies, Malcolm, *Bartók Remembered* (London: Faber, 1990)

Gillies, Malcom, ed., *The Bartók Companion* (London: Faber, 1993)

Racy, Ali Jihad, 'Historical Worldview of Early Ethnomusicologists: An East-West Encounter in Cairo, 1932', in Stephen Blum, Philip V. Bohlman, and Daniel M. Neuman, eds, *Ethnomusicology and Modern Music History* (Chicago: Illinois University Press, 1991), 68–91

Riggs, Kirsty K., 'Bartók in the Desert: Challenges to a European Conducting Research in North Africa in the Early Twentieth Century', *Musical Quarterly*, vol. 90, issue 1 (March 2007), 72–89

Suchoff, Benjamin, ed., *Bartók: Turkish Folk Music from Asia Minor* (London: Princeton University Press, 1976)

Suchoff, Benjamin, ed., *Béla Bartók Essays* (London: Faber, 1976)

Suchoff, Benjamin, ed., *Béla Bartók: Studies in Ethnomusicology* (London: University of Nebraska Press, 1997)

Suchoff, Benjamin, ed., *The Hungarian Folk Song, By Béla Bartók* (Albany: State University of New York Press, 1981)

19 John Lomax shaking hands with blues musician 'Uncle' Rich Brown, best known for his recording of 'Alabama bound'.

10

Girdling the globe

The empire of the Lomaxes

THE TITANS OF song collecting were a charismatic Texan double-act: John A. Lomax (1867–1948) and his son Alan (1915–2002). John grew up among what he called 'the upper crust of the po' white trash', and a burning sense of mission led him to become Twenties America's most influential folklorist; his musical discoveries among cowboys and black convict singers spanned the end of oral transmission and the dawn of recording. Alan Lomax became his father's co-recordist at seventeen; after John's death, he carried on the torch in the Mississippi Delta, before extending his activities worldwide.

John brought celebrated singers including Lead Belly into the limelight; the classic songs he collected and anthologised helped redefine American culture. Alan Lomax's effect on that culture was seismic, as he made his own discoveries, and as a singer-collector-impresario led folk-blues revivals in both America and Britain. His books, plays, and radio programmes championed the music of the dispossessed; he played a leading part in the musical revolution which threw up Bob Dylan, the Rolling Stones, and the Beatles. Meanwhile with his researches in Haiti, Spain, and Italy he opened up new fields in musicology. And drawing on his archive of films, videotapes, and sound recordings he promoted 'Cantometrics', a system of song-classification which he himself had created, and which he messianically believed could unify – musically at least – the world.

* * *

One for the blackbird, one for the crow
One for the cutworm, and two to grow ...

This was what six-year-old John Lomax chanted as he ran barefoot through freshly turned furrows, doling out seed-corn from his bucket. His autobiography, *Adventures of a Ballad Hunter*, depicts a rural Texan childhood in which folk songs, revivalist hymns, and the recitation of English poetry were all part of daily life. His best friend was a young ex-slave whom he taught to read, and who taught him plantation songs and dance steps in return. Lomax didn't grow up a cowboy because his father didn't have enough livestock, but cowboy culture was all around him, and cowboy songs got into his soul. His father had bred him up to be a farmer, but he was determined to study, and sold his beloved pony to finance himself. Setting out for Granbury College, Texas, at twenty in a mule-drawn wagon, he had in his trunk a roll of cowboy songs he'd jotted down on scraps of cardboard.

A compulsive autodidact, he spent the next two decades immersed in literary and linguistic study, teaching, and working as a university administrator. One day he plucked up the courage to show his roll of songs to a kindly disposed Anglo-Saxon specialist, but the response was crushing: such 'cheap and tawdry' stuff couldn't compete with Beowulf, he was told, so he meekly burnt his roll. But at Harvard, where he went to study American literature (and where a budding musicologist named Charles Seeger and a fledgling poet named T. S. Eliot were among his classmates), professor George L. Kittredge – a former acolyte of the ballad collector Francis James Child – encouraged him to write a dissertation on those cowboy songs. The intellectual soil at Harvard was fertile, and he soon found himself writing, with university backing, to a thousand local newspapers, soliciting examples of the native ballads and frontier songs he wanted to preserve from extinction. 'Crudity, incompleteness, or coarseness', he wrote, would in no way diminish their interest. The result was a flood of letters from all over America, out of which he created a lecture with his own sung illustrations. In 1910 he published his ground-breaking anthology, *Cowboy Songs and Other Frontier Ballads*.

Persuading people to sing into the cumbersome horn of his Edison machine was not easy, even with the blandishment of copious shots of whisky: he was often reduced to writing down the songs he had elicited, or singing them into it himself. Few cowboys saw the point of his researches, most sharing the general contempt for their music. But he could also strike lucky. He was directed to a broken-down saloon in the red-light district of San Antonio where a putative singer waved him away saying he was too drunk to perform. Returning the next day, Lomax was able to make the first-ever cylinder recording of 'Home on the range'; he'd come across partial versions of the song in the mail he'd received, and its origin was as a Victorian magazine poem, but this was the first time he'd heard it in its entirety. In Fort Worth's stockyards he chanced upon a gypsy fortune-teller who provided a wealth of material, including the first blues he'd ever heard and the dreamily expressive 'Git along little dogies' (not dogs but orphaned, malnourished calves). After the last line 'Lay still, little dogies, lay still', she would give, he recalled, 'the night-herding yodel of the cowboy … like the croon of a mother trying to quiet a restless babe'.

President Theodore Roosevelt himself penned the introduction to *Cowboy Songs*, but Lomax was a lone voice in academe: one professor who did collect ballads limited his quest to transplanted English and Scottish examples. It took years for the penny to drop with regard to indigenous music, though when it did Lomax found himself suddenly in demand as a singer-lecturer. But with a wife and three children to support (plus his mother and impecunious siblings) he was forced to increase his earnings by selling bonds for an investment bank. His song collecting went on the back burner, where it remained until tragedy (the premature death of his wife) and financial disaster (the disappearance of his job in the Great Depression) plunged him into a paralysing depression of his own.

IT WAS John's seventeen-year-old son Alan who coaxed him back to life in the early 1930s by persuading him to resume the trade he had pioneered. John was a Republican conservative, and Alan a fiery Communist, but the bond between them was unbreakably strong. Alan argued that with his father's practical experience in the field, and with his own bent for setting folk music in its socio-political context, they would make an unbeatable team. Thus galvanised, John persuaded the Macmillan Press to commission a collection of songs for a new anthology, and he convinced the Library of Congress to lend their support, which gave him the status to raise funds from scholarly organisations. In return, he would deposit his recordings with the LOC, in order to found the folk-song archive which the library had so far failed to establish.

The new anthology would be entitled *American Ballads and Folk Songs*, and would include everything from French creole songs and dances to songs everybody knew like 'Yankee Doodle', 'Amazing grace', and 'Swing low sweet chariot'. For John, American ballads were the preserve of miners, lumberjacks, soldiers, sailors, blacks, and down-and-outs. As John Szwed observes in his biography of the Lomaxes, 'There was a male roughness, a focus on work and the outdoors that had never been seen in the songbooks that emerged from the collectors who toiled in the parlours of the local nobility and church rectories in Britain.' Lomax was implicitly tilting at the then-prevalent notion that England had all the best tunes.

In the event, although the book was well received, the Lomaxes had to fend off the criticism that they had edited and smoothed the songs they had gathered on field trips; John replied that since the originals were stored intact at the Library of Congress, such liberties in a book designed to reach a wide public were legitimate. Moreover, his introduction raised questions about ownership which still resonate today:

> Although much of the material [in this book] represents actual fieldwork, a considerable portion we 'went and took' from indulgent and generous

correspondents and, by permission, from collections already in print. The previous collectors in turn picked up the songs somewhere. The real author or authors remain unknown ... Worse than thieves are ballad collectors, for when they capture and imprison in cold type a folk song, at the same time they kill it.

The Lomaxes' fundraising proposal to the Carnegie Foundation included these words:

> The Negro in the South is the target for such complex influences that it is hard to find genuine folk singing. His educational leaders [are] making him ashamed or self-conscious of his own art; his religious leaders [are] turning away from revival songs, spirituals; the radio with its flood of jazz, [was] created in tearooms for the benefit of city-dwelling whites. These things are killing the best and most genuine Negro folk songs.

They proposed to go 'where such influences are not yet dominant; where Negroes are almost entirely isolated from the whites ... Where they are not only preserving a great body of traditional songs, but are also creating new songs in the same idiom'.

* * *

They were by no means the first collectors of African American blues, and they were coming in on the back of a thriving commercial game. Radio had turned the phonograph industry's initial boom into a slump, and record companies were forced to seek new consumers in rural areas where the lack of electricity limited listeners to hand-cranked machines. And they found those consumers: the phonograph industry was saved by the music of immigrant communities, and by what we now call 'country' and rhythm & blues.

After the success of W. C. Handy's 'Memphis Blues'– issued as sheet music in 1912, and two years later in a recorded version by a military band – the blues as an art form, with its West African roots and its ancestry in minstrel shows, became a national craze. With Bessie Smith, Ma Rainey, and Ethel Waters as its African American leading lights, and Marion Harris as its pre-eminent white star – initially the blues public was largely white – the record industry cashed in, as it did with the jazz craze triggered by the Original Dixieland Jazz Band's first hit in 1917. 'Race' records – the word was then a respectful synonym for 'negro'– became a major marketing genre.

The record producers depended partly on tips from song collectors like Henry Columbus Speirs, who ran a music shop in Jackson, and who channelled so many singers towards them that he became known as the Godfather of the Delta Blues. But most of the tips came from talent scouts whom producers despatched all over the South.

Their search could demand persistence. Bob Stephens, a scout for the Okeh company, recalled a long hunt for

> some wild blues singer called Mississippi John Hurt. Finally we tracked him down late at night. It was blacker than a whale's belly and we had to put the headlights onto the door of his shack before we knocked. This guy came to the door wearing just a pair of trousers and he damned near turned white when he saw us. He thought we were a lynching party.

Thus was one great voice found, only to be lost again when the Okeh label was discontinued. (Three decades later a record collector came across his final release, and Hurt – who no longer even possessed a guitar – was once more tracked down, put onstage at the Newport Folk Festival, and, like the Cuban band Buena Vista Social Club in the Nineties, ended his unexpected second career in a blaze of glory.)

Frank Walker, a producer for Columbia, described the wholesale nature of the operation. You would let it be known when and where you would be recording, he said.

> It would be mentioned in the paper and the word would get around in churches and schoolhouses. You'd talk to everybody around: who did they know that could fiddle, could play guitar, could sing. And these people would show up from sometimes eight and nine hundred miles away. They never asked you for money. They were just happy to sing and play, and we were happy to have them – and mostly we saw that they had something to go back with.
>
> In Atlanta we recorded in a little hotel and we used to put the singers up and pay a dollar a day for their food and a place to sleep in another little old hotel. Then we would spend all the night going from one room to another … it was a regular party. We'd sit up all night long and listen to them. You said 'We'll use this' and 'We won't use that', and you timed it, and you rehearsed them next morning, and you recorded them in the afternoon. It was a twenty-four hour deal, seven days a week.

* * *

The Lomaxes' very different agenda set them apart. They were the first to record African American folk music systematically, and the first to see the value of a national archive; grants from the Carnegie and Rockefeller foundations allowed them to set out on the road. And it was no surprise that they should find their best material in Southern penitentiaries, since those dismal prison-farms fitted their musical requirements all too accurately. Black culture there, the Lomaxes reported, was uncontaminated by its popular white counterpart. Living in constant fear of the lash, the black inmates were segregated from the whites, cotton-picking and tree-felling in different areas, and sleeping in different dormitories. Many of the guards were sadistic, to the point where convicts would sometimes self-mutilate, cutting off a hand or a foot to get out. Yet they sang. 'In the burning hell of the penitentiaries,' Alan wrote, 'the old comforting, healing, communal spirit of African singing cooled the souls of the toiling, sweating prisoners, and made them consolingly and powerfully one.' Weekend visits from wives, girlfriends, and prostitutes were another palliative designed to prevent anger boiling over.

Their first recording, made in a prison near Dallas, was of a baptism song from a black washerwoman:

Wade in de water, wade in de water
Wade in de water, chilluns;
Gawd goin to trouble de water ...

This was a revelatory moment for Alan. 'She started slow and sweet,' he wrote,

but as the needle scratched her song on the whirling wax cylinder, she sang faster and with more and more drive, clapping her hands and tapping out drum rhythm with heel and toe of her bare feet, and as the song ended she was weeping and saying over and over 'Oh Lord have mercy, O Lord have mercy'. I wondered what made her voice soar so beautifully, and what sorrow lay behind her tears.

His next revelation came in a schoolhouse where a man called Blue was prevailed on to sing, reluctantly at first, about the lot of the tenant farmer. But he broke off halfway through, and began to speak as though addressing Franklin Roosevelt: 'Now Mr President, you just don't know how bad they are treating us folks down here. I'm singing to you and I'm talking to you so I hope you will come down here and do something for us poor folks in Texas.' That moment changed Alan's life, he told an interviewer fifty years later: 'I saw what I had to do. My job was to try and get as much of these views, these feelings, this unheard majority onto the centre of the stage.' Their recording machine would be 'a voice for the voiceless'.

In Jackson they recorded spirituals and hymns: 'Wave after wave of melody flowed from the group with never a false note, the voices blending exquisitely,' wrote John. 'Were it possible for the world to listen to such a group singing, with no vestige of self-consciousness or artificiality, the songs that seem to have sprung full-panoplied with beauty and power from the emotional experiences of a people, I say the world would stop and listen.' When they arrived in what was known as the Negro Republic of Sandy Island, off the coast of Carolina, they found that Ben Small, the leader of the church choir they had been invited to record, had just that day been shot dead after being caught in flagrante with a neighbour's wife; Brother Ben's surprisingly amicable 36-hour funeral wake provided an unexpected recording opportunity. Elsewhere riverside baptisms and revivalist sermons yielded glorious, rough-hewn poetry.

Some of the songs the Lomaxes collected were ballads about lynchings, others were English ballads from way back; one was an amalgam of the cowboy song 'The streets of Laredo' with the English ballad 'Barbara Allen' which the diarist Samuel Pepys had collected in London in 1666. There were witty and high-spirited efforts like the much-covered 'Rock Island Line' with its human hooter sounding at the end of each stanza. And there were songs reflecting institutional sufferings like this call-and-response evocation of a whipping, with the captain on horseback bearing vengefully down on his victim:

> *Ridin in a hurry*
> *Good Godamighty!*
> *Bull whip in one han'*
> *Cowhide in de udder*
> *Good Godamighty!*
> *'Bully, low down yo britches!'*
> *Good Godamighty!*

When that song was recorded, punctuated by the thud of axes, everyone within earshot was reduced to mutinous silence.

Work songs loomed large, with their tireless, pounding rhythms:

> *Eighteen hammers fallin, get on line,*
> *There ain't no hammer here ring like mine ...*

In the swamps of East Texas they noted how songs could both reflect and direct the finer points of railway track-laying. And they were fascinated by the 'field hollers' they found, with Alan applying precise musicological analysis to these improvised musical shouts by men working alone: 'They are solos, slow in tempo, free in rhythm, composed of long, gliding, ornamented and melismatic phrases, given a melancholy character by minor intervals as well as by blued or bent tones, sounding like sobs or moans or keening or pain-filled cries.' The best holler they heard came from a man named Enoch whose cry, in John's view, placed him among folk-singing's immortals:

> From far off in the darkness, long, lonesome, full-voiced, brooding notes pierced the stillness of a perfect night, indescribable and unforgettable. Starting on a low note, the cry reached a crescendo in such pervasive volume and intensity that it seemed to fill the black void of darkness. The sound came from everywhere and nowhere. Then the cry shaded downward, with the lower notes thrice repeated. Suddenly silence.

When asked what his holler was designed to express, Enoch replied with elegant simplicity: 'Blues done gone! Song done carried de blues away.'

Nicknames were an antidote to prison anonymity, and the Lomaxes collected thousands of them. The Texan singer James Baker was christened Iron Head, when a tree fell on him and he allegedly never lost a stroke of his axe or a phrase of his song. Lead Belly (aka Huddie Ledbetter) earned his name thanks to his strength, his unapologetic recidivism after several convictions for homicidal violence, and the bullet permanently lodged in his stomach. And he was to become, for a time, part of the Lomax team.

*　*　*

Lead Belly was the self-styled King of the Twelve-String Guitar, having learned his art from the celebrated blues guitarist Blind Lemon Jefferson. Blind Lemon combined quicksilver instrumental virtuosity with theatrical wit and an irresistibly arresting voice. Lead Belly didn't possess Blind Lemon's sophisticated musicality, but he had the charisma of an outlaw and

20　Prisoners in Angola, Louisiana, with Lead Belly (Huddie Ledbetter) in the foreground, photographed in 1934 by Alan Lomax.

inexhaustible musical and verbal inventiveness. John and Alan recorded him on a Louisiana prison visit in 1933, but their original cylinder recordings had a painfully primitive sound-quality. Arming themselves a year later with a gigantic aluminium-disc machine built into the back of their Ford, they were able to record with much higher fidelity, and, with a cactus needle or thorn as their stylus, they could use playback to check if second takes were needed. Travelling south again to recapture the sound of their original singers, they found Lead Belly still in prison, but with a freshly written song addressed to the state governor requesting his release.

He was indeed released, though that was thanks to automatic remission for good behaviour. Lead Belly and the Lomaxes remained convinced, however, that the song had played its part, and thus was the Lead Belly legend born: the murderer who sang his way to freedom. So appealing was the fiction that it was widely believed, surfacing in Tennessee Williams's play *Orpheus Descending* in 1957, and in a Lead Belly biopic in 1976.

Destitute, Lead Belly persuaded John to take him on as his driver and recording assistant: as Szwed tells it, the story of his turbulent six-month employment has a cautionary inevitability. His impressive prison cred helped smooth the path for many further recordings; he and John started giving joint performances for gatherings of folklorists, writers, civil rights campaigners, and well-heeled New Yorkers. Moses Asch, the crusading boss of Folkways Records who would later issue many Lead Belly recordings, was not so impressed. 'John Lomax – I hated his guts, but he was a terrific guy,' he recalled in 1986. 'He dressed [Lead Belly] up as a convict, and he would drag him round to show what a great guy John Lomax was, because he was his guardian.'

Suddenly all the rage, Lead Belly started interlarding his blues and work songs with pop and jazz, and with help from the country singer Tex Ritter (a friend of John's) he got his first recording contract. The legend grew and grew, with the *Herald Tribune* heading an article with the capitalised words: 'Sweet singer of the swamplands here to do a few tunes between homicides ... Why, he himself has sung to 2 prison pardons.' The infuriated Lomaxes did all they could to ensure that, despite the sensationalising of his image, he didn't abandon what they regarded as his true vocation, as a spokesman for black culture. Bringing out a book entitled *Negro Folk Songs as Sung by Lead Belly*, with scholarly annotations and an in-depth interview with the singer, was their way of keeping ideological control. However, the relationship between Lead Belly and John Lomax gradually fell apart, with the singer insisting on going his own way and hiring a string of lawyers to get back the money he believed John owed him. Yet the book was a flop, the record earned no royalties, the joint performances barely covered their costs, and John's protective support for his headstrong co-performer had been unstintingly generous; the evidence suggests that in financial terms John had behaved impeccably.

Meanwhile a debate was brewing over Lead Belly's authorship. A corner of the curtain concealing his art was lifted by the folklorist Fred Ramsey, who described how he acquired his songs: 'He stated that he took a melody from any given song, combined it with words of another, or of his own free rhyming, and then had the piece he was ready to sing. "I just take 'em and fix 'em," he said.' When Lead Belly heard Bessie Smith's recording of 'Nobody knows you when you're down and out', 'he sat very still at first, listening to the introduction and the chorus. By the time Bessie was on her second go-round, Lead Belly was humming along with her. Then, right after hearing the record, he sang it through.' Two weeks later he came back, announced that he had 'learned' the song, 'and proceeded to run through it in a style completely his own'.

The Lomaxes' habitual scrupulousness about authorship was intensified when they invited George Herzog to annotate the songs in the Lead Belly book. Herzog was a Yale professor with a rigorously anthropological approach, and he disconcerted them by suggesting that only three of the book's songs were Lead Belly originals, with the rest coming from white American tradition. John's introduction acknowledged this criticism in terms which could apply to much of the music discussed in this book:

> We present this set of songs, therefore, not as folk songs entirely, but as a cross-section of Afri-American songs that have influenced and have been influenced by popular music; and we present this singer, not as a folk singer, handing on a tradition faithfully, but as a folk artist who contributes to the tradition, and as a musician of a sort important in the growth of American popular music.

* * *

Alan's appointment, at twenty-two, as assistant archivist of American folk song at the Library of Congress – with John as his boss – heralded his emergence as one of the cultural leaders of New Deal America. Folklorists were integral to the campaign to help Americans reconnect with their culture, and Alan became a member of an avant-garde group of artist-activists which included the musicologist Charles Seeger and the playwright Nicholas Ray; film directors Joseph Losey and Elia Kazan, and architect Frank Lloyd Wright, were among their allies.

Despite near-deafness in one ear, Alan began to carve out a career as a ballad-singer for audiences in both labour unions and smart society. His day job meant classifying records, typing out lyrics, and answering scholarly enquiries, but he gave talks, wrote articles, and continued to record as part of an ambitious project to document folk music in every American state. Following in the footsteps of the British collector Cecil Sharp, Alan and his wife Elizabeth went off to record in Kentucky, braving hard conditions to bring back 1,502 discs for the archive; their aim, he said, was to help 'the home-made music of the mountains' reassert itself. And despite his father's bust-up with Lead Belly he retained links with the singer, inviting him to record more songs for the library. Meanwhile Alan was collaborating with John on a new anthology for a scholarly readership entitled *Our Singing Country*, for which Seeger's pupil and second wife Ruth Crawford Seeger was making transcriptions with a fastidiousness which would have impressed Bartók, and which drove Alan and his publisher mad.

Ruth Crawford Seeger was a modernist composer who, after a deep study of Bartók's transcription techniques, took the transcription of folk-song recordings to a level of sophistication which is still unsurpassed. Her appendix to *Our Singing Country*, in which she set out her transcription philosophy, was deemed by Alan Lomax to be too long and finicky to be published, and it had to wait sixty years before the music theorist Larry Polansky, aided by Seeger's biographer Judith Tick, brought out an annotated edition. According to Seeger's stepson Pete Seeger, she regarded her transcriptions as her art, and Lomax's refusal to publish the appendix came as a devastating blow.

Entitling it *The Music of American Folk Song*, she opened with the graphic illustration of a point at once obvious and hugely significant. She juxtaposed a 'correct' staff notation of 'Swing low, sweet chariot' with a line consisting of curves within curves representing all the little moments of vibrato in a recording; she presented other possible transcriptions on a spectrum in between. 'Notation with a view to readability and singability often strips the song of many or most of the finer subtleties of its particular style of performance, and leaves not much more than a skeleton of the original singing,' she wrote. She went on to survey the numerous possible styles of rendering the same sung melody on the page, taking into account such things as the degree of 'blueness' on the flattened blue-notes, and vocal mannerisms like 'the half-sung, half-spoken drop of the voice so characteristic of Negro singing, and the quick upward flip heard frequently among both white and Negro singers'. Tick describes this as 'a small book about small things. Sharps and flats, ties, dots, and rests, flags added to note-heads here not there, movable bar-lines, tiny curved lines called phrases, words altered by consonants added or subtracted, breaths taken in and let out later rather than sooner.' It's easy to see why this sort of thing didn't fit with Alan Lomax's impatiently headlong campaign, but the ideas in Ruth Crawford Seeger's book continue to echo in ethnomusicological debate today.

Jazz, Alan was to say later, had in those days seemed his worst enemy: 'Through the forces of radio, it was wiping out the music that I care about.' But the British journalist Alistair Cooke, who had been making radio programmes with LOC material, persuaded him to invite the ageing Jelly Roll Morton to come to the library and record a few numbers. 'I looked at him with considerable suspicion. But I thought, I'd take this cat on, and see how much folk music a jazz musician knows. The first recording began by [my] asking if he knew "Alabama bound". He played me about the most beautiful "Alabama bound" I had ever heard.' This man, he realised, was a 'creole Benvenuto Cellini', so he embarked on a recitation of Homeric proportions. The recordings, still to be heard courtesy of the Library of Congress and amounting to a brilliantly analytical history of early jazz piano, went on for a month: oral history had never taken this form before. Alan's title for the project was 'Autobiography of Jelly Roll Morton' and he would go on to do more autobiographies (most notably with the Dust Bowl singer-guitarist Woody Guthrie). Such interviews, he said, were 'almost like an analytic interview (only there was no couch). What I had decided on was a twelve-foot shelf of unknown America recording its life in prose.'

His next conquest was of the radio. In 1942, pointing to what the BBC and Radio France had done with folk music from the LOC archive, he and the Library persuaded CBS to commission a series of twenty-five programmes on folk music, with a huge production team plus a fifty-piece symphony orchestra; Alan would be the principal singer, commentator, and script adviser, and classical composers would be commissioned to base new works on folk songs. The programmes, broadcast to classrooms all over the country, were a success, though Alan had reservations about the classical works, and in particular Aaron Copland's. To inspire Copland, Alan had played him field recordings of the Southern ballad 'John Henry', but he was contemptuous of the result. 'His composition spoke for the Paris of Nadia Boulanger,' Alan complained, 'and not for the wild land and the heart-torn people who had made the song. The spirit and emotion of "John Henry" shone nowhere in this score because he had never heard, much less experienced them. And this same pattern held for all the folk symphonic suites, for twenty boring weeks.' On the other hand, Alan successfully brought an ex-football player named Burl Ives onto the programme after teaching him how to sing in country style, and he had no trouble harnessing Woody Guthrie's gritty musical evocations of John Steinbeck's novel *The Grapes of Wrath*, John Ford's film of which had just been released.

Guthrie hailed from Indian territory in Oklahoma, and he'd worked as a reporter before a series of family tragedies caused him to hit bottom. Alan was lost for words when he first witnessed Guthrie's seamless amalgam of speech and song: 'This little tiny guy, big bushy hair, with this great voice and guitar … just electrified us all.' He recorded Guthrie's autobiography on an even more massive scale than Jelly Roll's, then made him the focus of a book entitled, in Guthrie's phrase, *Hard-Hitting Songs for Hard-Hit People*. Put together by Alan, Guthrie, and Charles Seeger's son Pete, this book included protest and workers' songs from the Lomax collection, and mimeographed song sheets from union labour schools; it was a triumph for Alan's kind of song collecting, and would be, as Seeger put it, 'a testament to an unknown America, the folk poets who had been politically active and still kept their gift for song-making'.

But no publishing house would touch it, and nearly thirty years elapsed before it found a publisher in Moses Asch. Alan had in the meantime got Guthrie a contract to write a song suite based on John Ford's film of Steinbeck's novel, and he also put Lead Belly and Guthrie together: two singers from similar cultural backgrounds, whose art predated the advent of studios and amplification, and who instantly hit it off.

But Alan remained uneasy about his Southern interviews: blacks, he felt, would never properly confide in a white folklorist. He suggested a collaboration between the LOC and Fisk, the most distinguished black university in the South; thus it was that he and a team of Fisk researchers headed off to Coahoma, the cotton capital of the Delta, in 1941. Among the singers they recorded one hot July afternoon was a shy, barefoot farm-worker named McKinley Morganfield whose nickname, Muddy Waters, would go on to have talismanic significance for the Beatles, and one of whose songs (which Alan recorded that day) would provide Mick Jagger with a name for his new pop group. Muddy's songs were all about sexual desire and frustration, but, as Alan observed, 'they were more than blues, they were love songs of the Deep South, gently erotic and sentimental … He sang and played with such finesse, with such a mercurial and sensitive bond between voice and guitar.' Muddy's first song – 'Well, it's getting late in the evenin/ I feel like, feel like blowin my horn' – was in Alan's view 'as artful, as carefully structured as an eighteenth-century love lyric'. We can check on the truth of that by listening to it on YouTube: the singer begins by announcing the sorrows caused by his inconstant mistress, and ends with his death from grief; the guitar becomes a sympathetic confidant, while the regretful singer is constantly pausing, repeating wounded phrases, and dwelling on the occasional key word with a faint touch of yodel. The artistry is serenely accomplished.

'I realised I had recorded a masterpiece, and there was space for talk in the magic moment just at the end of a performance,' Alan wrote of this recording. So he asked Muddy some questions, beginning with – how had he been impelled to create that blues? 'I was changing a wheel on my car,' Muddy replied, 'I had been mistreated by a girl, and it got running in my mind to sing this song. I just felt blue … and I started singing.' The rest of his story is history: quitting the farm job when Alan sent him the discs of his songs, catching the train to Chicago where he became king of the blues, leading his own band and patenting his sentimental pop-blues style, with Alan remaining his friend and supporter throughout.

In 1947, as his father's health deteriorated (John Lomax would die the next year), Alan went back to the notoriously violent Parchman Farm penitentiary they had visited in 1935. He wanted to see how songs had changed there over the previous twelve years, and the prison's singing tradition had indeed gone into a decline. But while there he recorded what was to become a celebrated collection of work songs and delicately inflected hollers called *Murderers' Home*. The pun in the title – murderers held in a murderous place – remained apposite; Alan's sleeve note to the album, which stressed the inhumanity of the conditions under which the black convicts had to labour, breathed a Dickensian crusading fire. One track was of a freshly composed tree-felling song whose polyrhythmic intricacy closely reflected the rhythm of voices and bodies. Four men in stripes standing in a square round a tree, each facing inwards, with the two on opposite corners chopping together on beat one, and the other pair on beat two: in this way all four axes could be constantly in motion, without colliding or causing injury: 'Two golden chips were started by one pair of blades, then immediately carved out as the next pair struck … the chips sometimes ringing against the microphone.' The contrapuntal choral style enriched the rhythm, with each man adding his own touch of harmony or making improvised comments like 'Let me hear you' or 'Yes, my Lordy'. The lyrics alternated between sad and cheerful thoughts, and as Alan pointed out, while most work-song stanzas were short, these stanzas could run to a minute and a half, 'like an art song, or a Far Eastern improvisation, or a bebop solo'.

On the last chorus he reported,

> the live oak came crashing down. 22 [the leader] and his buddies stepped back, blew on their hands, and grinned. There was back-slapping when they heard their recording. Much later, when the record was released, somebody in Harlem found it and without a word to 22 or myself used it to orchestrate Alvin Ailey's *Work Song Ballet*. It is a pity [theatre goers] could not see the dovetailed pas de quatre for axes performed that day by 22 and his friends Little Red, Tangle Eye, and Hard Hair.

Alan's commentary, passionately arguing the need for prison reform, may have been the reason why this sweetly sung album, like the Guthrie book, took years to find a publisher. It was released in 1957, but he still preserved the anonymity of his singers, as he did with another politically controversial album he had recorded at the same time.

That arose out of a series of midnight concerts he had been fronting in New York's Town Hall; for the most successful event, entitled 'Honkytonk Blues at Midnight', he drafted in three household names: singer-songwriter Big Bill Broonzy, pianist Memphis Slim, and harmonica virtuoso Sonny Boy Williamson. After the show, lubricating the conversation with sour mash, he got them talking into his disc recorder. They discussed life in the levee camps, the plantations, and the penitentiaries waiting to receive rebels; they explained how the blues were their metaphorical revenge. Naming names, they swapped lynching stories, quoting the infamous adage governing life down South: 'If you kill a mule, I'll buy another one. If you kill a nigger, I'll hire another one.' This was a group autobiography of an incendiary kind never recorded before. Alan regarded the session as a triumph, but his interviewees were appalled when they listened back to themselves; they first demanded that the records be destroyed, then settled for a promise that their identities would never be revealed. When *Blues in the Mississippi Night* was released as a mixture of songs and interviews in 1957, it was with an invented name for each musician. Their fear was that if their names were known, family members still living down South would be punished in their stead. The full story was only made public in 1990, by which time all three men were dead.

* * *

Alan's American exploits have tended to obscure his parallel achievements further afield. In 1935 he made a recording trip to the Bahamas, where the descendants of several African tribes – Ibo, Ijo, Yoruba, Mandingo – had melded their own musical traditions with New World variants; freed slaves who settled there after the American Civil War brought yet more material to the mix. Alan's haul included sea shanties as well as 'rushing', jumping, and ring dances, and the polyphonic 'rhyming spiritual' anthems of the sponge fishermen, a convivial art form which had at that time reached the apogee of its development.

His trip to the Bahamas had been made on the assumption that, as Szwed puts it, it offered the chance to view the culture of people of African descent as it might have been in America at the end of the eighteenth century. His trip to Haiti the following year was inspired by the conviction that people there were closer to Africa than any others in the New World; his primary aim was to record the music of *vodou*, at the time enjoying notoriety in America thanks to a rash of films with titles like *Crime of Vodou* and *Revolt of the Zombies*. But in this quest he depended on guidance from the Roman Catholic Haitian

21 Alan Lomax and singer Raphael Hurtault listening to playback in Dominica in 1962.

bourgeoisie; he and his co-researcher, the black anthropologist Zora Neale Hurston, had to join other researchers on well-beaten tracks. When Hurston discovered to her fury that she was herself being studied by rival anthropologists while she participated in a tribal dance – a hotel bell-boy had sent them all to the same place – Alan struck out into the bush alone.

Just outside Port-au-Prince he found an intoxicating alternative realm: 'We came around the corner of a shanty and saw four couples dancing a slow one-step in the alley-way between a high candelabra cactus fence and the house. Hanging from the fence was an old bicycle tire, burning slow and orange, throwing a golden flame across the dancers … I wish I could tell how beautiful this scene was, how melancholy, how restrained and graceful.' The music – a melange of marches, blues, *meringues*, and *bals* – was 'click, chatter, tinkle, and deep throbbing thump-thump'. The instrumentation of the band comprised, in addition to intricate and sophisticated drumming, 'a pair of bones, a three-string guitar, a pair of Cuban *cha-cha*s and a *manoumba* – a rectangular box with a circular opening across which are ranged, in an iron bar, eight-inch iron tongues … Each of the instruments had a distinct rhythm which fitted into the rhythmic pattern of the whole, and the four players sang. It was deliciously lovely.'

The denizens of this vodou spirit-world, he said, moved with such sudden shifts of attitude that they seemed to become Cubist sculptures. Haiti, he declared, was 'all folklore', with every peasant being a potential anthropologist's informant. His haul, after a four-month stay, consisted of 350 feet of film and fifty hours of recorded sound: interviews, children's game songs, and folk tales as well as full-blown vodou rituals, all of which were deposited with the Library of Congress.

The immediate post-war years saw Alan remaking himself as America's first folk-music radio DJ and giving popular songs an increasingly political twist. He provided the music for Henry Wallace's presidential campaign in 1948, roping in Woody Guthrie, Pete Seeger, and Paul Robeson, and after the campaign's failure he masterminded a brilliantly successful radio series in which 'radio ballads' were used to spread the word about penicillin as a cure for venereal disease; he became the go-to man for musical events on behalf of many good causes. But the crunch came in 1950 with the publication of an article by a group of ex-FBI agents entitled *Red Channels: the Report of Communist Influence in Radio and Television*, in which Alan was named along with Orson Welles, Leonard Bernstein, Dorothy Parker, Aaron Copland, Burl Ives, and Arthur Miller. Alan hadn't hidden his partisan anger in a review of his friend Ben Botkin's politically sanitising book *A Treasury of Southern Folklore* published in 1949, and which carried no mention of lynching. Meanwhile the FBI had long been keeping tabs on him. Insisting that his exit wasn't in response to McCarthyite persecution, he set sail for Europe.

In London he became – together with folk-singer Ewan MacColl and folklorist A. L. Lloyd – a leader of Britain's folk-song revival, with Alan and MacColl forming their own skiffle group. And at the same time he was embarking on a hugely ambitious project which was to become the focus for the rest of his life. The idea for the project had been sparked by Columbia's perfecting of the LP record, which seemed to Alan the ideal vehicle for a folk-music album, and then, by extension, for a series of albums representing all the folk traditions of the world. He had proposed this idea at a folklore conference at Indiana University, but since nobody rose to the bait he decided to do it himself. Columbia, to whom he took the idea, commissioned thirty LPs for a series to be called the *World Library of Folk and Primitive Music*. In Szwed's words, Alan would become 'a one-man foundation, operating without benefit of the usual academic credentials and support, stepping uneasily between the world of commerce and entertainment and the abstemious, hermetic life of scholars'.

At the instigation of the anthropologist Claude Lévi-Strauss, the Musée de l'Homme in Paris invited Alan to use it as the base for his research, but he found its atmosphere stiflingly academic, and he also realised he would have to round out its exiguous holdings with music freshly recorded by himself. Hence his move to London in 1953, where he had already established links with the BBC through his wartime broadcasts (and where his activities were to be jointly monitored, without his knowledge, by the American embassy and the London police). He started the research for his new venture with a recording trip to Ireland, accompanied by the folk singer Robin Roberts who became one of his long succession of girlfriend/assistants; recording in bars and private houses, they gathered enough for an album, which in turn inspired him to compose an Irish ballad opera. The prospect of collecting songs for a Scottish ballad opera then drove him north where, supported by a BBC commission, he investigated the music of the Hebrides. And there, in the call-and-response of weavers and cattle herders, he encountered music which seemed startlingly akin to the work songs in Deep South prisons: 'I started the recording machine one night and the people around it looked like ordinary shopkeepers, but suddenly, every one of them joined in on the phrase exactly at the right time … They sang *together* as well as any Negro congregation I've ever heard.' But he was shunned by Scottish folklorists, who regarded him as an intruder on their patch.

In 1952 Alan was told by Columbia that publication of his series depended on the inclusion of a Spanish record. Armed with a commission from the BBC Third Programme to provide music for a Spanish radio series, he reluctantly agreed to run the project. To find an editor he went to a folklore conference in Mallorca, but the professor in charge was a refugee Nazi who had taken over the Berlin folk-song archive after Hitler had removed its Jewish director; that professor was now directing folk-music research in Barcelona. 'When I told him about my project,' Alan wrote later,

> he let me know that he personally would see to it that no Spanish musicol-
> ogist would help me. He also suggested that I leave Spain. I had not really
> intended to stay. I had only a few reels of tape with me and I had made no
> study of Spanish ethnology. This, however, was my first experience with a
> Nazi and, as I looked across the luncheon table at this authoritarian idiot, I
> promised myself that I would record the music of the benighted country if
> it took me the rest of my life.

The poet Robert Graves, then living in Mallorca, was one of the friends who encouraged him to persevere.

The Franco regime's attitude to folk music was reminiscent of the Soviet regime's in Central Asia during the Twenties; in both places, folklore was seen as a tool for bolstering nationalism. In Spain, politically correct styles were laid down – with mobile units of women educators sent out to 'rescue' and rearrange songs in accordance with the prevailing fascist ideology – while the language and music of troublesome sub-groups was proscribed; thus were Galician, Catalonian, and Basque elements repressed. Alan Lomax's policy was to collect *lo popular* – the people's music – in all its forms, and to interview and photograph the musicians; since local musicology was in its infancy and skewed by politics, the three thousand items he recorded were of great interest. And since many songs – like the stone-cutters' song from Galicia – were tied to traditions which have now disappeared, the importance of these recordings remains perennial.

'For a month or so,' Alan wrote,

> I wandered erratically, sunstruck by the grave beauty of the land, faint and sick at the sight of this noble people, ground down by poverty and a police state. I saw that in Spain, folklore was not mere fantasy and entertainment. Each Spanish village was a self-contained cultural system with tradition penetrating every aspect of life; and it was their inherited folklore that the peasant, the fishermen, the muleteers and the shepherds I met found their models for that noble behaviour and sense of the beautiful which made them such satisfactory friends. It was never hard to find the best singers in Spain, because everyone in their neighbourhood knew them and under-stood how and why they were the finest stylists in their particular idiom. Nor, except in the hungry south, did people ask for money in exchange for their ballads.

The areas he found richest in music were not in the Gypsy south but 'the quiet, sombre plains of the west, the highlands of northern Castile, and the green tangle of the Pyrenees where Spain faces the Atlantic and the Bay of Biscay'. And on this trip he developed a recording technique which would shock ethnomusicologists today: 'I hold the mike, use my hand for shading, volume ... Empathy is most important in field work. It's necessary to be able to put your hand on the artist while he sings. They have to react to you. Even if they're mad at you, it's better than nothing.'

Alan's notes evoke a sense of place, as with the aged shepherd's straw hut in Extremadura as he sang an old Romanian ballad: 'An oil lamp, a three-legged frying pan in a little square hearth ... forks and spoons stuck in a wall of rushes, rush beds of aromatic branches ... no windows, airy and clean ... low stools of cork and knotted branches.' Many of the ballads Alan found derived from a vigorous anti-clerical tradition; some hailed from England. When he recorded a mother in Valencia singing a lullaby, he made sure the listener heard the creaking of the cradle. The work songs by women, which often doubled as wedding songs, were pure fun, as was the *jota*, complete with shouts and whistles, which a shepherd from Andorra joyfully sang to his dog and flock.

Some of the ploughing songs have a Middle Eastern modality; when a group of girls in Extremadura sing a subversively satirical song whose scale ascends in the minor mode and descends in the major, the pitch control is effortlessly perfect. What strikes the listener about all these singers is the purity of their intonation, and their intense musicality. Meanwhile the instrumental tracks have charm: no wonder Miles Davis was inspired, with Gil Evans as his arranger, to use Alan's recording of Galician pan-pipe melodies as the basis for 'The Pan Piper' in his 1960 album *Sketches of Spain*. The sound is pure Miles Davis, but the spirit is Galician.

* * *

Nearing fifty, Alan was now in creative overdrive. 'I live in a tiny room that swarms with plans, ambitious plans,' he wrote from London to his estranged wife Elizabeth. 'For a ballet, for a play, for a book about Spain, for three television series, for my two books about America, for a book about England, for continuation of my series of records ... All the imaginative qualities that were repressed all my life are beginning to merge now ... I can tackle literally anything I choose.' The next thirty-five years would see the thwarting of many of those ambitions, but the fulfilment of others in a constant frenzy of activity.

And he still had time for one more major exploration. To compile the Italian volume of the Columbia series he'd been given the run of the archives at Radio Audizione Italiane, but its patchy holdings indicated that, as in Spain, he would have do the collecting himself. Armed once more with a BBC commission, he set off in 1954 on a meticulously planned journey, justly claiming later to have been 'by chance' the first person to record over the whole country: 'I was a kind of musical Columbus in reverse. Nor had I arrived on the scene a moment too soon.' What film-maker Pier Paolo Pasolini described as 'a limitless pre-industrial and pre-national peasant world' proved a musical cornucopia; Alan's tribute to this, collected on a nine-month journey, would fill sixty miles of tape.

When he and his assistant Diego Carpitella started that journey in Sicily, the sum total of existing Sicilian folk recordings amounted to just one hundred items. In three weeks they compiled a musical panorama which – thanks to Alan's detailed notes, and to interviews in which one can sense his persuasive charm – was also a document reflecting every aspect of life on this dirt-poor, politically oppressed island. Recording wasn't easy: irate husbands might gatecrash sessions where their wives were singing and drag them home; in one town some local mafiosi decided to murder the recordists and sell their equipment, and were only deterred by a senior mafioso from Palermo. And they nearly came to blows when Alan asked Diego to question suspicious Sicilian peasants about their sex lives and their voice production: 'He told me he didn't care personally whether Italian peasants made music through their throats, out of their ears or blew it out of their backsides – he just liked the music,' Alan wrote home. But the resultant recordings – tuna-fishermen celebrating their catch, salt-diggers humping their forty-pound sacks, reapers and threshers, and a blood-and-guts recitation by the last *jongleur* in Palermo of the *Chanson de Roland* – had a gripping immediacy.

Next stop Calabria, even poorer than Sicily and, after a series of floods and earthquakes, in the middle of an irreversible exodus to the cities. Here they caught a culture literally on the point of disappearing, including mischievous polyphony sung by women in a dialect no longer spoken, a *sdegno* song (expressing disdain for the faithless lover), and a children's tarantella accompanied by a bagpipe, with struck pebbles marking the rhythm. 'Neither the gaiety of Neapolitan song nor the tarantella can conceal for long the sorrowful voice of southern Italy, which has been the prey of Rome and Naples for a score of centuries,' Alan wrote in a radio script. 'You will understand this if you allow this razor-edged voice to cut at your heart – a woman, her throat clenched, with the sorrows of a lifetime of oppression and possessive, jealous love, her face a mask of sorrow, rocks back and forth in a straight-legged chair and sings a lullaby to her child.'

In Venice they recorded the chants of the *battipali*, men whose ancestors had sunk the oak logs on which the city was built; in a village in Emilia-Romagna they caught May plays and songs of Boccaccio-style bawdiness; in Liguria, where the polyphony was based on drones in a manner reminiscent of Georgian music, they recorded medieval French ballads. And in Genoa they encountered the *trallalero*, a five-part a cappella form: 'Here was an improvised, multi-part counterpoint as complex as anything in music, yet as easily achieved by these rough, tough characters in their wine-soaked bar-room along the docks of Genoa as the sound of the spiritual was for the African Americans in my Southern churches.' The men stand in a closed circle and are directed by complex hand signals; the leads are taken by a tenor and a falsettist called *la donna* who has been trained since childhood to sing in the pure, high register of the ecclesiastical boy soprano; one of the two baritone parts is called *la chitarra* ('the guitar'), while the basses, described as 'Slavic', provide the grounding. It generates a heady excitement: no surprise that today's Genoese musicians are preserving this extraordinary tradition.

* * *

Done on a minuscule budget, this had been a gruelling trip, and it was marred by thefts, the most serious of which saw the disappearance of most of Alan's notebooks. As a result, the book in which he'd planned to compare folklore traditions in Spain and Italy could never be written. On the other hand, a much bigger idea which he had been nursing finally jelled in his mind, and in a letter home in 1954 he spelt it out.

It concerned a new science which would correlate musical style and regional culture:

> The music of your place stands for everything that has ever happened to you when you were a kid ... it is a quick and immediate symbol for all the deepest emotions the people of your part of the world share ... So far as I can tell there are between [eight] and a dozen main musical families in the world – styles of making music. Each of these styles is characterised by a way of placing the voice, a way of moving the body, a relation of the song to the dance, an attitude toward music, a kind of melody ... All this gathering of folksongs, besides putting a lot of good tunes back into circulation, will serve in increasing man's knowledge of himself ... Folk music can become a historical touchstone like the radioactive substances studied by geologists ... Out of this could grow a proper way of relating art to society, or deciding what kind of art you want to have in what kind of world.

With the aid of his long-time supporter the anthropologist Margaret Mead, he floated this visionary idea, which he called Cantometrics, at a meeting of the American Anthropological Association; in 1962 he would be appointed Director of the Cantometrics and Choreometrics Research Project at Columbia University. But he was determined that it should not be colonised by academe; whenever possible it would abjure specialist terminology. Yet this new theory of song would be underpinned by Alan's reading of Freud, Marx, Darwin, and Emile Durkheim: it would be nothing if not intellectual. Alan's thumbnail analysis of the nursery rhyme 'Cock Robin' nicely illustrates his psychosocial approach: 'Oppressed, humiliated, denied, bullied and talked down to by a race of strong giants, [children's] fantasies have naturally run to violence and death', while their dreams and nightmares are of revenge and punishment for their 'guilty thoughts'.

Alan's new science was never espoused by ethnomusicologists, many of whom questioned its underlying assumptions. But that mattered less than the fact that he'd used it to open up a debate about singing and culture which broke new ground. And he didn't let its failure deflect him from his flamboyant civil-rights campaigns, nor from his plan to create a cultural database – a 'Global Jukebox' – which would anticipate the internet's predictive algorithms, nor from making further musical explorations. Accompanied by the folk singer Shirley Collins, his girlfriend in 1959, he went on a recording trip to the American South in the course of which they discovered the until-then obscure blues singer Fred McDowell. Three years later, with another female helper, he spent a summer scouring the Caribbean for folk music on behalf of the Rockefeller Foundation; on a trip to trawl archives in Moscow he found time for a spot of recording in Transylvania: he just couldn't stop. And the world played up to him: a 1957 issue of the London magazine *Punch* carried a cartoon of a ragged farmer sitting outside his shack and disconsolately singing 'I've got those Alan-Lomax-ain't-been-round-to-record-me blues'.

It was inevitable that a man with such an outsize personality – and enjoying such success – should have his detractors, though Alan's seem to have been driven by pure professional jealousy. He could indeed be arrogant and overbearing, he needed at all times to be the belle of the ball, and it was not always clear when he crossed the line between championing his musicians and patronising them. The most serious criticisms made of him were – and still are – that he occasionally stole credit from other folklorists for his musical 'discoveries', and that he denied Lead Belly's heirs some royalties to which they were entitled for the song 'Goodnight Irene'.

But the question of copyright in folk music is a thorny one, as he freely acknowledged. In 1950 he roughed out an article in which he described folk-song collecting as taking place within 'a free enterprise system', and he identified four agents in the process of bringing a song to the public. First was the singer, who might well also be creative; secondly the collector, who found the singer, recorded the song, maybe also arranged it and found a publisher; thirdly the arranger who might make it more saleable; and fourthly the publisher and record company. All, he suggested, might legitimately make a copyright claim. He himself was firmly on the side of the singers: in the early 1940s, when the American copyright office declared that 'a folksinger could not claim to be an interpretive performer', Alan insisted that the Library of Congress needed releases from singers, and that they should be paid if recordings were sold. There is no evidence that he was anything but scrupulous in his own dealings with musicians, even in the often chaotic circumstances of recording in the wild.

And he was incensed by his discovery in 1958 that the Scottish singer Lonnie Donegan was copying Lead Belly's songs complete with his performance style and introductory remarks, and passing them off as his own. Ironically, Donegan's rendition of 'Rock Island Line' became celebrated in its own right in America, inspiring cover versions. Lead Belly did not write 'Rock Island Line', but he very much owned his performance of it, in the same way that he owned his performance of 'Goodnight Irene', a song which he had learned from his uncles, and which the Weavers turned into a hit in 1950. Donegan's appropriation, Alan thundered, was 'outright knavery'.

'Alan did not himself file for copyright,' Szwed writes, 'but signed Popular Songwriter Contracts that allowed publishers to copyright those songs ... Alan's name, along with the singer's, would come under the title "Writer", but with added language that said "Collected, adapted, and arranged by".' The most pertinent comment on this whole controversy came from Charles Seeger, in an article in *Western Folklore* entitled 'Who Owns Folklore – A Rejoinder': 'the folk song is, by definition, and as far as we can tell by reality, entirely a product of plagiarism.'

In 1978 Alan was invited to join the committee advising NASA on which pieces of music to send into space aboard the Voyager spacecraft. He thus had the satisfaction of eternalising the music he had championed, from the Solomon Islands, India, and Japan to Peru and Mexico, and to tracks from Blind Willie Johnson, Louis Armstrong, and Chuck Berry. It was appropriate that in 2000 the Library of Congress should crown him with the title 'Living Legend'. It would take the best part of a non-stop year to listen to all the recordings on his website; he was a consummate showman, and a Utopian visionary with an unerring instinct for musical beauty. 'He loved his musicians,' says Shirley Collins. 'And they loved him back.'

Sources

The Lomaxes were superb writers, and their respective autobiographies make the perfect starting point. In *Adventures of a Ballad Hunter* John tells the story of his childhood and youth, his ground-breaking recording trips to the penitentiaries, and the gallery of characters he encounters down South. Alan's *The Land Where the Blues Began* covers the same terrain from a more politically engaged angle, then continues the story after John's death; both accounts include extensive interviews with musicians. John Szwed's magnificent *The Man Who Recorded the World* is as close as we will ever get to a definitive biography of Alan Lomax; as a professor of music, African American studies, and anthropology, Szwed is well placed to chronicle Alan's career (he also knew him) against the backdrop of a constantly changing political and cultural landscape. Billy Bragg's *Roots, Radicals and Rockers* gives a British perspective on Alan's activities in London.

The dawn and early decades of the American recording industry are brought to life in illuminating detail by *American Epic*, written by Bernard MacMahon and Alison McGourty with Elijah Wald, together with its four accompanying CDs of early tracks. Among the many histories of the blues, Paul Oliver's *The Story of the Blues*, published in 1969, is still the best thanks to its musicological underpinning, while Elijah Wald's *The Blues: A Very Short Introduction* offers useful insights. Virtually all the recordings by John and Alan Lomax are now housed on the Lomax website in the Library of Congress, with many also on release as CDs from the Rounder label; each comes with a covering musicological and historical commentary. Ruth Crawford Seeger's *The Music of American Folk Song* opens a musicological by-way on the art of transcription.

Bibliography

Asch, Moses and Alan Lomax, eds, *The Leadbelly Songbook* (New York: Oak Publications, 1962)

Bragg, Billy, *Roots, Radicals and Rockers: How Skiffle Changed the World* (London: Faber, 2017)

Cohen, Ronald D., ed., *Alan Lomax: Selected Writings 1934–1997* (New York: Routledge, 2003)

Lomax, Alan, *The Land Where Blues Began* (New York: Knopf, 1993)

Lomax, Alan, Woody Guthrie, and Pete Seeger, *Hard-Hitting Songs for Hard-Hit People* (New York: Oak Publications, 1967)

Lomax, John A., *Adventures of a Ballad Hunter* (Austin: University of Texas, 2017)

Lomax, John A., *Negro Folk Songs as Sung by Lead Belly* (New York: Macmillan, 1936)

MacMahon, Bernard and Alison McGourty with Elijah Wald, *American Epic* (New York: Touchstone, 2017)

Lomax, John A. and Ruth Crawford Seeger, *Our Singing Country: Folk Songs and Ballads* (New York: Macmillan, 1941)

Oliver, Paul, *The Story of the Blues* (London: Barrie and Jenkins, 1969)

Polansky, Larry, ed., *Ruth Crawford Seeger's 'The Music of American Folk Song' and Selected Other Writings* (London: University of Rochester Press, 2001)

Wald, Elijah, *The Blues: A Very Short Introduction* (Oxford: Oxford University Press, 2010)

22 Theodor Strehlow in 1932, dreaming of exploits to come.

11

'I am a white-skinned Aranda man'

Theodor Strehlow's divided self

AUSTRALIAN ABORIGINAL CULTURE, with its mystical dream-links between humans and their ancestors in both the sky and the earth, has been largely hidden from history. This is particularly true of the songs, dances, and sacred objects which form the ceremonial core of that culture, because many of them are 'closed', and secret. Aboriginal children must come of age before they can be allowed to hear certain songs: the words may not be written down, and absolutely mustn't be published in a book; to market recordings of them in performance would be anathema.

While the European settlers of the nineteenth century carved up the continent, a handful of whites with an ethnographic bent took an interest in the culture of its indigenous inhabitants, and they found their music arresting. One observer saw a resemblance between Aboriginal chant and Judaeo-Christian plainsong, both being 'conducive to the expression of solemnity and grandeur, as well as mystery'. Another described its sound as 'euphony ... due to the gentle and even way in which the voices, naturally melodious, fade away to absolute stillness'. Most of these observers shared the fashionable Darwinist assumption that the Stone Age Aborigines were destined for extinction, but in 1899 two energetic enthusiasts – a biology professor named Baldwin Spencer and his drinking companion Frank Gillen, who ran the telegraph station in Alice Springs – published a major study of Aranda ceremonies entitled *Native Tribes of Central Australia.*

One of the white community's self-appointed tasks was to convert the Aborigines to Christianity, and Lutheran missionaries from Germany, who learned the native languages to translate the Gospel into them, were in the vanguard of this earnest offensive. A scholarly pastor named Johann Reuther was part of it, but the 130 Aboriginal songs he translated into English are now lost. It is with Pastor Carl Strehlow, who arrived to assist Reuther in 1892, and went on to run the Hermannsburg Mission on the Finke River, that the story which is the subject of this chapter begins. And that this story, which focuses on Strehlow's son Theodor (1908–1978), can be told at all is thanks to a revelatory biography by the Australian poet Barry Hill. This book – *Broken*

Song: TGH Strehlow and Aboriginal Possession – deploys the disciplines of psychology, philosophy, anthropology, and poetics to shed light on the life and thought of an extraordinary song collector, and on his epic achievement.

Carl Strehlow was a caring pastor and a dedicated scholar. The situation he inherited at Hermannsburg – and tried to ameliorate – was one of endemic hostility between the small and dispersed Aranda clan and the white settlers in the region, whose attitude was genocidal: shooting parties went out into the bush to keep the male Aboriginal numbers down, and Aboriginal women were seen as sexual game. While discharging his pastoral duties, and having learned the local native languages, Carl Strehlow profited from the goodwill of his Aboriginal parishioners to collect, translate, and interpret large numbers of Aboriginal songs and myths on behalf of the Frankfurt Städtisches Völkermuseum, where ideas of the divine in 'primitive' societies were currently fashionable. Yet there was a reciprocal trade-off in this relationship: the Aranda loved singing Lutheran hymns, and still do – with the Hermannsburg choir still going strong today.

Carl married a Bavarian teenager named Frieda, and they had six children; exhausted by mission life, Frieda persuaded her husband that they should go back to Germany to recuperate for a while. When they returned it was only with their youngest child Theo. Carl's rule as a teacher was enforced with savage beatings, but Theo was clever: his home-schooling was in English, Greek, and Latin, while his everyday talk was in German and Aranda – and all his childhood friends spoke Aranda. This collision of two worlds, Lutheran and Aboriginal, would frame his life and work.

Initially, education drove him and his playmates apart, as did the moment when his father took him into his study to show him some *tjurunga* – pieces of wood and stone bearing sacred Aranda inscriptions – which were at the time puzzling white anthropologists. As Barry Hill points out, Theo's young playmates, as yet uninitiated, would have looked at those objects on pain of death. Watching his father patiently extract information from four men who regularly came to visit – sitting on the floor, singing, reciting, and spitting out their tobacco juice on the rug – Theo was drawn into the ethnographic mindset as an outside observer of the tribe of which, as a young child, he himself had been a member. He imbibed his father's respect for Aboriginal culture, and for the creative Aboriginal mind: both of them found ways to evade their duty as Lutherans to condemn pagan culture as taboo.

Worn down by the stress of his job – exacerbated by accusations during the 1914–18 war that he was turning his congregation into pro-German sympathisers – Carl fell ill, set off on a marathon desert journey to hospital, and died *en route*. The shock of this event on fourteen-year-old Theo was profound. He was packed off to boarding school in Adelaide, where he excelled in Classical and Shakespearean studies, and developed impressive skills as a pianist, horn player, and literary parodist; he won a scholarship to Adelaide University where his charismatic brilliance marked him out as a star. After graduation in 1931 came the question of what he would do his MA in. Norse mythology was his first idea, then Shakespearean tragedy, but he also began to feel the tug of the past. His Classics professor pointed out that no book had been written on Aranda language and culture, and that as a quasi-native speaker he was uniquely equipped to write one. A grant came through, and Theo didn't hesitate: armed with the money, he went home to pick up where his father had left off.

The first thing he did was to compile a list of Aranda names for plants and animals. Then he started to deepen his father's work on the origins of Aranda myths, and to extend his collection of songs. He was aware of the need for all this to be done quickly. 'The past is vanishing fast,' he wrote, 'soon I shall be a stranger in the land that bore me.' His father had established some basic principles: that the literal meaning of the word *tjurunga* was 'one's own secret thing', and that these objects had to be stored in secret-sacred places; that they united the person who possessed them with their ancestors; and that ownership of them was both personal and collective. Carl had also learned that *tjurunga* songs were believed to have been taught at night to their sleeping owners by 'hidden people' living in the earth.

As he set out on his first foray into the bush, Theo carried in his saddlebag a copy of Freud's *Totem and Taboo*, which was at that time a key text for anthropologists working in the field. Freud's assertion that the foundations of culture are to be found in parricide chimed with Theo's thinking at both the theoretical and personal levels: the primal-horde member's murder of his rival for food and women, and that rival being his own father. Theo would be haunted all his life by the feeling that he was the usurper of his father's realm.

Between 1933 and 1935 he covered 7,000 miles with an Aboriginal informant, mostly riding on camels and under constant threat from marauding Aboriginal groups looking for whites to rob and kill; that he could even contemplate this journey was thanks to his childhood immersion in bush survival techniques. After a year he reported success: 'Over seventy full-length myths have been carefully noted down in phonetic script, and some 1,250 double-lined verses of native chants have been recorded with full notes concerning their tempo and their metrical structure.' He had also witnessed 166 totemic ceremonies by participants in body-paint and feather-down. All this was to provide the foundation for his magnum opus, *Songs of Central Australia*, forty years later.

Strehlow was also hunting for *tjurunga*, despite his awareness that the buying and selling of such objects was sacrilege. But the trade was in full swing, as collectors for museums in Aldelaide, Frankfurt, and London bought the objects from starving Aborigines. Initially Strehlow himself thought it made sense: 'What was the use of men hanging on to the sacred objects of their forefathers?' he asked in his diary. By selling them they would free themselves both from hunger and from religious restrictions, he argued. But his first visit to a sacred cave brought a Damascene moment, and taught him how deeply he'd incorporated the Aboriginal world-view.

An old man had been trying to recount a myth for him, but kept forgetting how it went, so he suggested they go to the cave where the story belonged, and where the drawings on the rock would act as prompts. The story concerned a woman who had been the sweetheart of the moon, which had there been united with her, and had finally crept away leaving the imprint of its fingers and knees in the rock-plate. Eagerly the man led the way to the cave where he promised the *tjurunga* would be resting, but they had vanished. 'Nothing, nothing,' he murmured. 'He suddenly looked old and broken,' Strehlow recalled. 'An overwhelming feeling of hatred and disgust swept over me when I thought of the white man who had stolen from an old native even the last and most precious things that still remained to him ... We ate tea in silence, and the old man wept quietly afterwards.'

Tjurunga were often the focus of Strehlow's song-collecting sessions, their magic power unlocking memory. On one occasion, after he had written down some songs, the men took the *tjurunga* and rubbed them with sacred oil,

> chanting in a wailing tone that went right through me, some of the verses I had noted down, one verse for each tjurunga ... they started off from high-pitched notes and dropped down to a solemn chant in the middle of each verse. Then as the stone glistened in the blazing shine of the noonday sun, they dropped into the lowest note of the bass register, where the voice ceases to vibrate, and only a few poor broken accents then melted away into the distance.

Strehlow routinely fed the men who came to stay at his camp and assist in his research, and he expected them to sing for their supper, though they didn't always oblige. 'Gave neither tea, sugar nor tobacco to those men who had not chanted last night, or stolen away to the camp without singing,' he noted crossly after one failed session. 'I felt I had to be firm with these men, but it hurt me terribly to be so.' When he asked, the next day, if they were tired of this song-collecting business – would they rather work for the gold prospectors nearby? – they assured him they had many more songs to sing to him. 'So we had our little evening's reading [from the Gospel] as usual, and then I gave them that withheld tobacco, and the flour, and the peach stew ... My own heart felt free again, and I was happy with my great old men.' He had become their *ingkata* – ceremonial chief – as his father had been before. When one of his informants took him to a cleft in a rock where his personal *tjurunga* were lodged, and formally presented them to him together with some secret knowledge – explaining that he had no son or grandson responsible enough to be trusted with the information – that bond was confirmed.

Strehlow was already aware of his true mission, spelling it out in his diary:

> I am recording *the sunset of an age* that will never return – every act that I see is being performed for the last time, and the men who are with me have no successors. When they die, they will take all their knowledge to the grave with them – except that part which I have recorded. Hence I am writing down everything in full detail, so as to give the clearest picture of an age and of a culture that no one else but I have been privileged to witness.

In 1937 the London *Times* published a report drawing attention to the fact that, after 150 years of white settlement, the indigenous Australians had been almost wiped out. Malnourishment and the diseases introduced by Europeans (especially venereal) were the main causes, it said, of this progress towards extinction. A fierce debate ensued in Australia, with a handful of anthropologists trying to counteract the racist reflexes of officialdom; all this played into a concurrent debate over police brutality in the bush.

And Strehlow, newly married, found himself in the thick of it. In 1936 he was appointed patrol officer on behalf of the quaintly named Department of the Protector of Aborigines (which had existed for a century, without offering protection of any kind). His job would require him to keep tabs on Aboriginal affairs over 15,000 square miles of territory, and his appointment made headlines. 'Playmate of Blacks becomes Protector', as the Melbourne *Herald* put it.

His excitement at the thought that he might be able to ameliorate the Aborigines' lot was soon tempered by the discovery that his powers were very limited. And the first case he had to deal with was a shock: Lukas, his closest childhood friend, had been beating his wife, and Strehlow found himself having to sentence him to a whipping. Standing by while the punishment was administered by two of Lukas's relatives, Strehlow suffered agonies of remorse. His new job as a colonial bureaucrat may have put him among the 'khaki gentry', but in spirit he belonged with the Aranda.

This was underlined by the fact that his 'dark friends' were increasingly pressing him, as a reincarnation of their ancestors, to accept custody of their *tjurunga*: he was now the keeper of Aranda communal memory. But he could still make gaffes like an outsider: when he showed the Hermannsburg community a film he had shot with them, in which *tjurunga* figured prominently, women grabbed their children in horror and rushed out into the night. He made more films, but stipulated that they should only be shown in universities.

His first book, *Aranda Traditions*, was published in 1947; he could have published it ten years earlier but, in deference to Aranda sensitivities, he wanted to wait until certain old men had died. The book's first scholarly review cut him to the quick, criticising it for not acknowledging the work of other scholars, for not being scientific enough, and, above all, for being too literary; that his prose was genuinely poetic didn't help. But the directness with which he translated the native verse into plain English could not be faulted:

Red I am as though I was burning in a fire,
Red, too, is the hollow in which I am lying.
Red I am like the heart of a flame of fire,
Red, too, is the hollow in which I am lying.

He pressed on. In 1950, armed with his ethnographic films plus draft chapters of *Songs of Central Australia*, he set sail for London, hoping to gain the doctorate which would secure his academic future. But London's anthropologists closed ranks against him: he didn't have kosher anthropological credentials, and he wasn't following the theoretical orthodoxy laid down by the London School of Economics. After four dispiriting weeks he gave up and set off for Germany, which was in a deep sense home, and there he found the recognition he craved. Many of the sacred objects which his father Carl had sent to the museum in Frankfurt had been destroyed in the war, but Theo's films were a hit, and he took them on tour round the continent.

Strehlow saw stylistic similarities between Aranda verse, the *Epic of Gilgamesh*, and the Hebrew Psalms; he believed that the modern counterpart to the oral poetry which Homer is said to have written down was the verse of the Aboriginal poets (indeed, Hill regards Strehlow as their Homer). And it's no surprise that Strehlow's distillation of the Aranda creation-myth in *Songs of Central Australia* should have echoes of the *Book of Genesis*, and even stronger ones of the *Gospel According to St John*, since he was at the same time devoutly translating the Gospel into Aranda:

According to the aboriginal theory, the ancestor first called out his own name; and this gave rise to the most sacred and secret couplet or couplets of his song. Then he 'named' the place where he had originated, the trees or rocks growing near his home, the animals sporting about nearby, any strangers that came to visit him, and so forth. He gave names to all of these, and thereby gained the power of calling them by their names; this enabled him to control them, and to bind them to his will. In each instance he not merely gave them a name, but also described them briefly ... in this way a series of couplets was brought into being; and this series constituted the song that each ancestor left behind for the benefit of those human beings who were to be reincarnated from himself and from his own supernatural children.

The cross-cultural resonances of this canon – for it is indeed a canon, as in any other musical tradition – are huge.

Strehlow had once been fond of declaring that in Aranda song 'music is the servant of the words', but in *Songs of Central Australia* he rowed back on that. The first part of the book is musicological, emphasising the fact that this poetry was always sung, and never performed without music. And this music may in itself embody mysteries. Catherine Ellis, the musicologist who helped Strehlow notate the songs, saw it as an expression of 'non-linear time', as 'moving from past to present to future; it is one in which the long past is ever-present and ties both future and past to the moment when a correct reproduction of a Dreaming performance takes place.'

But at the same time her research showed that song leaders needed many years of training, not only to learn the mythological and religious significance of any performance, but also to master the structure of each musical form. And those structures were detailed and precise. The process was hierarchical: the songline itself was a symbolic map showing the journey of the ancestor celebrated in the song, and the 'small songs' within it represented places or actions involving that ancestor. Melodies typically descended in pitch, with intermittent upward leaps; rhythmic figures were almost always divisible by six, with the heartbeat as the fundamental time unit. Yet performers could exercise creativity, as Ellis concluded: 'It is within this subtle structural iridescence that the performer has great scope, without affecting adversely the timeless communication [with] the ancestor.'

Hill discerns a Spenglerish quality in the world-view expressed through Strehlow's crowning work, which he describes as 'a summa as conservative as could be. Anti-rational; anti-critical; anti-Enlightenment'. Strehlow now abjured all reference to the primal horde in Aranda culture, to the cruelties of initiation, and to the belief in murderous spirits. 'He is leading his reader,' says Hill, 'towards an appreciation of orderly unities, not of dancers who are lost in a frenzy of excess.' Strehlow's pronouncements on the decline of civilisation, and on the uniqueness of his role in preserving the embattled Aranda culture, may indeed have a tinge of megalomania. But he really did believe in the redemptiveness of the art he was chronicling, and in its power to help shape the sung poetry of the future. Whatever its inherent contradictions, his great book changed the musicological landscape, allowing new generations of scholars to build on its foundations. For today's ethnomusicologists in Australia, the primary task is to revive those indigenous chants and give them back to the people whose heritage they are. A heritage of course, now largely lost.

* * *

It was Strehlow's misfortune that the publication of *Songs of Central Australia* was delayed for fifteen years, not appearing until 1971: in the meantime, although he was finally awarded a professorial chair, he'd become increasingly embittered by his lack of academic recognition. A negative (and not at all perceptive) review in the *Times Literary Supplement* rubbed salt in his wounds.

But he was regarded as a leading advocate in Aboriginal matters, as witness a legal *cause célèbre* in 1958. An Aboriginal circus-hand named Rupert Max Stuart was charged with the rape and murder of a nine-year-old girl. He was the grandson of Tom Ljonga, who had been Strehlow's faithful companion on his first song-collecting trip in the desert. Stuart had also been, as a small boy, one of Patrol Officer Strehlow's charges at a station he commanded. Strehlow didn't contact him during his trial, subsequent conviction, or sentencing to death, but four days before he was due to hang, Strehlow was persuaded by a Catholic priest, who was convinced of Stuart's innocence, to give an informed judgement on the language of the evidence by which he had been convicted.

Strehlow interviewed Stuart in prison, and found no compatibility between the English of the confession and the vernacular dialect which Stuart spoke. 'Rupert Stuart just does not talk like that,' he declared. Strehlow's voice was thus added to those of the civil rights groups who had questioned police evidence: Stuart's conviction was never revoked, but he was spared execution. Strehlow took a dim view of Aborigines of Stuart's generation, who in his opinion did not cherish their traditions as their fathers had done, so his participation in this protracted battle was for political rather than personal reasons; and since the conviction was not overturned, he felt he had failed. As he wrote in his diary, 'All that effort came to nothing. Perhaps it is a consolation that Stuart's life has been saved' (as Hill wryly observes, it was certainly a consolation for Stuart). Had he lived longer, Strehlow would have been cheered to learn that Stuart later remembered his family secrets, stayed faithful to them, and became a leading figure in the campaign for Aboriginal land rights. Strehlow's pessimism about the future of Aranda lore was shown – by this case as well as by subsequent events – to have been exaggerated.

In 1969 he wrote a moving memoir of his childhood and the death of his father, *Journey to Horseshoe Bend*. But his last years were a story of mounting paranoia, as possession of the films and recordings he had made, and of the sacred objects he had collected, seemed to turn his brain. He ditched his wife of thirty years in favour of a younger woman, with whom he developed a bunker mentality as custodian of this hoard of musicological treasure, Strehlow brazenly falsifying the record to bolster his claim to ownership.

This was a time when Aboriginal land rights (which Strehlow passionately supported) were at last being publicly debated, as were their ramifications as to which specific Aboriginal families should benefit, and who should control the newly registered sacred sites. Strehlow broke many a lance in righteous battles to prevent white anthropologists from taking control of these matters, and he fell out with the Australian Institute for Aboriginal Studies which was desperate to get its hands on his collection. 'I will not hand over what I have for the glory of greedy white imposters who have leapt upon the Aboriginal bandwagon,' he wrote to an anthropologist friend. 'It is better for Aboriginal culture to die than to be prostituted in this shameful way.'

When the clamour for Strehlow to yield up his collection started to come from Aboriginal groups as well, he became even more stubborn, at one point threatening to burn everything. The crunch came when he lent hundreds of photographs to *Stern* magazine for a big feature which was then syndicated to the Australian magazine *People*. He had made this loan to raise money for his new foundation, and he had stipulated that the pictures should not be reproduced in Australia. Their presence in an Australian magazine irreparably damaged both his reputation, and his precarious self-image. 'I had no right to trust anyone with what I had been entrusted by the only completely loyal friends I have ever known – those black men who were guardians of a great culture not affected by white values,' he wrote in his diary. Three weeks later, shortly before he died – of a heart attack as he was opening an exhibition of his collection – he added: 'Perhaps it is best that all I have, and all my knowledge too, should die with me and be lost forever to mankind.' His collection is now on public display in the Strehlow Research Centre at Alice Springs.

With two mother tongues, German and Aranda, and owing allegiance to two profoundly incompatible religious traditions, and with the perennial burden of responsibility for a secret-sacred culture, was Strehlow's crack-up inevitable? The self-description he penned in his last days might suggest so: 'I am that complete anomaly – a white-skinned Aranda man of the old sort.' A tragically divided self.

Sources

Barry Hill's magisterial *Broken Song* is the definitive biography, setting Strehlow's life and work in its political and intellectual context. Strehlow's own account in *Journey to Horseshoe Bend* is atmospheric; copies of his magnum opus *Songs of Central Australia* are hard to find. Scholarly works on Aboriginal music are thin on the ground, but Catherine Ellis's *Aboriginal Music Making* is a key musicological study, while Allan Marett's *Songs, Dreamings, and Ghosts* is an in-depth musical and social study of a tradition parallel to that of the Aranda.

Bibliography

Ellis, Catherine J., *Aboriginal Music Making: A Study of Central Australian Music* (Adelaide: State Libraries Board of South Australia, 1964)

Hill, Barry, *Broken Song: TGH Strehlow and Aboriginal Possession* (Vintage, Knopf: Sydney 2002)

Marett, Allan, *Songs, Dreamings, and Ghosts: The Wangga of North Australia* (Middletown, CT: Wesleyan, 2005)

Strehlow, TGH, *Aranda Phonetics and Grammar, Sydney*, Oceania Monograph 7 (Sydney: University of Sydney, 1944)

Strehlow, TGH, *Journey to Horseshoe Bend* (Sydney: Angus and Robertson, 1969)

Strehlow, TGH, *Songs of Central Australia* (Sydney: Angus and Robertson, 1971)

12

The stirring of a thousand bells

Jaap Kunst, Colin McPhee, and gamelan

IT'S NO SURPRISE that *le kampong javanais* – the Javanese village – should have been the most popular colonial attraction at the 1889 Exposition Universelle in Paris. People were charmed by the grace of the dance and the magic of the music, which might have been designed to represent Caliban's sounds and sweet airs that give delight and hurt not. The resident dancers at the Exposition became tabloid celebrities; Saint-Saëns declared that gamelan 'dream music' had hypnotic powers. Debussy, having attended performances at the kampong, would later extol the music as being 'as natural as breathing: their conservatoire is the eternal rhythm of the sea, the wind among the leaves, and the thousand sounds of nature.'

Yet the English were the first Europeans to appreciate it. One of Sir Francis Drake's entries in the logbook of the Golden Hind in 1580 describes a musical exchange on the south coast of Java between the local ruler and his English visitors. First Drake gave a performance with his musicians in honour of Raia Donan, king of Java, then he listened to the king's 'country-musick, which though it were of a very strange kind, yet the sound was pleasant and delightfull'. European interest was rekindled in the nineteenth century with the collecting expeditions of Sir Thomas Stamford Raffles and others, but the melodic and harmonic nature of gamelan only came properly into focus when the English physiologist Alexander Ellis subjected Javanese music to tonal analysis in his pioneering study of 'the scales of various nations'.

Colonial links forged in the seventeenth century ensured that Dutch and Javanese scholars should lead the musicological enquiry. In 1857, students of the Royal Academy of Delft became the first Europeans to give a gamelan performance; the author of the programme note expressed an awareness of its microtonal modes, but gave a patronising explanation for them. Quarter tones, he wrote, were due to 'a deficiency of the instruments' because the Javanese had 'no knowledge of the mechanics necessary to make them all the same ... The variety of sounds and the simplicity of style cause all pieces to sound almost alike.' But Dutch scholarship was soon on the trail in a properly

23 Colin McPhee on a song-collecting trip to Sumatra.

scientific way, led by Isaak Groneman whose day job in Jogjakarta was as the sultan's personal doctor. And the discipline's presiding genius, Jaap Kunst, was also Dutch; after seminal work on the music of Java and Bali, Kunst would go on to become one of the founding fathers of ethnomusicology, and it was he who coined that term.

Born in 1891 and trained as a lawyer, Kunst was an accomplished violinist, and in early adulthood spent his holidays collecting folk melodies on the Friesian island of Terschelling, to which he introduced the fiddle; the three-volume song collection he made there is still used by Friesian musicians as a reference book. He took an office job in Amsterdam but found it stifling; leaving both it and the girl he was engaged to marry, he persuaded a singer and a pianist to form a trio with him to tour Indonesia. They presented a programme of French folk songs, for which he doubled as violinist and animal imitator. After nine successful months they disbanded, but he stayed on: he'd met his future wife – Katy van Wely, daughter of a colonial administrator – and he'd been entranced by a performance at the court of Prince Mangkunegoro VII in Solo.

'I do not recall ever seeing or hearing anything which, in all its different expressions, was so completely uniform, something in which music, song, gesture, colour and line were so in harmony with each other,' he wrote afterwards to the prince, only regretting his inability to understand the words and the symbolism. Financing himself through legal work, he embarked on a musical quest which would last the rest of his life.

The prince's wedding celebrations in 1920, which Kunst witnessed 'as in a dream', got that quest off to a mind-blowing start: 'It is both barbaric and magnificent, and at the same time refined ... some twenty gamelans mix their tones. I just don't know where I am.' He acquired an Edison Amberola machine and in 1922, using a long wooden funnel to catch the gamelan's wide-angle polyphony, made his first wax cylinder recordings. (Now held in the Berlin Phonogramm-Archiv, these still sing to us with a silvery sweetness.) While honeymooning with Katy in Bali, Kunst began a study of instrumental and vocal genres which bore fruit in their co-authored book *The Music of Bali*.

In contrast to many European colonies, the Dutch East Indies were run on relatively civilised lines. What interested the Dutch was the spice trade, and the Javanese courts, which survive to this day, were allowed to continue as symbolic rulers. And since their political role was curtailed, they focused their patronage on the arts, their rivalries resulting in ever-higher standards of excellence. The Dutch supported this – to them – politically harmless activity, and in Prince Mangkunegoro they found an ideal ally. He had studied in the Netherlands, served as a Dutch army officer in the First World War, and he'd been called back by the colonial administration in Java to succeed his uncle as the local ruler. Since his overriding desire was to preserve the indigenous culture, he in turn enlisted Kunst, inviting him to head the musical side of an institute devoted to Javanese culture.

Kunst's declaration of intent at its inaugural conference read like a manifesto: 'Let the development of Javanese music take place exclusively ... supported by indigenous elements,' he wrote. 'Let Western influence remain far removed from the art which is so very different in nature. Western infection is threatening to destroy the indigenous music.' Some people at the conference wanted to see a synthesis of Eastern and Western music, but most wanted Javanese music to retain its purity.

Kunst's study continued with the aid of a resident gamelan player, with the well-informed prince clarifying technical points; Kunst and his wife made a collection of instruments, and wrote a schoolbook on gamelan. He began pushing for the government to fund research, and in 1930 was rewarded with a post as its official musicologist. When that post was abolished in cuts following the global crash, he worked on until his return to Amsterdam, where he was appointed curator of the Royal Tropical Institute; the prince worked on too, triumphantly getting gamelan onto local Javanese radio. Kunst's magnum opus, *The Music of Java*, was published in 1934, and he spent the rest of his life refining it.

But as his pupil Ernst Heins points out, there was a glaring anomaly in this story. Kunst may have been a fervent string-quartet player, but the only time he ever touched a gamelan was to measure the instruments. 'We can only guess how different *Music in Java*, and perhaps even ethnomusicology itself, might have been if he had [played in one],' Heins writes. He attributes this abstinence to the social barrier which separated coloniser from colonised; before Indonesian independence in 1949, it had been unthinkable that a European should play in a Javanese gamelan, or even take lessons.

* * *

Other Western enthusiasts had no such inhibitions, most notably the Canadian composer Colin McPhee. Born in Montreal in 1900, McPhee was a pianistic child prodigy who lacked the will to realise his promise. Instead he became a prolific composer as part of the 'American school' led by his friends Henry Cowell, Aaron Copland, and Edgard Varèse. Many of his scores are now lost, thanks to his impatience to press on towards whatever goal he was pursuing at any given moment: petulant when he thought a work was undervalued, he was more likely to destroy a manuscript than work to improve it. Invited to submit biographical information for *American Composers Today* in 1945, he wrote back: 'The other day ... I tore up old programs and the reviews afterwards ... All this, of course, I bury. It's nobody's business, anyway, what I've chosen to make of my life.' Closet homosexuality was the key to his compulsive need for privacy; as his biographer Carol J. Oja observes, he became skilled in falsifying the chronology of his life.

Like other American composers in the Twenties, McPhee grew tired of writing esoteric music for small audiences. While some sought inspiration in American folk music, he was fired by some records released by the German Odéon company as part of its global sales drive. The company's aim was not musicological: it wanted to sell phonograph machines, and the records to play on them, to people in developing countries. In 1902 the British Gramophone Company sent their recording engineer Frederick Gaisberg on a trip taking in Calcutta, Tokyo, Shanghai, Hong Kong, Singapore, and Rangoon, with the fruits sold back to people in their countries of origin. Odéon, which dominated the Indonesian market, suffered a dip after Germany's defeat in the First World War, but bounced back to make the first commercially released recordings of Balinese gamelan – 98 sides for the Indonesian market. McPhee heard several of these.

Odéon's plan to develop an indigenous market flopped; since live performances were still taking place daily in temples and households, the Balinese saw little point in this new-fangled and expensive machine. One frustrated dealer reported that McPhee was the only customer in an entire year to buy his discs; the collection McPhee amassed contains most of the copies still extant, as the dealer smashed his remaining stock in a fit of anger. On a larger scale, Odéon did something similar by destroying the matrices of these records – an act which Béla Bartók described as an outrageous piece of cultural vandalism. These discs have an enduring importance: fifty years on, descendants of the musicians who made the Odéon recordings were able to relearn the music, and lodge tape-recordings of it in family shrines.

For McPhee, whose compositions had been tending eastwards with shifting rhythms and intricately layered textures, the arrival of those records was like the sun coming out. As he wrote later:

> The clear, metallic sounds ... were like the stirring of a thousand bells, delicate, confused, with a sensuous charm, a mystery that was quite overpowering. I begged to keep the records for a few days, and I became more and more enchanted with the sound ... How had this music come about? Above all, how was it possible, in this late day, for such a music to have been able to survive?

At twelve he had written a piece for a children's percussion band in which plates were dropped and smashed; he had wanted to create the impression of 'frail china splintered on marble – some idea of crystal sound, something aerial and purely sensuous. It is strange that another ten years should find me in Java and Bali where music sounded exactly like that.' All his life he'd been looking for a particular sound, and in the music which Odéon captured he found it.

In 1931 McPhee set sail for Bali in company with his wife, the anthropologist Jane Belo, plus a posse of artists and writers. Since Belo was rich, and regarded her husband's homosexuality as a challenge, McPhee's plan to immerse himself in Balinese culture could proceed smoothly; they built a house in a quiet and conservative village and put down roots.

This was a time when Bali was in vogue among the European and American intelligentsia, with books and plays proliferating, and Charlie Chaplin, Noël Coward, and Leopold Stokowski among the celebrities paying visits; Margaret Mead and her partner Gregory Bateson declared Bali a paradise for anthropologists, and produced a celebrated photographic study of local life. In contrast to the Westerners who built colonial-style houses, McPhee and Belo built a simple one from bamboo and thatch, complete with an auditorium for music and dance. Like the other expatriates they had a retinue of servants, but they sought to replicate the traditional way of life, particularly in the kitchen where McPhee, a virtuoso cook, was taught Balinese culinary magic.

His daily routine included several hours of piano practice, followed by several more of gamelan transcription; he kept a book for each of the main styles – some bare and rugged, others richly ornamented – which he photographed and filmed. Composing in the Western idiom now ceased to interest him: he felt 'free and happy, liberated from [something] in which I no longer believed'. And gradually he began to understand the new aesthetic: 'At first, as I listened from the house, the music was simply a delicious confusion, a strangely sensuous and quite unfathomable art, mysteriously aerial, Aeolian, filled with joy and radiance ... I began to have a feeling of form and elaborate architecture.' Despite the profusion of Indonesian treatises on literature and poetry, law, medicine, building, and shadow-play, McPhee could find no indigenous writings about gamelan performance, and he felt duty-bound to document it. *Music in Bali*, the monumental study into which he poured everything he discovered, and which scholars still routinely consult, would not be published until 1966, two years after his death.

* * *

He forged close friendships with his informants in circumstances which sound idyllic, and may also have had a sexual element:

> In the afternoon Lebah would sit down near the piano, to play phrase by phrase some *gendèr* [a Balinese marimba, with bronze keys suspended above bamboo resonators] melody while I wrote. Or he would pick up a drum to show the rhythm in a certain part of the music. Seriously, leisurely, we worked together till sundown ... At last we would decide to stop. We would walk down the hillside to bathe in the spring, or else in the pool far below, where through the ferns the water fell from overhead.

His first informant, a gamelan historian named Kaler, took umbrage when McPhee asked for help to meet the composer I Lotring whose music he had heard on the Odéon recordings. McPhee's field notes describe Lotring as 'short, slight, about 30, a mild, guileless smile, hair very thin "from so much thinking"; a goldsmith, a famous cook; lives by the sea in a very poor house; several wives; unreliable and a little tricky; dreams of pieces at night ... same style as Kaler, but Kaler a pedant and Lotring imaginative'.

Lotring's gamelan had been destroyed during internal strife among its performers, and he had been reduced to silence. McPhee resolved to restore the instruments and reform the group, with the result that Lotring started composing again and the group found fame. McPhee persuaded them to build him a thatched hut on the beach in which he could work; during rehearsals he would ask the player of the *gendèr* to let him take his place:

> This was enough for me to experience the sensation of being, at least for the moment, completely united, in close and absolute sympathy with the players, lost with them in the rhythm of the music … Here there was no conductor's stick to beat time, no over-eloquent hands to urge or subdue. The drumming of Lotring was at times barely audible; you felt it rather than heard it, and the music seemed to rush ahead on its own impetus. You were swept along the stream, no longer knew what you were doing. It was something free and purely physical, like swimming or running.

One of McPhee's assistants was an eight-year-old boy called Sampih who had gallantly rushed into a flash-flood to save him from drowning. McPhee discovered by chance that Sampih, whom he made his adoptive son, had remarkable talent as a dancer: 'I came home unexpectedly one evening to find the phonograph on the floor, playing the loudest and most syncopated

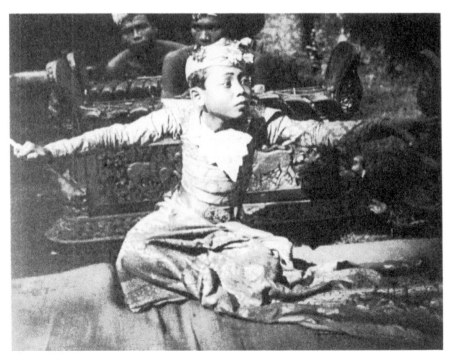

24 McPhee's protégé Sampih dancing.

gamelan record, and Sampih improvising a wild *kebyar* dance … Although he stopped the moment he saw me, it was not before I had a glimpse of melodramatic gestures, coquettish eyes and flashing hands that caught with surprising precision the violent and abrupt accents of the music.' Sampih was a wild child of the mountains with a serious streak of violence, but McPhee, like a devoted parent, got him proper teachers, formed a bamboo orchestra to accompany his dancing, and launched him on a career.

* * *

Packing up the fruits of his musical research before returning to New York in 1935, McPhee had the feeling of 'storing a folio of pressed flowers'. Back home he began to spread the gamelan gospel with missionary zeal. He brought the sounds of Bali to New York's Cosmopolitan Club, showing his films of Balinese musicians, and playing his two-piano gamelan transcriptions with the composer Marc Blitzstein. In an article for the magazine *Modern Music* he contrasted the functional craft of gamelan with the rarefied art music he and his fellow-composers were writing, and he asked how their music too might be made to fit into daily life. He had championed the work of the Mexican composer Carlos Chávez as possessing a 'primitive energy which has nothing of the exotic, but is a clear and forceful expression of racial vitality in primary colours'. Chavez returned the compliment by offering to conduct the premiere of *Tabuh-Tabuhan*, the work which would be McPhee's crowning attempt at an East-West fusion.

He described this work as 'a concerto for piano and large orchestra using Bali-jazz-and-McPhee elements', and its title as 'a Balinese collective noun, meaning different drum rhythms, metric forms, gong punctuations, gamelans, and music essentially percussive'; *tabuh* was the Indonesian for hammer. The heart of the work, which has a Western three-movement structure, is a flute melody which McPhee had transcribed, and the layering and ostinatos are quintessentially Balinese. The premiere took place in Mexico City and was a triumph, but McPhee's attempts to interest leading conductors – Serge Koussevitsky (for whom he played the work through), and Leopold Stokowski (to whom he sent the score) – came to nothing. As Carol Oja observes with an exasperation unusual in a biographer, this apparent rebuff – the sort of thing which all composers have to accept as par for the course – was enough to send him back in disgust to Bali.

'If I must function in life,' McPhee wrote, 'it is as a recorder, a preserver of musical ideas which we call primitive, but which will prove to be of great value to future musicians.' He wasn't happy to see how well-worn the trail had become – 'everyone wants to be Robinson Crusoe' – but he was delighted to return to his quest, even if 'the inner meaning of the music seemed to recede, the more I knew it'.

And he knew a lot. He had discovered early on that no two clubs played alike: 'the temperament of the village and its musicians is clearly revealed in performance. While one club may play with brilliant and almost feverish intensity ... the club two villages away performs with cold precision, or even apathy.' And he'd realised the centrality of rhythm. 'Without the drums,' he wrote,

> the music is lifeless, lacks direction. Without them the dancer cannot move. The drums are 'the heart of the music', 'the blood running in the veins'. The pair of drums, male and female, which infuse life into the abstract, formal structure of the musical composition, have a double function. They supply an elaborate cross-accentuation through alternating heavy accents produced by the drum sticks, and a light interplay of filling-in tones produced by the hands and fingertips.

After describing the abstracted look on the players' faces, he noted that 'the men performed their isolated parts with mysterious unity, fell upon the syncopated accents with hair's-breadth precision.' Moreover, close observation led him to a provocative and profound conclusion: 'The Oriental relies on rhythm to create dissonance; he is unconscious of it melodically (or harmonically). Polyrhythm means dissonance.'

Now he saw his role as pro-active. The *gamelan semar pegulingan* – Gamelan of the God of the Pillowed Bed – was an all but lost art form, and McPhee decided to found an ensemble to revive it: 'I was tired of going about the island with a notebook, asking questions like a government official. By forming a club not only would I have music near the house once more, but I could learn the forgotten court style of playing in the most natural way possible, by hearing it pass from teacher to pupils.'

He also founded an *angklung* ensemble with village children aged from six to eleven. Angklung is vigorous folk music, with the *angklung* itself consisting of three bamboo tubes of different lengths hung within a light wooden frame, and tuned to sound a single tone in three octaves when the frame is shaken. In his engaging memoir *A House in Bali* McPhee tells how this ensemble came into existence. His house was often full of children, and one day he heard them improvising their own gamelan: 'strange and lively music, uncertain drums, melody very out of tune, and the pathetic accents of a cracked gong'. He happened to have bought some miniature instruments from the local blacksmith, and when the children saw them they fell on them with delight. Initially they taught each other, attempting long and intricate compositions, and when they demanded a proper teacher, McPhee engaged one. The development of what

25 A photo by McPhee of *suling* players from the court of Tabanan in the
1930s; a *suling* is an end-blown flute.

he dubbed the Club of Small Men was swift and impressive, to the point
where, on the day of a temple feast, they led the main village gamelan in
procession to a sacred spring where they played through the night until dawn.

In 1938, with war on the horizon, McPhee left Bali for ever, but he
remained a passionate advocate for gamelan. He had the satisfaction of hearing Bartók include his piano transcription of some Balinese ceremonial music
in a recital in Amherst, Massachusetts, and of getting Benjamin Britten to join
him for a recording – now available on YouTube – of one of his two-piano
gamelan arrangements (for a time Britten shared a house with McPhee and
W. H. Auden in Brooklyn – the conversation must have been fascinating).
The American composer Lou Harrison, whose own music would become
deeply impregnated with gamelan techniques, copied down all the examples
in McPhee's influential essay *The Five-tone Music of Bali*. Composers at the
cutting edge were very much on his wave-length, and, with Steve Reich as
cheerleader, they remain so today.

Meanwhile he got down to writing, revealing a waspish tone as a music
critic, and evocative literary skills with *A House in Bali* which got excellent

reviews. Writing that book, he said, was 'like making bread – you let the dough rise, cut down, let it rise again'. But he was very ambivalent towards what he called 'that Other Book', his monumental study of music in Bali, which at times he feared would never materialise, and which he sometimes dismissed as 'drudgery'. 'I did not live in Bali to collect material,' he told Sydney Cowell. 'I lived there because I wanted to, for the pleasure of it.' He disdained the paraphernalia of scholarship, wanting to purge the book of 'all stupid jargon-like aeophones [*sic*], idiophones beloved by Sachs and Hornbostel'. Yet as Oja points out, his approach to research was fastidious and scholarly.

He later tried to get funding to do for the music of Peru and Bolivia, Haiti and Mexico what he had done for the music of Bali, but to no avail. He presented jazz programmes on radio, but hated the sound of his own voice – 'such an affected drawl, it sounded like some dreadful Museum of Modern Art fairy.' He orchestrated some Iroquois dances, despite what he called the 'lack of rhythmic interest and energy' in American Indian music.

And he did have triumphs, first when Sampih came over to New York at the head of his own *gamelan kebyar* (Sampih's subsequent murder in Bali affected him deeply). In 1953 Stokowski finally conducted *Tabuh-Tabuhan* at the Carnegie Hall. But apart from a brief but happy stint as a professor at UCLA, the rest of McPhee's career was blighted by disappointment, depression, and poverty (living out of suitcases in a single room without a phone). His greatest sadness was that he never managed to record the gamelans he worked with; the aural documents with which he had hoped to complement his transcriptions thus never materialised. He died in 1964, his health undermined by alcohol, while correcting the proofs of *Music in Bali*.

McPhee wrote his own oddly wistful epitaph in a letter to Cowell: 'The beautiful mystery is this: that my few friends admire or love me, not for what I've accomplished, but for what they think I might have done. A work of art which does not exist is the most beautiful of all.' And he was modest in estimating his achievement during his seven years in Bali. 'I had succeeded in helping prolong the past. To delay it even for a day was my one wish,' he wrote, despite feeling there was something necromantic about the project. 'Who had benefited? None. But at the same time, none were harmed by this look towards the past, and from it much pleasure had been derived; many evenings of diversion had been the result.'

Quite apart from his magisterial book, and his lead in opening Western music to Eastern influences, McPhee left a big footprint on Bali's musical scene. His protégé Lotring's compositions became central to the Balinese canon, and as recently as the Nineties his *gamelan semar pegulingan* was still going strong. Oja's picture of the Club of Small Men performing in a temple shows the original infant cast still playing together in advanced middle age. McPhee had called back disappearing forms, and infused them with new life.

Sources

Jaap Kunst still awaits a proper biography, but Ernst Heins's essay on him in *Ethnomusicology: Historical and Regional Studies* is a useful starting point. And in *Recollecting Resonances*, Madelon Djajadiningrat and Clara Brinkgreve contribute a revealing chapter on his long and fruitful relationship with Mangkunegoro VII. Carol J. Oja's *Colin McPhee: Composer in Two Worlds*, on which this chapter draws, is an excellent critical biography; McPhee's essay 'The Five-tone Music of Bali', published in 1949, summarises his first conclusions, while *A House in Bali* is a charmingly atmospheric account of his life on the island. His magnum opus, *Music in Bali: A Study in Form and Instrumental Organisation in Balinese Orchestral Music*, is now a rare item. Neil Sorrell's *A Guide to the Gamelan* is a useful pocket introduction; the Odéon recordings from 1928 are available, remastered in 2015, with an accompanying essay by Edward Herbst, on the World Arbiter label. Lotring's performances of his own compositions in 1972 have recently been re-released, entitled 'Indonésie Bali: Hommage à Wayan Lotring', by Ocora. Annegret Fauser's *Musical Encounters at the 1889 Paris World's Fair* gives the context for gamelan's introduction to Paris.

Bibliography and recordings

Djajadiningrat, Madelon and Clara Brinkgreve, 'A Musical Friendship: The Correspondence between Mangkunegoro VII and the Ethnomusicologist Jaap Kunst, 1919 to 1940', in Bart Barendregt and Els Bogaerts, eds, *Recollecting Resonances* (Leiden: Brill, 2014), 179–201

Fauser, Annegret, *Musical Encounters at the 1889 Paris World's Fair* (New York: University of Rochester Press, 2005)

McPhee, Colin, 'The Five-tone Gamelan Music of Bali', *Musical Quarterly*, vol. 35, issue 2 (April 1949), 250–81

McPhee, Colin, *A House in Bali* (London: Periplus Publishers, 2000)

McPhee, Colin, *Music in Bali: A Study in Form and Instrumental Organisation in Balinese Orchestral Music* (Boston: Da Capo Press, 1976)

Myers, Helen, ed., *Ethnomusicology: Historical and Regional Studies* (New York: Norton, 1993)

Oja, Carol J., *Colin McPhee: Composer in Two Worlds* (Washington, DC: Smithsonian, 1990)

Sorrell, Neil, *A Guide to the Gamelan* (London: Faber, 1990)

Bali 1928 – Anthology: The First Recordings, World Arbiter 2018

Indonésie-Bali: Hommage à Wayan Lotring, Ocora France Bo7XW8DX6H

26 Paul Bowles and his team – plus interested bystanders – with their Volkswagen in the Atlas Mountains.

13

Hot mint tea and a few pipes of kif

Paul Bowles in Morocco

THE FLAMBOYANT PAUL Bowles is best known as author of the novel *The Sheltering Sky* – made into a film by Bernardo Bertolucci – but he also had other talents. Born in 1910, he was musically gifted and his initial ambition was to be a poet; at twenty he was making his mark with the reigning literary deities, first in New York, then in Paris where he charmed the celebrated literary tyrant Gertrude Stein. She introduced him to Jean Cocteau, Ezra Pound, and André Gide, but she didn't rate his poetry: she thought he should stick to music, and propelled him and his mentor-lover the composer Aaron Copland towards Tangier, where a summer in the sun might, she hoped, feed his muse.

Copland hated Morocco, but for Bowles it was the *coup de foudre*. He would go on to have considerable success in New York as a composer of instrumental works, scores for ballets and films, and incidental music for theatre productions by Orson Welles; his sound experiments with words would be harnessed by William Burroughs for his novel *The Naked Lunch*. And he would go on other travels – he briefly owned and lived on an island in the Indian Ocean – but that initial taste of Tangier triggered a lifelong addiction.

The Sahara, he declared, was a place where the sky's shelter was anything but comforting: 'a great stretch of earth where climate reigns supreme, and every gesture man makes is in conscious defence from, or propitiation of, the climatic conditions. Man is hated in the Sahara ... But where life is prohibited, it becomes a delectable forbidden fruit.' In the 1930s he made several trips to Morocco and Algeria, collecting 78rpm discs of local music. At the suggestion of the composer Henry Cowell he made copies of these and sent them to Béla Bartók, who worked some Berber material into a piece. 'When I heard the *Concerto for Orchestra*,' Bowles wrote later, 'there was the music, considerably transformed, but still recognisable to me, who was familiar with each note of every piece I had copied for him.' In 1947 he settled permanently in Tangier, and spent the remaining fifty-two years of his life writing, composing, and giving interviews to literary pilgrims at his house in the Medina.

But collecting commercial 78s was not enough. Bowles wanted to record his own tribute to the music of the western Maghreb, and in 1959, after years of lobbying, he got a Rockefeller grant to collect for the Library of Congress examples of every major musical genre to be found in Morocco. Bowles's proposal stressed the urgency of the project. 'Public apathy,' he wrote, 'is destroying the performing traditions [of art music] … It is the folk music, however, which is most in danger of disappearing quickly, and it is upon that that I should concentrate.' The project would be 'a fight against time and the de-culturizing activities of political enthusiasts'.

The south of Morocco was dangerously close to the war of independence then raging in Algeria, but the rest of the country, having won its own independence three years previously, would be fertile recording territory, and Bowles would traverse it in four journeys totalling 25,000 miles. With a Moroccan fixer and 'a level-headed Canadian with a Volkswagen and all the time in the world' Bowles set off from Tangier, armed with an Ampex 601 reel-to-reel tape machine weighing forty-two pounds, and an official permit to record.

But Moroccan officialdom was ambivalent. Halfway through the project the permit was suddenly withdrawn. Bowles ignored that and went on recording, but in Fes he encountered an official with precisely the attitude he had warned of in his proposal. 'I detest all folk music, and particularly ours in Morocco,' Bowles reported the official as saying. 'Why should I help you to export a thing which we are trying to destroy? You are looking for tribal music. There are no more tribes. We have dissolved them. And there never was any tribal music anyway – only noise.' This, said Bowles, was symptomatic of the 'irrational longing' of educated people in 'alien cultures' to 'cease being themselves and become Westerners'. Bowles argued that 'the very illiteracy of the [Moroccan] people through the centuries has abetted the development of music; the entire history and mythology of the people is clothed in song.' He took a romantic view of the purity of Moroccan musical tradition, with the music of the Berbers as its touchstone. 'It is a highly percussive art,' he wrote, 'with complicated juxtapositions of rhythms, limited scalar range (often of no more than three adjacent tones) and a unique manner of vocalizing. Like most Africans, the Berbers developed a music of mass participation, one whose psychological effects were aimed more often than not at causing hypnosis.' He made a distinction between 'static repetition and organic (or deceptive) repetition, in which the reiterated rhythmical or melodic motif is merely a device for capturing the attention, the music's ultimate aim being that of imposing itself totally on the consciousness of the listener. The effect is not monotonous but hypnotic … There is no quick way of listening to Berber music.'

He contrasted this with the music which the invading Arabs had brought with them – 'addressed to the individual seeking by sensory means to induce a state of philosophical speculativeness'. Arab culture was a contamination, he believed, and only in the High Atlas was Berber music left intact as 'a purely autochthonous art'. In Khenifra he recorded an enthusiastic antiphonal song by two groups of girls accompanied on a drum and *guimbri* lute, but after pointing out that the music represented two cultures with two unrelated scales, he dismissed the result as an 'ethnical monstrosity ... I found the combination highly displeasing, but this may be because I was aware of the music's basic degeneracy.' As Philip Schuyler, editor of Bowles's Moroccan recordings, acidly observes, 'change and hybridity, the very forces that keep music vital, were in his view signs of decay.'

The trips were arduous and fraught with problems. The Volkswagen Beetle couldn't always cope with the mountain tracks, while the generators on which the functioning of the Ampex depended were often impossible to find; piping hot Pepsi was sometimes the only safe thing to drink, and the fixer took generous advantage of the hash-jam they'd acquired as a lubricant for recording deals. Listening to a trance-song in Marrakesh, Bowles mused benignly on what he called the Moroccans' 'befuddlement music': 'They will sometimes describe it as "music that makes you play games inside your head". A glass of hot mint tea and a few pipes of kif along with this music can provide complete pleasure for the space of an hour or so for a Marrakchi.'

Bowles had to get used to unsettling behaviour from his performers. In one mountain village the singing girls sat in pairs with a shared towel over their heads which projected their sound through folds of cloth towards the floor, and they talked incessantly between verses: when he asked why, he was told that, as this was an improvised performance, they were simply making up what they were going to sing next. And he had to keep a close eye on his budget. One ensemble consisted of three oboes, four drums, and eight rifles, but he was told that if the rifles weren't fired the cost would be halved, so he accepted that. All went well until three climaxes in the performance, when the rifles went off in unison: it was explained the men had been so fired up they couldn't resist participating, and he was presented with a bill for twenty-four cartridges. His refusal was greeted with smiles, and the men went off to play (and fire) at a wedding.

Bowles was always ready to turn a technical disaster to artistic advantage. When Bowles tracked down the *zamr* – two reed pipes wired together, each with its own mouthpiece and culminating in a bull's horn – he found that it covered the sound of all the instruments it was teamed with, so he had to persuade his *zamr* player, deceitfully but diplomatically, to play beyond the

27 The celebrated *qsbah* player Boujmaa ben Mimoun holding his instrument, while the leader of the group plays the *zamr* double clarinet.

range of the microphone. But there was another reason why Bowles wanted to cut out the *zamr*. In the same ensemble was Boujemaa ben Mimoun, an outstanding player on the *qsbah*. This long flute with an exceptionally low register was a favourite instrument of the camel drivers, and Bowles had twice failed to record it satisfactorily. When he asked Ben Mimoun for a solo, the musician replied: 'How is anybody going to know what the qsbah is saying all by itself, unless there is somebody to sing the words?' Polite but insistent pressure – reinforced by large helpings of kif – was needed to persuade Ben Mimoun and his colleagues to record two versions, one for a *qsbah* solo and the other with a sung text.

Bowles was delighted with the resulting solo, which was so intricately virtuosic that it inspired him to poetry: 'In a landscape of immensity and desolation it is a moving thing to come upon a lone camel-driver sitting beside his fire at night while the camels sleep, and listen for a long time to the querulous, hesitant cadences of the qsbah. The music, more than any other I know, most completely expresses the essence of solitude.' But as Schuyler points out, Bowles had set up the whole thing to suit his personal taste, 'conjuring up an image of a place that didn't quite exist': the piece was actually recorded outside a town on the coast, and, rather than sleeping camels, the audience consisted of local musicians, a recording crew, and some government officials. However, Bowles was honest about his interventions, and as Schuyler concedes, 'from the selfish view of a Western listener' he was right to describe this track as one of the best things in his collection. Was Bowles, as some have asserted, a 'colonialist'? Schuyler replies that though his opinions may have been romantic, Orientalist, 'or simply wrong', his admiration and affection were sincere.

Texts were of secondary interest to Bowles; for him, capturing the sound was the thing, and he was content to leave its analysis to others – he simply wanted to share the music he loved. As he wrote to the head of the folk-song archive in the Library of Congress, 'My principal interest in the collection of tape is in seeing as much of it as possible reach a large public.' He wanted the Library to issue six LPs but they could only afford two. But he did have the satisfaction of seeing his recordings of *jilala* trance music in a Tangier wedding procession – which reminded him of Stravinsky – released on LP, and also of seeing the Joujouka village musicians, whom he had co-discovered with the Beat poet Brion Gysin, made world-famous thanks to their championing by the Rolling Stones musician Brian Jones. A major compilation of Bowles's recordings, with Schuyler's commentaries on his field notes, had to wait for release until 2016.

* * *

Some of Bowles's predictions about musical extinction were borne out by events, others proved overly pessimistic. The Moroccan government has woken up to its cultural responsibilities and supported the Fes Festival of World Sacred Music. Record companies, including Rounder and the Paris-based Institut du Monde Arabe, have sponsored excellent Moroccan recordings, including the trance music of *gnawa*, Imazighen 'Berber blues' from the Middle Atlas, and songs from the Tafilalet oases which suggest cross-fertilisation with the blues of the Mississippi. But many of the 250 tracks which Bowles recorded in 1959 now constitute unique musicological evidence.

'I found a goldmine right there in Meknes in the Jewish music,' he wrote to the Library of Congress, 'so I stayed on there and made three recordings, including one evening in the largest synagogue, where I got the entire service.' This was after clearing yet more official hurdles, since at that time the Moroccan government was opposed to allowing Americans to record that music. And here Bowles's warnings *were* prophetic, in that after the Middle East wars of 1967 and 1973 the Jews he recorded in Meknes and Essaouira either moved to Casablanca, or left Morocco entirely.

The Sephardic-Jewish tradition of which he caught the sound is inextricably intertwined with Arabo-Andalusian music, and it traces its descent back to Moorish Spain. It consists of a huge repertoire of musical settings of medieval Arabic poetry, with new texts being substituted as time went on. One of Bowles's most engaging recordings has a twenty-year-old cantor leading his synagogue flock through a craggy musical landscape with gazelle-like grace; another is of a soaring Andalusian chant by an older cantor in what Bowles calls the 'antique style'. He also recorded *malhun*, Andalusian love songs at once human and divine, and movements of a *nuba* suite which in its full form lasted seven hours.

Bowles's recordings speak to us vividly across the decades. Some indicate musical styles now lost, others remind us of the unforgiving slog of desert life which lies behind music which we can, if we're lucky, still hear today. But his greatest legacy went beyond music to celebrate a sound-world which he evocatively described in a letter to Glanville-Hicks, who later wove it into a song-cycle entitled *Letters from Morocco*:

> Wind, water, birds and animals, and (here) human voices make a fine auditory backdrop. The human voices make the most beautiful sound of all, when the muezzin calls during the night, especially the one for dawn, which begins about five fifteen and finishes a little before six. They preface the actual *mouddin* with religious remarks, sung in freely embroidered florid style, each man inventing his own key, mode, appoggiatura and expressive devices. And when you have a hundred or more of these incredibly high, piercing, birdlike voices doing flamenco-like runs in different keys, from different minarets, against a background of cocks crowing, you have a very special and strange sound.

Sources

Paul Bowles's letters and his autobiography are colourful and revealing, and *The Sheltering Sky* embodies his implicit credo; *Their Heads Are Green* reflects his life on the road during his global travels. The beautifully produced Dust to Digital box of his Moroccan recordings from 2016 comes with his own photographs plus an authoritative commentary by the recordings' editor Philip D. Schuyler.

Bibliography and recordings

Bowles, Paul, *The Sheltering Sky* (London: Penguin, 1949)
Bowles, Paul, *Their Heads Are Green* (London: Abacus, 1990)

Bowles, Paul, *Without Stopping: An Autobiography* (London: Peter Owen, 1972)

Miller, Jeffrey, ed., *In Touch: The Letters of Paul Bowles* (London: Flamingo, 1995)

Music of Morocco from the Library of Congress, Dust to Digital DTD-46

28 Domna Samiou on location with Yehudi Menuhin.

14

A voice for Greece

Domna Samiou's crusade

To THOSE WHO have nothing, music comes like a gift from the gods. Like Gershwin's Porgy, Domna Samiou grew up with plenty of nothing, and she too lived in a shack. Her parents were Greeks who had been expelled from Turkey in 1922, six years before she was born, and the shanty town on the outskirts of Athens where they lived with fellow-refugees, under the disapproving eye of the police, had neither water nor electricity. Music was Samiou's passion, but there wasn't much of it around – just a man carrying a gramophone with a flower horn, who would stop on his rounds and play a song for half a drachma; otherwise it was the singing in a nearby church where, every Sunday, she and her father would attend service. 'Not out of religious zeal,' she later explained, 'but for the music. To me it was like going to a concert or the theatre, and I learned all the liturgies by heart.' Being female, she was not allowed to sing inside the church, but she made up for it back home: 'My sister, my mother, my father and I would all sit round the brazier, and my father and I would chant – he would be the priest and I would be the deacon, or he would be the left choir and I would be the right. In Easter week I was in my seventh heaven.'

She loved the all-night vigils which women would hold in their shacks, to pray for a sick child or absentee husband. 'They would borrow an icon of the Virgin Mary from the church, and beside it they would place a tin of sand in which guests could put their candles. And they would tell us children to chant, saying that God would listen to us, because we were young and innocent.'

Life didn't get easier as time went on. Her father died of malnutrition when she was twelve, and the rich lady in whose house she found employment as a cleaner took her in as a lodger, 'so that I could eat a plate of food and not starve to death as well'. The German occupation was followed by civil war in the streets, during which the shanty town was burnt to the ground, leaving the remainder of the family homeless. But a ray of light came: her employer, who had registered her fine voice, sent her to Simon Karas, the country's leading champion of traditional music. 'What can you sing?' he asked her. She was at first too embarrassed to speak, and finally answered 'a tango'. One verse was enough for him to sign her up for lessons, and to send her to night school: 'Without an education, he said, I could not properly learn music.'

Studying ecclesiastical chant with Karas, she went deeply into the Byzantine modes, and as a member of his choir recorded them for the new state-run radio station. Karas was a song collector who spent his summers on safari in the mountains, armed with pencil and paper in the quest for village songs which he would then teach his choir; he got Domna a job as a radio programme-maker.

Greece's post-war upheaval saw mass migration to Athens, and Domna and her mentor hoovered up the music thus brought in from Crete and Thrace, Macedonia, and the Peloponnese. They were also charged with the job of vetting for authenticity the 45rpm singles which the record companies were putting out: this search for ethnographic purity – in the Seventies a less contentious concept than it is today – became her guiding principle. She saved up, bought an Uher recorder, and struck out on her own as a collector-broadcaster, carving a career as a producer of records, stage plays and films; she also began assembling what would become a massive folk-music archive.

Her other big turning point came in 1971, when the left-wing singer-songwriter Dionyssis Savvopoulos invited her to sing at a students' club. Savvopoulos's reasoning was simple: 'She had been scrambling up mountains and gathering unknown songs from grandfathers. The only thing left was to come to the microphone and sing them herself.' Until then, she said, it had not even crossed her mind to sing in front of an audience. 'Everything I had done until then was done out of my love for folk song. It had never occurred to me that I myself could sing.' With her distinctive voice and her persuasive advocacy, says Savvopoulos, 'she made us understand the difference between the great tradition of her art, and the cheap folklore of the colonels' – this being the era of Greece's rule by a military junta. It wasn't long before she had become a singer feted across Europe, setting a trend for folk music among young Greeks who had hitherto regarded it as something to be ashamed of. Her records, notably *Folk Fables in Song*, testify to her impeccable musical taste; her monument is the Domna Samiou Greek Folk Music Association.

Her posthumous torch-bearer is the *lyra* player Sokratis Sinopoulos. His teacher was Ross Daly – the British musician who put the three-string *lyra* on the map – and his choirmaster was taught by Karas, so the apostolic succession has been a neat one. Samiou had spotted Sinopoulos's talent when he was a teenager, installed him in her band, and finally made him her co-producer; he is now working on a definitive collation of her recordings. Karas's archive, he adds, is even larger than Samiou's, and he agrees that ideally the two archives should merge.

Well, why shouldn't they? He grins wryly: 'It's not easy, because there are egos involved, and the directors and collectors of the Karas archive want to keep control. As an associate professor at Thessaloniki University, I am constantly trying to bring them together. I am trying to create a space where they can co-exist.'

Online source

The website of Domna Samiou – domnasamiou.gr – provides copious links to her CDs, her career, and her autobiography.

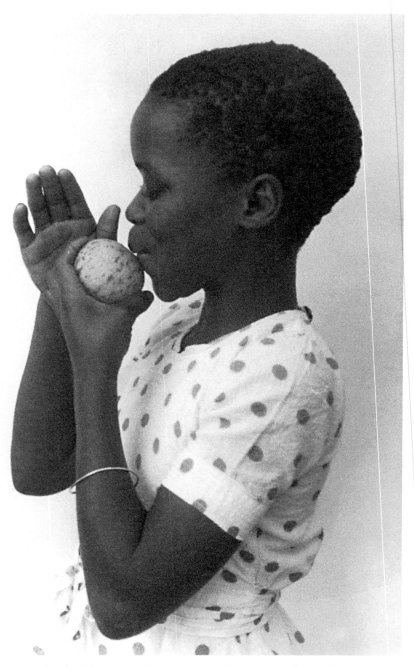

29 John Blacking's photo of a girl playing the spherical flute.

15

Things that are made to cry

John Blacking and the Venda

FOR ETHNOMUSICOLOGISTS, SONG collecting *per se* is not usually the primary goal. But some combine scientific rigour with a collector's love for music in a way which neither Percy Grainger nor Béla Bartók could have faulted. So let one example of this breed stand for many: John Blacking's *Venda Children's Songs*, published in 1967, is still a classic of the academic genre.

Best known for his definition of music as 'humanly organised sound', and for his influential book *How Musical Is Man?*, Blacking initially aspired to be a concert pianist. But he began his career with service in the Coldstream Guards, leading a platoon of Malay irregulars in the campaign against Communist insurgents in 1948–9. He read anthropology at Cambridge, went back to work in Malaya as a government advisor on the place of 'Aborigines', got sacked because he disagreed with the official policy of removing them from the rainforest, and went instead to work for Hugh Tracey, who was at that time compiling the International Library of African Music in Johannesburg. Accompanying Tracey on recording trips to Mozambique and Zululand, he developed his own theory about the role of body-movement in the making of music.

In 1956 Blacking embarked on twenty-two months' fieldwork with the Venda of the Sibasa District in Northern Transvaal. Singing Venda songs and playing their instruments, he pioneered the participant-observer method that was then becoming fashionable. As his obituarist John Baily points out, he tended to idealise the egalitarian aspect of Venda society, ignoring their division into noble and commoner classes, but his romantic characterisation of the Venda as 'the musical people', whom we should all emulate, gained traction worldwide. His ideas chimed with those underpinning the new Society for Ethnomusicology which had been established in the USA in 1955, but with one exception: he took issue with their analytical separation of music from its cultural context. Blacking was worried – and with hindsight, how right he was to worry – that ethnomusicology could reduce music to a mere sociological exercise. He saw music and its cultural context as inextricably interrelated, and this was his approach with the Venda; he christened it 'cultural analysis'. In his trim and soldierly way, he taught generations of students at the Queen's University of Belfast, who in turn carried his method round the world.

Venda Children's Songs is gracefully evocative, even when at its most analytically rigorous. Here it is on basic definitions:

> The term 'songs of the Venda' ... includes all tunes that are 'sung' or 'played on instruments', as well as patterns of words that are recited to a regular metre. It is its rhythm, therefore, that distinguishes 'singing' (*u imba*) from 'talking' (*u amba*), from 'reciting praises' (*u renda*), and from 'narrating' (*u anetshela*). Even a single tone blown on a stopped pipe or horn comes into the Venda category of music: the performer 'plays' it (*-lidza*), or more literally 'makes it cry', since *-lidza* is the causative of *-lila* (to weep, cry). Musical instruments are thus known as *zwilidzo*, 'things that are made to cry'.

When Blacking likens Venda music to a waterfall, one immediately senses its character: 'It is for ever moving, and yet its overall pattern never changes, and from a distance it even appears as solid and immovable as a stone statue.' And he admires the music's force: 'Quite often a drum skin is torn and a ritual postponed for some hours while it is replaced ... leg rattles disintegrate during a dance; the leather supports of xylophone keys break.' Such accidents don't upset people, he says, 'since they are evidence of good, vigorous playing, and the intense excitement that goes with it'. He notes that most Venda children are competent musicians, each playing at least one instrument, and that although they have no explicit grasp of melodic pattern, they can instantly spot a wrong note in a solo or chorus.

His first priority in making an ethnomusicological analysis was, he said, 'to be sure that transcriptions of the music represent what is *intended* by the performers'. The fifty-six songs in this collection reflect the transcriptions and texts of over four hundred recordings, plus notes made in conversation with the musicians; he recorded some songs in a dozen different versions.

His analyses of modality, melody, and speech-tone are laid out with diagrammatic precision, but his commentaries on the songs are miniature essays on village life. Some of these begin with a complaint that none of his informants have been able to explain a text, but that only acts as a spur to his learned detective work. Three examples can illustrate his method, as he comes at each song from many different angles, employing an eclectic range of analytical tools:

1.

'Maovhelwa'

Maovhelwa a a tanga tshikona (Storks are dancing *tshikona*)

Children sing this ditty when they see *maovhelwa* (sing. *Liovhelwa* = Abdim's stork, *Sphenorhynchus abdimii*) flying overhead. These birds fly round in circles anti-clockwise, so that the Venda are reminded of their national dance, *tshikona*. The birds do not merely 'dance' (*-tshina*): they 'dance in stately fashion' (*-tanga*), as do old women and important persons. The Venda have good reason to honour the birds, as they eat locusts and army worms and are therefore regarded as protectors of crops. One informant even suggested that the birds were ancestors who returned every year to look after their descendants' welfare, and that was why they danced *tshikona*. The birds appear only during the season when crops are growing, after which they migrate northwards: thus one does not hear this song between June and September, when most children's songs are sung.

2.
'Nyamulemalema'
Nya-mulemalema, (Madam Bat)
Ida u dzhie goko. (Come and take some food)
Goko a si lau (The food is not yours)
Ndi la Malogwane (It belongs to Malogwane)

This may be sung towards nightfall by boys, as they wave sticks around and try to attract bats. If a boy catches a bat he may give it to a girl, even if she does not ask for it. Girls who are nearing the age of puberty want bats for *u kwevha* (stretching the labia minora). Some male informants have said that the girls take the bats and hold them, with wings stretched, against their labia. Van Warmelo reports that girls use the powder obtained from charred and pulverized bats' wings ... to help the labia to stretch well, like the wings of a bat ... the Reverend Diether Giesekke reports that boys also sing this as they hang upside down by their knees from the branch of a tree. They sing the song and perform the action of milking.

At the *domba* initiation I saw girls and boys hanging in the same way: the purpose of the ritual is to teach them that babies should present the head first during parturition.

The singer calls the bat, enticing it with food; but when it comes he kills it, arguing that it has stolen another's food. There is an element of hunting magic in this song.

3.
'Mvula'
I a vhuya mulobilo, Kolongonya! (Here the rain comes, pouring down)
Vho-mmane mbebeni, Kolongonya! (Carry me on your back, Auntie)

171

Ni nnyise lufherani, Kolongonya! (Let me shelter in the verandah)
Nndu khuludzi na biko, Kolongonya! (Big houses are warm)

'Mvula' is sung when children see the rain sweeping across the fields, especially boys who are out herding. Although the song expresses the desire to shelter, some children like to run outdoors into the rain to sing.
Mulobilo = an ideophone describing the rain when it is falling very hard.
Kolongonya = an ideophone describing the water falling off the edge of the thatched roof.
Mmane = wife of father, junior to the speaker's mother: mother's younger sister: wife of one's father's younger brother or one's elder sibling. In this context probably the brother's wife, who is often a favourite, since she may cook food for her husband's younger sibling. The father's younger wife would, on the other hand, tell the child to go to his own mother for food. The mother's younger sister would not be living with the mother in normal circumstances, because marriage is virilocal.

All this was sixty years ago. John Blacking has gone, as has the meticulously organised society he was observing, but his book remains eloquent testimony to academic song collecting in its most dedicated and scrupulous form.

Sources

John Blacking's short book *Venda Children's Songs* is an exemplary piece of ethnomusicology; John Baily's essay in the *Yearbook for Traditional Music* sets Blacking in context.

Bibliography

Baily, John, 'John Blacking and his Place in Ethnomusicology', *Yearbook for Traditional Music*, vol. 22 (1990), xi–xxi
Blacking, John, *Venda Children's Songs* (Johannesburg: Witwatersrand University Press, 1967)

16

Record companies as collectors

From Folkways to Muziekpublique

MANY OF THE earliest field recordings of non-European music were made not by musicologists, but by scouts from British and German record companies. Having sold gramophones to well-heeled Third World listeners, they wanted to sell records of their local music to be played on them. Today these records are precious evidence of music which has since been lost, but their original purpose was commercial. Yet record producers have perennially been fired by the romance of capturing music before it dies, and the list of labels dedicated to ethnography is long. Those dealt with here reflect the variety of ways in which such companies can emerge, whether in response to politics, to changing public taste, to personal crusades, or simply by accident.

'I thought I had a large concept of documentation,' wrote the American song collector Samuel Charters, 'but in Moses Asch I met a man whose concept was large enough to contain mine and all the others.' Asch himself recalled telling Albert Einstein about his intention to found the company which became Folkways Records, and getting an emphatic thumbs-up from the great physicist. Asch's vision was of a record company which could 'describe the human race, the sound it makes, what it creates'.

Son of the politically radical Yiddish novelist Sholem Asch, Moses Asch was born in Warsaw in 1905. Anti-Semitism drove the family to Paris, and when France was engulfed by war in 1915 they migrated to the Bronx where Leon Trotsky, a friend of Sholem's, lived next door. Moses was fascinated by sound electronics, and went into business as a designer of public address systems, but when the socialist *Jewish Daily Forward* newspaper commissioned him to create a transmitter for its Yiddish-language radio station, he discovered a market for Yiddish music, and began to produce records for it.

He also recorded Lead Belly, which led to recording relationships with left-leaning singers including Burl Ives, Woody Guthrie, and Pete Seeger, and with jazz musicians like Mary Lou Williams, Art Tatum, and Coleman Hawkins. Over-extending his operation, he went bankrupt; he resurrected his business as a new company, Folkways Records, registered in his secretary

Marian Distler's name, but with himself designated as 'consultant'; he ran the company from its formation until his death in 1986, notching up two thousand titles. Many of these were what he called 'tribal' music, until the ethnomusicologist George Herzog suggested that 'ethnic' might be a less insulting term. Herzog's tales of the destruction wrought by Allied bombing on Berlin's sound archive persuaded Asch to build up his own ethnic archive, the first album of which was *Music of the Sioux and Navajo*, followed by albums of music from Haiti and Cuba.

When one of his contributing anthropologists suggested booklets giving social and historical context, a pattern was set from which Asch would never deviate. Henceforth every record had its own academic documentation, with Asch decreeing that none should ever be deleted. 'Just because the letter J is less popular than the letter S, you don't take it out of the dictionary,' he sardonically observed. And whenever he had a hand in the making of a recording, he insisted that one single mike would not only suffice, but actually be better than two or three. 'That's how I hear it,' he said. 'Mixing can never give you the accurate sense of the original sound. I hate stereo recordings.' On his death the entire Folkways collection was deposited with the Smithsonian Institution; hence the creation of Smithsonian Folkways Recordings, which has honoured Asch's vision by building on his library to create a massive ethnographic collection. This has been achieved partly through the acquisition of the backlists of other independent labels, in a policy begun by the Smithsonian's former curator Anthony Seeger. Thus did the out-of-print or unpublished albums of UNESCO's collection – recorded in seventy countries – become part of the Smithsonian archive, as did the 350 records of the Arhoolie label. As Seeger points out, without their efforts much of the music which independent labels have produced would not have been heard at all. 'They've often done things which the popular record industry discovers only belatedly, and capitalises on,' he says. And since the record market is now geared to producing hits, the queue of independents wanting to transfer their materials to Smithsonian is lengthening all the time.

But the growth of the Smithsonian-Folkways archive is also due to the commissioning of new recordings. Notable among these have been two series on Latin American and African American music, and a majestic ten-CD survey of the musics of Central Asia. However, such projects require external subsidy – the Central Asian set was backed by the Aga Khan Trust for Culture – and a hoped-for African series will only materialise if comparable support is found.

As a branch of the US National Museum, the Smithsonian has a uniquely privileged position, but despite its non-profit status it's not immune to the ills affecting its competitors. Its ways of reaching its audience without breaking the bank include cleverly focused digital marketing through iTunes and Spotify; its liner notes are available free as downloadable pdf files. Without those, CDs would be as useless as museums without labelling or signing.

By inducing Americans to take an interest in the music of other cultures, Moses Asch had lit the fuse for a new fashion. In 1965 Teresa Sterne took time off from her work as a classical record producer to launch the ground-breaking Nonesuch Explorer Series, which under her stewardship grew to comprise ninety LPs of traditional music, recorded in some of the remotest – and for recordists most difficult – corners of the earth. The initial album, a concert of Balinese gamelan entitled *Music from the Morning of the World*, was recorded by the British musician David Lewiston, who became the company's most prolific collector. 'Whenever I came back from a trip,' he told me, 'she'd simply ask what I'd got for her, and twenty-eight Nonesuch LPs were the result.'

This was the first taste of gamelan for most Western listeners, many of whom as a result got hooked on what was not yet called 'world music' (that label was put into general parlance in 1987, by a group of London marketing men desperate to find a way of selling non-European music). In 1977 Sterne received the ultimate accolade of seeing an Explorer recording sent aboard Voyager into space, but in 1979, amid furious protests from composers including Elliott Carter and Aaron Copland, she was abruptly defenestrated.

This did not deter Nonesuch from continuing its non-Western strand, but it was now in attenuated form, and on the back of pioneering work done by others. Thus it was that in 1987 Nonesuch released *Le mystère des voix Bulgares*, reissuing recordings which had originally been made by the Swiss ethnomusicologist Marcel Cellier and released on his own label; having made a killing with this record, Nonesuch cashed in further by making more Bulgarian-voice albums. And they cashed in again on the sudden success of Buena Vista Social Club. But that's another story: the credit for rediscovering those incomparable Cubans goes to the guitarist Ry Cooder and his producer Nick Gold.

It's hard to overestimate the importance of Gold and his company World Circuit in discovering – or rediscovering – artists from Mali, Senegal, and Cuba during the last decades of the twentieth century. First they brought the Senegalese band Orchestra Baobab's *Pirates Choice* to the world's delighted attention: this music had been recorded in 1982, but became forgotten during the funk-inspired *mbalax* craze. Gold and his colleagues then did the same for the singers Oumou Sangare and Cheikh Lo. They teamed Ry Cooder with the Malian singer Ali Farka Touré to make the award-winning album *Talking Timbuktu*, and then, intending to record two Malian high-life musicians in collaboration with some superannuated Cubans in Havana, Gold and Cooder did strike gold.

30 The Senegalese Orchestra Baobab, whose music Nick Gold's company
World Circuit rescued from obscurity in 1989.

The Malians had visa problems and couldn't make it to Havana, so instead
Gold and Cooder assembled the Cubans, who had assumed their solo careers
were over. After cheerily christening themselves Buena Vista Social Club
(after a popular music venue in Havana in the 1940s), they recorded enough
music for three albums which, on their release in 1997, took the world by
storm. Thus was the music of pre-revolutionary Cuba given a new lease of life,
and thus did singer Ibrahim Ferrer, pianist Ruben Gonzalez, and ninety-year-
old *trova* guitarist Compay Segundo shine brightly, if necessarily briefly, each
unique and unforgettable.

* * *

It's appropriate that Paris, long a melting pot for Asian and African musics, should be home to two of Europe's most significant ethnographic labels. Yet record production for both Ocora and the Institut du Monde Arabe was an accidental by-product, rather than what they had been set up to do. Ocora – Office de COoperation RAdiophonique – was established by Radio France in 1957: its prosaic purpose was to train sound engineers in the French colonies so that they could set up their own radio stations after independence. The Institut du Monde Arabe (IMA) was created by the French government in 1980, in an attempt to tame the tiger of racism with the aid of sober information. With a French president, an Arab director-general, and six Arabs balancing six French members on its governing board, strict equality is written into the IMA charter. The titles of the records it has put out – including *Trésors de la musique algérienne* and *Chants d'allégresse: Les Femmes de Tétouan* – reflect a cultural pride which was much in evidence when I visited the company in happier days before the Arab Spring had triggered first hope and then despair. Dorothée Engel, presiding over its record production, wanted to side-step my questions about countering the French racism which was then already in the ascendant. 'We're a cultural institution, not a political one, nor even a religious one,' she insisted, pointing out the multi-faith nature of the Arab world. 'I don't think we can reach people like Le Pen's followers – they don't just want to purify France from Arabs, they want to purify it from everyone but themselves. All we can hope to do is reduce people's fear of other cultures, by saying "This is who we are, and how we live. Come and share a few moments of your time with us."'

And that was the spirit in which their record-producing activities began: 'We'd always invited travelling groups to perform, and initially we recorded them just for the archive, to preserve their heritage. But some of these concerts were so exceptional that one day we thought, why not make CDs?' They produced a CD of Cheikha Remitti, the grandmother of *rai*, and it sold thousands; they began to discover that their CDs could help hitherto-unknowns get invited to tour. That was how the Sudanese singer and band-leader Abdel Gadir Salem got onto the circuit, after being invited to perform at the IMA; that was how the Tunisian lutenist Yousra Dhahbi – whose first CD the IMA had put out – made her mark. When I asked why superstar Khaled didn't figure on the Algerian compilation, Engel's reply made perfect sense: 'He has no need of us. We want to help people whose music might not otherwise survive.' Likewise they didn't put out CDs of the 'city music' so popular in Lebanon and Egypt – not because they were hung up on ethnic purity, but because its booming market meant it could look after itself.

IMA's main markets outside France were Britain, America, and Japan: their CDs hardly sold at all to the Arab world. Piracy was the reason, though Engel ruefully admitted that this was poetic justice. Why should impoverished Arabs pay inflated Western prices to listen to their own music? At least the IMA didn't have to make a profit: 'We're lucky not to have to meet sales targets,' she said. 'We can afford to take our public on a voyage of exploration. We choose the best music we can find, without obeying the dictates of fashion.' But she admitted there was increasing pressure even on them to break even; this problem was compounded by the fact that the Arab countries which sponsored the IMA were falling behind with their promised annual contributions.

All this was in 2003: how profoundly, and how dreadfully, the Arab world has changed since then, and how hollow the silence of the ancient city out of which the celebratory triple-CD entitled *The Aleppo Suites* had emerged in 2009. It's no surprise that in recent years the IMA's rich stream of CDs has all but dried up.

Meeting, on the same day in 2003, the Malagasy boss of Ocora, Serge Noelranaivo, I got a similarly worried story about sales, despite the vast sweep of the Ocora backlist from which, as with Folkways, no record is ever deleted. From cautious beginnings – producing just one symbolic record per year in the early Sixties, before they realised what a goldmine they were sitting on – Ocora's output grew dramatically to cover every part of Africa and the old Silk Road, plus parts of South America, but it had recently hit an unexpected snag in the form of the 'world-music' boom.

Why so? 'Because traditional music hasn't shared in this boom. Because the shops want stuff they can pile high and sell fast, and we're getting squeezed off the shelves. The so-called world music that is currently fashionable is not world music at all – it's just mainstream pop from somewhere else.' What labels like Ocora needed, said Noelranaivo, was an equivalent to the recommended retail price for books. 'It's saved the book in France, and it could do the same for our CDs. We have to get them back into the shops. I know there's a market for them – there are plenty of people like me around.'

Hence one of his marketing gambles: a seven-CD box covering the traditional musics of every continent for a mere 15 euros. The title sounds dull – 'Collection Ocora Catalogue Album' – but the contents are riveting. From the moon guitar in Hanoi to the *kora* in Gambia, from *bouzouki* in Greece to the *koropatia* dance in Honduras, here are the fruits of ethnomusicological forays spanning half the globe over half a century.

Eighteen years on, Noelranaivo is still in the saddle, and still grappling with problems of distribution. The shops are now even more resistant to selling ethnographic CDs, and digitisation – which Ocora may reluctantly have to embrace – is not something to which the musicological booklets essential to their products are suited. The label is still state-funded, but each time Radio France gets a fresh board of directors Noelranaivo has to make the case anew for this support. 'Survival means a daily struggle,' he says, 'but our concerts are as well-attended as ever, and our potential market is still there.'

* * *

Topic Records may be a tiny outfit, but it's the oldest independent label in the world. And it represents a quixotically heroic strand of British song collecting. In 1936 the Workers' Music Association (WMA) was founded as an educational offshoot of the British Marxist Party, and in 1939 the Topic Record Club was created to bolster the WMA's campaign against European Fascism. Its first record was a 78rpm disc bearing a song (delivered in a mischievous middle-class voice) entitled 'The Man that Waters the Workers' Beer'; on its B-side was a full-throated arrangement of 'The Internationale' performed by the Topic Singers and Band. When war broke out, shellac supplies were diverted to military use, and Topic's release schedule became sporadic; no attempt was made to promote its records beyond the confines of the WMA because the operation was done on a shoestring, as it has been ever since. A mimeographed newsletter from 1941 to the club's 800 members indicates just how strapped it was for cash:

> A final word of appreciation to all those members who have responded to our last month's appeal for a 1/6d levy to help us meet that dreadful bill of £40 we have to face for unexpected purchase tax imposed on certain back numbers. But we haven't nearly enough in yet to meet it – remember that many members have left to join the forces, or have been bombed or evacuated. Have you done your bit by the club yet?

In the Forties and Fifties Topic's main thrust was pro-Soviet, with recordings being sourced from Eastern-bloc labels, and *Paul Robeson's Message of Peace* forming a fittingly Communist climax. Topic's post-war leading lights were the singer-songwriter Ewan MacColl and the singer-historian A. L. Lloyd, plus Pete Seeger and his sister Peggy. Lloyd's pamphlet *The Singing Englishman* and MacColl's folk-ballad record *The Shuttle and Cage* pointed the way which Topic was to follow, with *The Singing Sailor* (compiled in 1954 by Lloyd, MacColl, and the left-wing actor Harry H. Corbett, better known as half of BBC television's *Steptoe and Son*) cementing the policy: henceforth Topic's prime focus would be on folk song from the British Isles. No matter that the company's London studio had sandbags in the windows and egg boxes on the walls to drown out the sound of passing trains, or that, for recording on location, all that was required was, as production manager Bill Leader said, 'any decent room, with not too much traffic noise'. Musician Tony Engle, who took over direction of the company in 1973 and ran it for four decades, describes what Topic has always been after as 'music with dirt under its fingernails'.

Engle himself trained as a civil engineer.

> But my life changed when I heard a track by the Ian Campbell Folk Group on the *Family Favourites* radio programme – that was the string that led me to go to the record shop and find the record. I read the sleeve notes, which sent me on to something else, and within a year I'd sold all my Charlie Parker and Joan Baez records in order to buy Dubliners records. I then sold all those to buy Harry Cox, who had records on Topic and was the archetypal traditional musician.

The central problem he had to contend with was not only the fact that two world wars had gone like a scythe through Britain's working-class menfolk:

> Traditional music in Britain didn't get properly recorded until the Fifties. It couldn't develop the way the blues did, or even the way Irish music developed, both of which were available on record from the Twenties onwards. Back then, nobody thought to record Harry Cox, and when he *was* finally recorded – in the Sixties, in his old age – he was having to compete with the Rolling Stones.

Inspired by Lloyd's pioneering song collecting in the Balkans, Engle also produced an impressive series of field recordings from the Mediterranean, the Caucasus, and Asia, but his overriding aim – on a minuscule budget – has been to keep alive as long as possible what remains of the British song tradition. First with survivors like Harry Cox, Sam Larner, and Anne Briggs, and now with what he calls the 'revivalists' led by Shirley Collins (who drew much of her inspiration from the Topic archive of field recordings), and the trinity of Martin Carthy, Norma Waterson, and their daughter Eliza Carthy. The tradition represented by these latter singers still thrives in clubs and pubs, and its influence has been far-reaching: Paul Simon would never have stumbled on 'Scarborough Fair' had he not heard it sung by Martin Carthy. Topic can no longer afford to produce new records, and it survives thanks to digital publication from its backlist; the record industry which used to support these singers is now, in Engle's view, moribund.

Bernard Kleikamp, bravely sailing against the economic wind with his PAN record company in Amsterdam, attributes the death of the CD business to two things: saturation of the market, and illegal copies and downloads. His policy has always been to document living traditions, rather than dying ones:

31 Shirley Collins in the 1960s.

'I didn't want my company to release the last surviving Tierra del Fuego singer who at eighty-five was singing the songs of her youth. Music adapts to the flow of time, and that's what I aim to document.'

Streaming, Spotify, and YouTube are now transforming the whole scene, but musicians and producers will always go on finding each other, as evidenced by Real World's 'Big Room' studio which welcomes artists passing through, and by a small but promising portent from the 2018 Mediterranean migrations. Muziekpublique is the name of a Belgian not-for-profit record company, and Refugees for Refugees is the collective name for the musicians who appeared on its first CD. These musicians hail from Syria, Afghanistan, Pakistan, Tibet, and Iraq; all are virtuosi, all have been driven from their homeland by war and persecution. One couldn't imagine a better foundation for fusions, and so their music proves: an Indo-Pakistani raga melds sweetly with a Tibetan song, a classical Arabic suite incorporates a Hazari Afghan melody, Sufism unites singers from very different countries far apart. For its latest CD Muziekpublique has roped in seventeen *gnawa* musicians who have settled in Belgium: *Jola: Hidden Gnawa Music in Brussels* allows this expatriate Maghrebian minority a public voice for the first time.

Sources

Richard Carlin's *Worlds of Sound* sets the Folkways label in its cultural and commercial context; David Suff's beautifully illustrated history *Three-score and Ten* charts the development of Topic Records from 1939 to 2009 with the aid of seven CDs. *Vision and Revision* is a CD spanning Topic's current stars and its great voices from the past. Gene Bluestein's interview-essay on Moses Asch is detailed and informative. The Kleikamp quotes come from *Living Ethnomusicology*.

Bibliography and recordings

Bluestein, Gene, 'Moses Asch, Documentor', *American Music*, vol. 5, no. 3 (Autumn 1987), 291–304
Carlin, Richard, *Worlds of Sound* (New York: Collins, 2008)
Sarkissian, Margaret and Ted Solis, *Living Ethnomusicology: Paths and Practices* (Champaign, IL: University of Illinois Press, 2019)
Suff, David, *Three-score and Ten: A Voice to the People* (London: Topic, 2009)

Jola: Hidden Gnawa Music in Brussels, Muziekpublique, 2020
Vision and Revision: The First 80 Years of Topic Records, Topic Records TXCD597

Musical snapshots

The importance of sound archives

FOR MUSCICOLOGICAL RESEARCH, sound archives are the bedrock, and they go back to the birth of recorded sound; their primary impulse was scientific. The first was founded in Vienna in 1899 at the prompting of the physiologist Sigmund Exner; a year later the psychologist Carl Stumpf founded the Berliner Phonogramm-Archiv after recording a Siamese theatre group with the new-fangled Edison cylinders. Stumpf's pupil Erich von Hornbostel supervised the growth of this archive from 1905 until 1933, when he was sacked by the Nazis for being on his mother's side Jewish. Although he made field recordings in Oklahoma, Tunisia, and the South Sea Islands, it was his analytical and comparative work on the materials in the archive which earned him fame as the founding father of what was called 'comparative musicology'. 'All learning is comparative,' he wrote, and comparison would allow us to draw universal conclusions about 'the origins and growth of music, and the nature of the musically beautiful'. It was typical of Hornbostel's meticulousness that he should insist that his travelling researchers do every experiment twice.

Having started out as part of the Friedrich Wilhelm University's psychology department, the Berliner Phonogramm-Archiv relocated to the city's conservatory, after which it became, under the Nazis, part of the Museum für Völkerkunde. That then morphed – after being dismembered during the Second World War – into the Ethnological Museum of Berlin. The Phonogramm-Archiv now hosts 350 separate collections, and holds 150,000 recordings, 16,000 of which are on wax cylinders, many complete with multiple-use metal negatives.

At around the time when the Vienna and Berlin archives were being founded, Franz Boas was persuading the American Museum to house the recordings he had made on his anthropological expedition to Siberia and Alaska. Thus were sound recordings enshrined as academically collectible, and the Smithsonian Institution's Bureau of American Ethnology quickly followed suit. Today the Library of Congress and the Smithsonian – a university in all but name – are the dominant American players in the game, with the LOC holding 3.6 million sound recordings, of which the Alan Lomax Collection alone – one of the LOC's many sub-collections – includes 6,400 sound recordings and 6,000 pieces of film.

In Eastern Europe in the Fifties, many post-war nations set up sound archives of folk music as an affirmation of their identity. A similar process began in Britain, though it had very different roots. Back in 1906, the Gramophone Company had started donating metal masters to the British Museum, which was collecting audio recordings of poets and statesmen. But the museum had no proper sound archive until the British Institute of Recorded Sound was set up in 1955, its collection boosted by thousands of shellac discs which had been sent in, following a public appeal. Now known as the British Library Sound Archive, this institution is the biggest of its kind in the world, currently holding six million recordings in every form of technology from cylinder to digital. Its collection of traditional and 'world' music is vast.

But these archives are not mere repositories for mummified artefacts. All stress their educational function, and all are striving to reflect the music of the moment. For Janet Topp Fargion, curator of traditional and 'world' recordings at the British Library Sound Archive, music is living history which needs to be documented. 'Music doesn't die, it simply changes,' she says. 'And it's changing so fast that we have to hurry to catch it, to take snapshots of its evolution. Capturing things now is more urgent than it's ever been. And as communities round the world realise the importance of capturing their own history, we can help by collecting musical evidence of their past, and sending it back to them.' As an example of this, Topp Fargion cites 1,500 rare Indian recordings which, under the sound archive's 'endangered musics' programme, have recently been put online, after being digitised by a Mumbai record collector. They were originally part of a series of shellac discs made by the German Odéon record company in 1912–16 and 1932–8, and much of their music is no longer performed today. Hence this project's importance, to Indian musicologists in particular.

One striking demonstration of the British Sound Archive's international usefulness is the story of the Golha project. Towards the middle of the twentieth century, Persian classical music was at a low ebb, thanks to the combined influence of Turkish and Arab music plus Western pop; Persian music was seen as irrelevant to the state's modernising policies. This was a time when there was no Persian TV or film industry; radio was the only available form of mass entertainment. In 1956 an assistant prime minister named Davud Pirnia had a patriotic idea: to open the airwaves to the country's best musicians, singers, and poets for performances in the classical mode. And over the next twenty-three years the *Golha* – 'Flowers of Persian Song and Music' – became a cult, with people all over the country making a weekly tryst with the programme; a total of 850 hours were broadcast. As the classical singer Muhammad-Reza Shajarian put it, Golha 'rescued our music from perdition'.

The music was never archived, but in 2004 Jane Lewisohn decided to try and recover it. She chased up sections of the *Golha* in countries all round the world, and got a grant from the British Library's Endangered Archives Programme to digitise it; the resulting Golha Project Website now allows the public free access to the entire collection.

Many recordings have a limited life-span, thanks to the obsolescence of the equipment needed to play them: as Topp Fargion points out, the machinery to play reel-to-reel and digital audiotape is now hard to find, and its transfer to CD requires special software. Stimulated by an awareness of this problem, the archive has launched a programme called Save Our Sounds, to encourage people to send in their 'obsolete' recordings before they degrade irretrievably.

Meanwhile the archive still sends people out to record, supporting them with grants, and giving them tuition on how to negotiate the licences without which commercial reproduction is an infringement of intellectual property rights. Thus, even in these citadels of scholarship, does the art of song collecting, in its humble time-honoured form, live on. The chapters which follow look at how present-day collector/conservationists are carrying the torch.

Bibliography

Lewisohn, Jane, 'Conservation of the Iranian Golha Radio Programmes and the Heritage of Persian Classical Poetry and Music', in Maja Kominko, ed., *From Dust to Digital: Ten Years of the Endangered Archives Programme* (Cambridge: Open Book Publishers, 2016), 587–616

32 Nurlanbek Nyshanov, who brought some of Kyrgyzstan's oldest instruments back to
life after the lifting of the Soviet yoke, plays the jew's harp.

17

Magic in two strings

Central Asia awakes

WHAT IS 'CENTRAL Asia'? Denoting neither a language nor a nationality, the concept is a European one, devised to package a vast and multifarious region which disappeared from the political map during the Communist period. For the purposes of this chapter it comprises the republics which the Soviets carved out in the 1920s, and which are now known as Uzbekistan, Tajikistan, Turkmenistan, Kazakhstan, and Kyrgyzstan, plus Uyghur Xinjiang. For most of the twentieth century the region was resistant to outsiders: only now is the international spotlight moving back onto it, thanks partly to its new geo-political importance, and partly to a new awareness of its traditional culture, and in particular its music.

In Kyrgyzstan, Kazakhstan, and Turkmenistan the traditional music is nomadic, reflecting the cycle of the seasons and the fauna of the steppes, with the same few instruments creating a musical lingua franca linking players thousands of miles apart. We're talking principally about the jew's harp, many kinds of lute, and the shamanic fiddle: with a mirror set in its bowl to ward off evil spirits, plus its haunting cello-like timbre, the last of these is a commanding presence. The two-string Kazakh *dombra* and the three-string Kyrgyz *komuz* are Central Asia's answers to the guitar, their airy magic impregnated with the sound of horses' hooves. To play at speed while waving your instrument balletically in the air – or behind your back, or upside down – is a routine mark of virtuosity.

These instruments can also have serious artistic purposes. What the Kazakhs call a *kui* and the Kyrgyz a *küü* is a wordless instrumental piece which may tell a story – perhaps about the winged horse Tulpar, cousin to the ancient Greeks' Pegasus – or it may simply be a tone-poem. But the glory of this nomad-pastoralist music lies in its self-accompanied singing by bards; this is folk music of the most sophisticated sort.

It's essentially a solo art, whose sound-world is permeated by Turkic and Mongolian influences. Urban influences from Iran, meanwhile, gave rise to the classical style of Uzbekistan and Tajikistan, which is rooted in a tradition of music theory that goes back to tenth-century Baghdad. Known as the *shash-maqom* ('six maqoms', a *maqom* being a modal form), this is the Central Asian equivalent of the European suite or song-cycle. It goes at a stately pace, it's powered by sophisticated poetics and complex melodic modulations, and it culminates in a peak of intensity with a vocal duet 'in one single breath' as its audiences demand. Each major city traditionally had its own style, and the art form's heyday was as part of the extraordinary flowering of painting, poetry, and music in fifteenth-century Herat. Sedentary versus nomadic, written versus oral, Muslim versus shamanic, lyric versus epic: on every level, Central Asia's two musical traditions are in sharp contrast.

When the Communists took control of the lands which the Tsars had colonised as 'Turkestan', their attitude to music was best expressed in Stalin's motto, 'nationalist in form, socialist in content'. The emirs who had acted as patrons of the *shashmaqom* were gone; the Communists were happy to support it as a manifestation of Tajik and Uzbek identity (although those countries have fought over its ownership ever since), but in other respects the Communist support for music was more the kiss of death than a new dawn. Yunus Rajabi was a lutenist and conservatoire-trained composer who in 1927 was invited to found a national folk-music ensemble for the fledgling Uzbek radio. Over the years he transcribed the entire *shashmaqom* repertory, culling different versions from different performers; splicing them together, he then created the versions he considered most 'authentic'. His distillation became the one taught at the conservatory, and long remained canonical, reinforced by a biennial competition to see who could reproduce it most faithfully, down to the smallest details of ornamentation. As the American ethnomusicologist Theodore Levin scathingly observed, this was frozen music kept artificially alive, though recently the competition has become more open to experiment.

Meanwhile the socialist rationalisation of folk music was proceeding apace. It hit a problem with the Kazakh tradition of sung-poetry contests, for example; these were so deep-rooted that the Soviets gave up trying to stamp them out, harnessing them instead to their cause, and substituting collective farms for villages as the competing entities. Much of the work done by local cultural commissars in the Twenties and Thirties – establishing choirs and music theatres – was laudable, but the Soviet conviction that European art forms held the key to the future for the indigenous peoples of Central Asia increasingly cast a blight.

In 1952 the chairman of the Union of Composers of Uzbekistan declared that monophonic *maqom* was a relic of the country's feudal past and could not 'properly reflect the new Soviet reality', so he disbanded the radio's folk-music ensembles, and for a while traditional Uzbek music was officially discouraged.

A more insidious threat came from government-run music schools where oral transmission was replaced by notation-based learning, extinguishing improvisation in the process. In the *maqom* ensemble set up by the government in the 1950s, an army of traditional instruments was used for arrangements which flew in the face of the purposes of the music: getting sixty musicians to play music designed for five brought fundamental changes in both tuning and instrument technology. Traditionally unfretted instruments acquired frets and appeared in new forms, with bass, alto, and soprano versions, and the requirement that everyone should play 'in tune' – sometimes in five-part harmony as a backing for a traditional melody – led to the adoption of the Western chromatic scale. The microtonal intervals which had been one of the defining characteristics of *maqom* were thus replaced by semitones, and as a result its delicately calibrated sound-world was blurred.

The damage was patchy rather than total – musicians in remote areas continued as before – but the result of all this was a major rescue-and-recovery job awaiting song-researchers. Yunus Rajabi hadn't been the only Soviet musicologist to research in Central Asia: Viktor Uspensky was one of a dedicated group who carried on the Russian Empire's huge survey of the culture in its southern fastnesses, and in 1925, fired by patriotic zeal, he went on an expedition through Turkmenistan recording thousands of folk songs and chants from devotional Sufi gatherings. In 1928 he and his colleague Viktor Belyayev published the first volume of a fastidiously transcribed collection entitled *Turkmen Music*; this triggered a new Orientalist vogue among Russian composers – plus the ever-exploratory Paul Hindemith – who wanted to weave Turkmen melodies into their compositions.

The second volume of this collection drew criticism for its alleged failure to acknowledge 'democratic moments' in the feudal history of *shashmaqom*; Belyayev himself accused the intellectually incorruptible Uspensky of adopting an 'archaeological' approach, rather than one which celebrated post-revolutionary musical developments. Belyayev went on to become the Soviet Union's prime authority on the music of Central Asia, but the collection of essays which he published as a summation of his work reflected a neatly Stalinist carve-up of the territory which didn't reflect cultural, linguistic, or musical realities. The boundaries of traditional music were not congruent with the national ones, and Belyayev's analyses took no account of the microtonal refinements which are the essence of Central Asian music. He was aware of those refinements, but regarded the Western tempered scale as a more appropriate medium.

The first serious challenge to this constricting orthodoxy came from a French musicologist named Jean During. He had entered the Central Asian musical scene via an unorthodox route, starting as a guitar teacher, first in

France and then in Teheran whither his fascination with the 'mystery and profundity' of Persian classical music had drawn him. His proficiency on the guitar gave him a head start with the *tar* and *setar* lutes, on which he took lessons with leading Iranian masters including the blind guru Nur Ali Borumand; as the latter's prize pupil, and having renounced the guitar, During won the *setar* award in a national TV competition. This feat was all the more notable given the Iranians' traditional assumption that only they could understand the spirit of their music.

During had arrived armed with a master's degree in philosophy from France, and in Teheran he got a grant to study Iranian philosophy; he also began writing a series of books on Sufism, shamanism, Kurdish culture, and on every aspect of Iranian traditional music. Some of these books were translated into Persian, notably *La musique iranienne: tradition et évolution*, which by the time of its publication in Teheran had acquired historical importance. 'I had been a witness to the last chapter in the story of Persian court music,' he explains, 'because the musicians who I'd studied with were now all dead. And they had never chased publicity – they hated the media, never went on the radio.' He spent eleven years in Iran, followed by periods in Baluchistan and Azerbaijan; his string virtuosity earned his recordings a place in the archives of the Baku conservatory, and opened doors to collaboration with local players.

I meet him at his house in Paris which, with its tapestries and rugs, seems the purest embodiment of austerely classical Persian culture; clusters of string instruments, some venerably old, lurk in every corner. A fine museum, I say, but he demurs: it isn't a museum, because he and his Iranian wife play these instruments every day. And as he talks and plays it becomes clear that his overriding concern is for *maqom* – or *mugam*, *mugham*, or *maqam*, depending on whichever corner of Central Asia you're dealing with – to be understood by its practitioners as a science, as much as an art. 'I don't want to criticise Central Asian players, because many of them are fine musicians,' he says. 'But they've lacked the analytical tools. Since the seventeenth century there has been no theoretical treatise on maqom. In my opinion a musician must have at least a minimum of theoretical knowledge about what they are playing.'

It needed a foreigner with During's boldness to break that charmed circle. From his vantage-point as director of research at the Centre National de la Recherche Scientifique in Paris, he has promulgated his view of a half-lost sound-world through workshops with Central Asian chamber groups, and he's supported that view with dozens of recordings and compositions of his own in the Middle Eastern style. Some of those recordings show how much fine traditional music went on discreetly despite the Soviet directives: for this music the mid-twentieth century was a golden age.

Other CDs reflect During's work on behalf of local song collectors, as with some richly ornamented music from Ili and Kashgar: a celebrated *tanbur* player had transcribed from memory all the *muqam* he had learnt in his youth, and During persuaded Radio France to commission a one-off performance which he recorded for posterity. With his commentaries on modes and scales, his records open up worlds within worlds: the grave power of the Persian *radif* system; the lute music of Kazakhstan and Kyrgyzstan; the decorous sweetness of Sufi chant set off by the contrasting silk and bronze strings of *tanbur* and *dutar*, or by the spike-fiddle and flute descanting above. Yet despite his reverence for tradition, During doesn't want this music to stand still. He's more than happy to see new instruments brought into the *shashmaqom*: 'It worked perfectly with the oud in Iran, though that took many years to settle in. It had to lose its Arabic accent.'

During may not be a song collector in the conventional sense, but as an inspired talent-spotter – the Azerbaijani *mugam* singer Alim Qasimov was one of his discoveries – and as an advocate for the musics of Central Asia, he has made a huge contribution both to that region's musical life and to our knowledge of it.

* * *

The other dominant figure in recent musical research has been During's friend Theodore Levin. Professor of music at Dartmouth College in New Hampshire, the austerely rabbinical Levin trained as a classical pianist, discovered the banjo, and was then drawn inexorably eastwards. He'd gone to Israel just after the Six Day War to research his Polish-Russian Jewish roots, and in east Jerusalem he'd chanced to catch the sound of the muezzin, which struck him as the most magical thing he'd ever heard; that was his epiphany. While studying music history at Princeton he joined the Harmonic Choir – America's first throat-singing group – but his ethnomusicological baptism came in the form of a year studying the *shashmaqom* at the Tashkent conservatory; here he forged friendships with young musicians who would go on to become the leading figures in Central Asia's traditional-music revival.

Dropping out of academe, he was hired by the Smithsonian Institute to develop an exchange of folk musicians between America and the Soviet Union, and in 1987 he brought fifty of them over to the Smithsonian Folklife Festival in Washington. Among them was a group of singers from a Georgian village, with whose curator he co-produced a Georgian CD. He also brought over the Azerbaijani singer Alim Qasimov (who had not yet been heard in America), and a member of the Tuvan throat-singing ensemble Huun-Huur-Tu, whose road manager he became, and whose first American records he produced. It was he who put Qasimov and the Tuvans on the map, and launched their international careers.

Meanwhile in Moscow he'd met some Russian scholars who steered him onto a different track.

> I learned their approach to ethnomusicology, which they saw as ethnography, the study of folklore. The way they did their field-work, and the way they wrote about it, made a lot of sense to me – it seemed more in touch with what was happening in these cultures. I decided to write something which would be more a narrative than an analytical book. I also wanted to give something back to the musicians who had shared with me their intimate thoughts about their art.

The result, after five years of tramping through remote parts of Central Asia, was a book which triggered a small revolution in ethnomusicology: *The Hundred Thousand Fools of God: Musical Travels in Central Asia (and Queens, New York)*.

When it was published in 1996, Uzbekistan and strife-torn Tajikistan were *terra incognita* to virtually all foreigners barring cognoscenti, so Levin's musical and social travelogue was a revelation – and doubly so, thanks to the fact that Communist accretions were at that moment being scraped away to expose the

33 American musicologist Theodore Levin recording in a Tuvan yurt in 1987.

192

traditional culture beneath. Levin's 'fools of God' were the Sufi mystical saints for whom music is primarily a moral calling; one of his discoveries was that chanted devotional poetry – whether in the context of shamanism, Zoroastrianism, Islam, or Judaism – was still central to social life, as it had been seventy years before.

His method was not so much song collecting as musician collecting, analysing their styles and probing their thoughts. His prime instrumental informant was Turgun Alimatov, a self-taught string virtuoso whose rebellious originality had put him beyond the pale for the Rajabi school. But as Levin found, that originality proved elusive: any given piece would go through a process of improvisation which could take years before it found its definitive form. How did he create his music from *maqom*, asked Levin. 'I didn't create music,' Alimatov replied. 'I took what existed ready-made, and I played it. I listened, I played, listened, played. I didn't compose melodies. Why search for new music when there's so much ready-made?' Then he drew an analogy: 'One person builds a house, and leaves that house. I come to it and remodel it – and then an even better master will come along and do another remodelling.' His speech was studded with words like *dard* (passion), *kaif* (delight), and *saz* (harmony), and his oft-repeated motto had a sublime simplicity: 'First a musician must tune himself, then he must tune his instrument. Only then can he tune the listener.'

Levin's account is full of such homespun poetry. A singer-healer tells him, 'When I see a sick person the spirits come like jewels on a string. They give me the sound. They tell me how to play, and what to play.' The contralto Munajat Yulchieva, who went on to become one of Uzbekistan's most celebrated female *maqom* exponents, said she sang to God 'with a chest voice, a Sufi tone, like a prayer' (her very name means 'prayer').

One theme running through Levin's book is the vulnerability of Central Asia's musical traditions – caught at the moment of their re-emergence, and threatened in that same moment by encroaching globalisation. He quotes a Bukharan-Jewish classical musician talking about the 'infection' of synthesisers and the pop vernacular, but is reluctant to share that musician's pessimism. The same question was raised in a hundred different ways by Levin's next project, which picked up in the post-Soviet Nineties where his earlier collaboration with Huun-Huur-Tu (under Communism) had left off. Now international stars with one foot in Tuva and the other in California, they would act as his guides in an exploration of their art on their home turf.

The Communists had done their best to eradicate Tuvan religion in the Thirties, shooting shamans and Buddhist priests, and they made folk music a tool of politics; the Tuvans' salvation lay in the fact that there were enough of them (200,000 in the mid-Nineties) to stave off the total annihilation of their culture. Having come of age in the Soviet era, Levin's musicians – after that culture had been profoundly ruptured – regarded his quest as their quest too.

His report on this voyage of discovery takes the form of a book co-written with the Tuvan ethnomusicologist Valentina Süzükei. Entitled *Where Rivers and Mountains Sing*, it offers a series of revelations, the first of which comes as Levin watches one of the singers fishing:

> Tolya was lazily casting his line into the boulder-strewn river when I first heard him sing to the water. The soaring harmonics of his high, flute-like melody were seemingly amplified by the hissing and gurgling of the water flowing over and around the rocks … 'In the old days, herders used to sit by a stream in the evening and throat-sing,' he said matter-of-factly. 'The stream itself showed them how to sing. Listen.' Tolya began again … Starting with a long drone note, he introduced rhythmic articulations with movements of his lips and tongue, shaping the drone into a pulsating, roiling tone … A piercing overtone melody rose out of the thick texture of the fundamental pitch, and the gyrating rhythm of the overtones interlocked with rhythms created by the swiftly flowing water. Tolya sang a couple of breaths of melody at a time, pausing between breaths to listen to the river, like a jazz musician momentarily dropping out to listen to a fellow band member take a solo.

Tolya explained that this was his offering to the local spirit, or master, of the river. 'The river is alive. Rivers sing.'

This animist faith surfaces constantly in Levin's account, with its personification of trees, waterfalls, and rocks. Even the wind could play its part, creating an Aeolian-harp effect on a zither left out to dry its gut strings in the sun. One singer ringingly called forth the reverberant qualities of a towering rock-face, saying he loved to hear the voice of the cliff answering his own. Levin filmed a shaman whose costume was an orchestra of bells, beads, teeth, feathers, and a wolf skull; his chanted purification ceremony left Levin convinced that something benign had taken place during his own trance as a patient. You might dismiss all this as incurably romantic, but equally you could argue that this close interaction between humanity and nature represents a lost world of feeling which we all might profitably rediscover.

The strictly musical implications of Levin's line of inquiry were at once simple and profound. Süzükei had been conducting her arrangements of Grieg and Tchaikovsky with a folk orchestra, and she wanted to record the pitches of a two-string *igil* fiddle, so she asked a player to bow the open strings. 'And he played both of the strings together. I said, "No, play them individually. I have to write down the tuning of the instrument." And again he played them together. I must have asked him five times, and always there was the same response. Finally he got angry, and I was also angry. Why is he so stubborn, I wondered?'

Only later did she understand that the absolute pitch of the strings meant nothing to him. All that mattered was their pitch relative to each other: he didn't hear the strings as separate pitches, but as part of one total sound. 'For him, pitch was subordinate to timbre – the specific quality of a tone determined by the presence, distribution, and relative amplitude of overtones.'

To illustrate her idea she drew a physical analogy, first showing a neatly closed fan, then opening it with a flick: 'When you make a sound on the igil, it's like spreading open the fan. Inside this one sound is a whole acoustic world created by the spray of overtones that results when you draw a bow across the instrument's horsehair strings.' Then she drew another analogy: 'In European music, sound is packed compactly into discrete pitches, with the fundamental frequency and overtones all perceived as one. Tuvan music is like loose snow, and overtones are like a spray of snow. The looser the bow, the more the spray effect – which is exactly what Western string players don't want. They want a sound that's perfectly focused, consistent, unified.' The jew's harp, ubiquitous in Central Asia, might have been designed to maximise timbral complexity; and singing in a resonant environment, or in concert with a natural sound-source, like moving water or wind, also enhances timbral richness. The world of the bagpipes, or the ecclesiastical Greek *iso*, where the drone is a separate instrument or singer, could not be more alien.

'You have to have inside your head this stock of sounds that's built up over the years of living in the grasslands,' says Süzükei. 'Timbral sound-making and timbral listening will survive as long as herders live in nature and listen to the sounds of the taiga [coniferous forest] and the steppe, birds and animals, water and wind.' This isolation of reinforced harmonics from their fundamental pitch – which is what throat-singing is – can be found in parts of Africa too. In Süzükei's view it requires a major readjustment of how you listen – and for those reared in the European musical culture, the ability to listen 'timbrally' is hard to acquire.

For Westerners, images of macho males simultaneously creating airy soprano sweetness and dark undertones, or of beautiful young women singing in a rasping chest-voice growl, are irresistibly intriguing; for Tuvans the international success of Huun-Huur-Tu has made their art form a national treasure to celebrate.

Levin sees this as just one element in a musical world where jew's harps, fiddles, flutes, and zithers all exploit the timbral dimension of sound: 'Perhaps, like the proto-Indo-European language whose existence is conjectured by linguists, a proto-Turkic musical language once existed as a comprehensive whole among the Inner Asian nomads, in the halcyon days of the Khaganate.' In other words, back in the days when all Turks were united in one nomadic super-state, from the sixth to eighth centuries CE.

* * *

Politically speaking, Central Asia's great awakening from the Soviet fantasy has not run smoothly: in most of its states, corruption and human rights abuses are the norm. But its musical awakening, particularly in Kazakhstan, Kyrgyzstan, and Uzbekistan, has been one of the region's big success stories. If this reflects the inherent strength of the music, it also reflects the resourcefulness with which its musicians are recovering their lost traditions, and making out of them something new.

Take, for example, the conservatoire-trained Kazakh pianist-composer Yedil Huseinov. I find him surrounded by instruments he'd made from the bones and feathers of the birds and animals whose sounds he evokes. He's turned his back on the Western classical repertoire to create an old-new one focused on the jew's harp, plus the resonances in his throat and the added resonance of a drum operated with his left foot; when our interview is over, he takes me off to watch him – armed only with his jew's harp – share the stage at a jazz club with his rock band.

Consider the Kyrgyz multi-instrumentalist Nurlanbek Nyshanov, whose work as a musical archaeologist has taken him to museums and recording archives where he has identified and reproduced instruments which had been forgotten: the *chopo choor* (a herder's ocarina), the *choor* (a soft-toned flute), and the wooden jew's harp whose sound is subtler than that of its metal cousin. But this man is also a composer and arranger, creating ensemble music with unusual instrumental combinations: that may go against the traditional solo nomad style, but he insists he's keeping faith with the spirit of the mountains where he grew up, and to which he returns on his horse whenever city life gets too oppressive.

One might also single out the man with whom Nyshanov and his players created the captivating fusion I witnessed in 2003 at a concert in the British Library in Bishkek. A wild-looking figure with a face as though carved in oak suddenly appeared from among the dark-suited crowd. He mused intently, took some deep breaths, rolled his eyes till only the whites were visible, then launched into song. Unpitched at first – just groans, shrieks, and hisses – it turned into an ecstatic chant which he amplified with warlike gestures. The *Manas* epic is Kyrgyzstan's martial answer to the *Iliad*, though several times longer, and Rysbek Jumabaev is a *manaschi*, a master-reciter of it.

After emerging from his trance he told me through an interpreter how he'd found his vocation.

A manaschi came to my house when I was four. I was frightened, so he took me on his knee and blessed me. When I was eight, he started appearing to me in dreams, and I realised I was destined to join him. But that work is a gift from God – it can't be taught. I started performing as an amateur when I was sixteen, but I stopped because public interest was drying up. Then I started having stomach pains – I couldn't eat, couldn't sleep. Doctors gave me drugs but nothing helped.

He went to a clairvoyant, who told him to visit a shrine, slaughter a sheep and spend the night there, and re-dedicate himself to the *Manas*. 'I took friends with me, and we were woken in the middle of the night by a great wind, which we took as a sign that God was visiting us.' At the time when he spoke to me, Jumabaev was well on his way to stardom, and within sight of being able to afford the cow he needed to help feed his family.

Popular interest in *Manas* recitation, which had indeed gone into decline, has now been rekindled by such feats of musical archaeology. But Jumabaev's performance at that concert had also been enhanced by a halo of sound on fiddles and flutes – a nice idea stage-managed by the two organisations sponsoring the event: the Silk Road Project and the Aga Khan Music Initiative (AKMI). The first of these organisations was dreamed up by Yo-Yo Ma as a contemporary equivalent to what he called 'the internet of antiquity', with musicians from every stop along the way working together to create new fusions. The second organisation is now having a bigger impact on musical life worldwide than any has had before, or will ever have again. And Levin, initially in tandem with During, was the musicological brain behind both.

The Silk Road Project came first; out of it emerged the AKMI, which derived much of its impetus from the Aga Khan's response to what he saw when he visited civil war-torn Tajikistan as spiritual leader of the Ismaili Muslims who lived there. He was shocked by the hunger and disease they were enduring, but entranced by their singers and dancers; he brought bread, money, and hope. This former playboy now devotes his energies to helping mend broken communities all over the Muslim world, with music at the heart of that process. And not just the music of the past: the forging of new musical languages and forms, as well as the re-learning of old ones. Tajikistan and the adjacent countries became the AKMI's initial focus, though it has since extended its operations to North and West Africa, and to the Middle East and South Asia, girdling the globe.

With the AKMI, musicians are expected to take the lead. Aided by the project's director Fairouz Nishanova, Levin and During drew on their contacts to assemble a posse of stars ready to sign up to the common objective. Nurlan-bek Nyshanov was one of these; others included the Kazakh *dombra* maestro Abdulhamit Raimbergenov, the Kazakh diva Ulzhan Baibussynova, and the Tajik string player Abduvali Abdurashidov, who had almost single-handedly revived the *shashmaqom*. Levin and During had tried to enlist the help of the conservatories in their search for potential leaders, but since those institutions were still fixated, Soviet-style, on technical excellence rather than experimentation and collaboration, they weren't much help.

The first job for the AKMI musicians was to establish a series of schools in which master-performers would pass on their art to young aspirants, and these schools – there's even one in Afghanistan – are inspirational. In a school in Bishkek I watch a fledgling *manaschi* learning the ropes – *pace* Jumabaev's assertion that it can't be taught – and I also watch groups of adolescents pursuing the effect which all Kyrgyz lutenists must master, the evocation of horses' hooves. In a snowbound village by Lake Issyk-kul I visit a school where eight pupils are living *en famille* with their tutor Zainidin Imanaliev and his singer-wife Kenjegul, who inculcate with genial ferocity the principles of finger-technique, posture, and breathing. In Almaty I watch Raimbergenov get fifteen young players to execute a unison *dombra* gallop with not a note out of place: his pedagogical method is now enshrined in a series of textbooks funded by the AKMI and used in Kazakh schools. Only the most talented children are let loose on the horse-hair fiddle, it being so hard to play, but in the hands of 22-year-old Zalina Kasymova, who graduated to it via its bastardised orchestral variant, it makes a sound as mysteriously expressive as the cello of Pablo Casals. Thus are seeds sown for the future.

The AKMI musicians' next task was to preserve their musical heritage: the ten CDs on the Smithsonian Folkways label, which cover the whole of Central Asia, would pay homage to the past, and indicate where the region's music might be heading next. There's a special poignancy in the CD by the Badakhshan Ensemble, which hail from the Pamir Mountains of Tajikistan once known as the Roof of the World. These resilient musicians continue to champion their Ismaili culture despite extreme privation and the intermittently hostile political atmosphere in which they have to work, and when civil war broke out in 1990 they feared for the future of their art. With mystical texts by Rumi, Hafiz, and Khusraw, plus accompaniment on strings and drum, their music has a rugged simplicity. 'These songs are the tears in our blood,' says Soheba Davlatshoeva, the singer-dancer who leads the group. *Falak* ('fate') is the name of the Badakhshani style of philosophical lamentation, and for the first song on their CD Davlatshoeva launches into the Tajik variant of a perennial poetic idea: 'The world is like a garden, and I am like the morning

34 Soheba Davlatshoeva and the Badakhshan Ensemble: singing stars from
the Pamir mountains.

breeze/ As I blew through it one day, my life passed.' A cappella, and occu-
pying an austerely narrow pitch-range of just two intervals, her singing has a
coiled intensity which grips the heart.

The Badakhshan Ensemble are not puritannical – they play Tajik pop
music for weddings – and neither is Homayun Sakhi, the Afghan *rubab* maestro who was another of the AKMI's original 'tradition bearers'. Born into one
of Afghanistan's leading musical families, he has twice been forced by war to
relocate – first to Peshawar, then to California – and in both places he has
founded schools for young players. He believes that every kind of music (even
guitar and symphonic music) can feed into the repertoire of his instrument,
despite its roots in North Indian classical music. As his Smithsonian CD
demonstrates, his virtuosity permits him to suggest symphonic richness while
staying within the bounds of the *rubab*'s traditional sound-world.

But it was the Chinese *pipa* lutenist Wu Man – for whom Western
composers like Terry Riley and Philip Glass have written pieces – who masterminded the most intriguing fusion in these recordings. Drawing on singers

and players from the Ferghana Valley, the Gobi and Taklamakan deserts, and the snow-covered peaks of the Tien Shan and Pamirs, she encouraged adjacent but very different musical worlds to meld. The results, however, are uneasy: microtonal Uyghur music can't absorb the influence of pentatonic Chinese music without losing its character, and Kazakh breeziness sits oddly with delicately inflected singing from the Uyghur composer Sanubar Tursun (who at the time of writing is imprisoned by the Chinese, along with hundreds of thousands of her compatriots, for the heinous crime of daring to celebrate their own culture).

There was even room for European classical musicians in this experiment. The AKMI roped in the Kronos Quartet – veteran collaborators with musicians from every land under the sun – to devise fusions with Homayun Sakhi on one hand, and with Alim Qasimov and his daughter Fargana on the other. Sakhi came armed with one of his own compositions, for which – since he doesn't work from scores – he had recorded his *rubab* part, while realising the string-quartet sounds on a Casio synthesiser; the whole piece was then transcribed into Western notation.

But the mechanics of the Kronos-Qasimov fusion were tortuous. They began with Kronos asking Alim Qasimov to record six songs for them to work on; then they got their arranger to create a score. But when they started work together, Qasimov's improvisatory instincts could not be restrained, as Levin recalls:

> When Alim sang the song, backed by his players on the *kemancheh* [spike-fiddle] and *tar* [double-chambered lute], and when he diverged from what Kronos had on paper, the Kronos leader David Harrington would say 'I think he put an extra beat in there' – and would ask his arranger to accommodate it. Every time Alim changed something, it had to be entered into the score. For him it needed to be different and fresh every time, but for the Kronos it had to be the same. He kept saying 'Don't play my melody – make up something of your own which goes with what I'm playing'. These were not complex songs, but we're dealing with very deep differences in terms of how the mind works. For the Kronos it's not real unless it's on the page. But for Alim the Ur-form is enough, which is realised differently each time.

The ideal partner, Levin says, would be a musician who had grown up hearing *mugam* in Azerbaijan, but who had also been trained in the Western classical style: 'They need to be bi-musical.'

Bi-musicality – a term coined as the musical equivalent to bilingualism by the American musicologist Mantle Hood in 1960 – is now accepted as a key qualification for fusions across major musical divides. The Sakhi-Kronos experiment works beautifully for the slow first half of their test-piece – it has poise and grace, and in the boisterous section which follows the musicians' respective ways of thinking it gels nicely. But it's hard to imagine the Qasimov-Kronos collaboration leading anywhere much: the logistics are hopelessly complex, and for all their good intentions, the two groups in this recording played and sang as though on different planets.

On a Tajik *dutar* lute there are only two strings, but there are five ways of tuning them, and an infinity of ways in which that instrument's sound can be made to open out like a flower: Sirojiddin Juraev is master of them all. His latest CD, recorded with back-up on *setar* and frame-drum, reflects both his reverence for the *shashmaqom*, and his determination to develop it further with a melange of traditional melodies and new compositions. And this too is a project from AKMI, which has supported Juraev throughout his career, and has produced this CD. You couldn't wish for a neater expression of the evergreen spirit of Central Asian music, or of the discreet but essential role which musicologists from the West have played in its revival.

35 Tajik virtuoso Sirojiddin Juraev accompanying Zumrad Samijonova (1981–2007) on the two-string *dutar* lute.

Sources

Theodore Levin's *The Hundred Thousand Fools of God* and *Where Rivers and Mountains Sing* are the requisite starting points for further reading; his narrative style is vivid and companionable, and he's rigorously informative on history, music theory, and the contemporary socio-political situation. *The Music of Central Asia*, sponsored by the Aga Khan Trust for Culture and edited by Levin et al., includes essays by musicologists from the region, and is the definitive guide. With its capacious website it offers a brilliantly detailed picture of every aspect of its subject. Jean During's *Musiques d'Asie Centrale* is an excellent short handbook. Razia Sultanova's *From Shamanism to Sufism* draws on fifteen years of fieldwork to trace how women have kept religious culture alive across the region: this is a unique study of a hitherto under-examined sphere. Sirojiddin Juraev's new CD is available on Amazon; all ten of the Smithsonian Folkways 'Music of Central Asia' CDs are first-rate, with *Borderlands, Badakhshan Ensemble, Tengir-Too*, and *Rainbow* illustrating specific ideas dealt with in this chapter. During's recording of rare Uyghur repertory is available from Ocora. Michael Church's *Songs from the Steppes: Kazakh Music Today* reflects the scope and variety of that country's folk music.

Bibliography and recordings

During, Jean, *Musiques d'Asie Centrale* (Paris: Cité de la Musique, 1998)
Levin, Theodore, *The Hundred Thousand Fools of God: Musical Travels in Central Asia* (Bloomington: Indiana University Press, 1996)
Levin, Theodore, *Where Rivers and Mountains Sing* (Bloomington: Indiana University Press, 2006)
Levin, Theodore, Saida Daukeyeva, and Elmira Köchümkulova, eds, *The Music of Central Asia* (Bloomington: Indiana University Press, 2016)
Sultanova, Razia, *From Shamanism to Sufism: Women, Islam, and Culture in Central Asia* (London: I. B. Tauris, 2011)

Borderlands: Wu Man and Master Musicians from the Silk Route, Smithsonian Folkways SFWCD 40529
Chine: Musique Ouighoure: Muqam Nava, Ocora C 560253
Music of Central Asia Vol. 5: Song and Dance from the Pamir Mountains, The Badakhshan Ensemble, Smithsonian Folkways SFWCD 40524
Music of Central Asia Vol. 8: Rainbow, Kronos Quartet with Alim and Fargana Qasimov and Homayun Sakhi, Smithsonian Folkways SFWCD 40527
Ouzbekistan, Turgun Alimatov, Ocora C 560086

Songs from the Steppes: Kazakh Music Today, recordings by Michael Church, Topic Records TSCD929

Tengir-Too: Mountain Music of Kyrgyzstan, Smithsonian Folkways SFWCD 40520

36 British musicologist John Baily practising the *dutar* with Khalifa Now Ruz on the *zerbaghali* goblet-drum.

18

Red badge of courage

Musicians in Afghanistan

THE LITERAL TRANSLATION of Farida's stage-name 'Mahwash', conferred when she was designated an Afghan musical master, is 'like the Moon', but the figure facing me on the sofa is more like a great golden sun, at once dignified and full of mischief. We're in a little corner of Afghanistan in north London, and she's just arrived to promote a CD which will confirm her as her country's quintessential voice. But *Mahwash: Radio Kaboul* will do more than that: it will also lift the curtain on a musical golden age which flourished briefly before the *mujahedin* – followed by the Taliban – snuffed it out. 'I want the world to know about the music we had, and must not lose,' says Mahwash. She was a noted singer at school, but family pressure forced her to stop when she went out to work. She got a job as a typist at Radio Kabul, was noticed as she sang at her desk, was quickly launched as a star, but soon hit the buffers. 'I got married and became pregnant, but still went on singing, which gave great offence. Some members of my family were so opposed that they put poison in my food. Luckily I got to hospital in time, had an operation, and survived. It was clear that God didn't want me to die so young.' She tells me this gaily, as she does the tale of her sacking by the first Communist government, her reinstatement by the second, her continued career under tightening censorship, and her eventual flight to Pakistan, where she no longer dared sing. 'Finally the UN offered to get me asylum, because as a female singer I was in increasing danger from the mujahedin.' She chose to settle in her married daughter's country, California, from where she tours the Afghan diaspora wherever family festivities demand her compelling voice.

But the new CD emanates from Geneva – hence the French spelling of its title – and there I find, in another little corner of Afghanistan, Mahwash's backing group Ensemble Kaboul. Led by Khaled Arman, and including his father Hossein and flautist cousin Osman, these instrumentalists represent a further hot-line back to that golden age. Hossein was one of Kabul radio's leading singer-composers, and Khaled started working there at fourteen, though his instrument at the time was the classical guitar. He went on to study guitar in Prague, and began a concert career in Paris, but was stopped in his tracks when guitar maestro John Williams dropped by, praised his Scarlatti, and asked why he didn't play his own music.

'That question sank into my soul,' says Khaled in his tiny studio. 'So I asked my father to send me a *rubab*.' He taught himself to play this Afghan lute, but found that its four frets and three melody strings limited its scope. 'I decided to expand its possibilities, and this is the result.' His customised instrument has an extra melody string and twenty frets: the tone-palette established with the aid of its drones and sympathetic strings is perfumed. He digs out a *tanbur* lute which he has customised too, adding frets to permit the quarter-tones which were integral to Afghan music before India's musical invasion. Then he produces a *dilruba*, a sitar played with a bow. 'There is only one other *dilruba* player left in Afghanistan now. I want to save this instrument from extinction.' In tandem with the Mahwash disc, he's releasing a solo one of his own – *Rubab Raga* – on which, with the aid of overdubbing, he recreates the authentic Afghan classical sound.

Khaled's father Hossein, a noted teacher, was forced to watch the destruction of his beloved music school. 'The flower of our musical culture had scarcely opened,' he says, 'before the storm destroyed it. All my former colleagues are dead. Some in war, some from a broken heart.' The Taliban, he adds, were merely the final straw. Is he now planning to go back? His face becomes suffused with sadness: 'I want to, but what could I do when I got there? There's no school, no pupils, no instruments, no music books.'

Khaled has inherited Hossein's didactic zeal, and is drumming up support for a scheme by which talented Afghan children may once again be inducted into their musical heritage. He has not been back since the fall of the Taliban, 'but when I go I want to have something in my hands to give my students. And in any case, music can only be appreciated by those who aren't worrying about how they will fill their stomachs.'

When I ask Mahwash about her musical future, I get a reply which confirms the truth of an Amnesty report on post-Taliban society. The day after the new government was installed, she says, Kabul television broadcast a programme including a clip – filmed some years previously – of her singing, decently swathed in a veil. Halfway through, the film was stopped on air, because complaints had been received from the mullahs.

When will she go back to her home town? 'Please publish my reply to this question,' she replies, after taking a very deep breath. 'It's not true that the position of women in Afghanistan is better since the Taliban departed. The present government is still absolutely opposed to women's liberation. I long to go back to Afghanistan – I miss it terribly – but I just don't dare.' Why? 'One of my friends, who is also a singer, went back, and found a letter waiting for her which said "If you don't get out today, tomorrow you will be killed". I think I would get the same threat.' She's speaking in an even tone, but tears are now streaming down her cheeks.

* * *

All this was in 2007, since when much has changed, and nothing has changed. Khaled Arman has diversified into Western styles, and Mahwash has gone from strength to strength as the Californian diaspora's favourite singer. Music in Afghanistan itself is in a convalescent state, after the most calamitous period of its war-ravaged history.

Music-loving emirs presided over the development of a truly Afghan style in the nineteenth century, and influences fed in from north India and Iran, resulting in the refined instrumental amalgam which can still be heard at the hands of virtuosi like Homayun Sakhi today. Meanwhile *ghazal* was becoming the dominant Afghan vocal genre: rhyming poems about a love at once human and divine, melismatically set to music. Radio Kabul, which was established in 1940, took over the torch of patronage, and in the Sixties – when the country was enjoying a brief period of quasi-democracy – musicians were riding high; a benign explosion of home-grown pop was spearheaded by the 'Afghan Elvis' Ahmad Zahir. Zahir's mysterious death in 1979, the year of the Soviet invasion, marked the beginning of a war of attrition against music in general. The Communists themselves supported music, and regional folk tradition in particular, as a symbol of the secular society they wanted to establish, but the *jihadi* movement and the onset of mujahedin rule subjected musicians to increasing censorship, as though in preparation for the scorched-earth policies of the Taliban. Musicians were forced to flee the country; many are now dead, or simply have not gone back.

* * *

It was serendipitous that two British musicologists should have been able to chronicle Afghan musical life during that short window of opportunity in the Seventies when the country was at peace. And without the heroic efforts of husband-and-wife John Baily and Veronica Doubleday we would have had much less information about the country's music than we now do. Since their sojourn in Herat, starting in 1973 and followed by frequent visits, they have produced a steady stream of CDs, books, films, and articles, tracking the lives of musicians first within Afghan borders, then further afield when making music there became too dangerous a thing to do. Moreover, they have immersed themselves deeply enough in Afghan music to win *shauqi* status, as respected amateur performers: she as a singer, he as a player of the *dutar* and the boat-shaped *rubab*, with its guttural-ethereal sound.

Baily trained as an experimental psychologist, and initially aspired to be a guitarist singer-songwriter. But during a stay in Nepal he began to play the tabla, and then went to study under John Blacking in British ethnomusicology's power-house at Queen's University of Belfast. 'His ideas about how music is rooted in the body were very similar to the way mine had evolved, after vainly trying to play Indian music on the guitar,' says Baily. Intrigued by the fact that the *dutar*'s original two strings had multiplied to fourteen, he decided to study its development: 'I wanted to examine the relationship between the changes in the instrument, the movements of the performer, and the music.'

After acquiring the necessary Farsi by working as English teachers in Teheran, Baily and Doubleday settled in Herat. Initially Baily didn't do any song collecting, though in the course of his instrumental research he was constantly recording. Doubleday, who had been working as his research assistant, suddenly found her métier: she'd realised there was a musical realm in Herat inaccessible to Baily because he was a man.

She had begun studying miniature painting with a Herati master, but since that kept her isolated at home, she took up embroidery – a communal women's art – which became her passport into Herat's closed female society. 'Now I could make my own study of women's music,' she says.

> And my interest was not limited to music. I wanted to find out about how women lived and worked, and about their family relationships. And I realised that if I could perform their songs myself, it would help a lot. I took my tape recorder into people's homes, drank tea with them, and induced them to sing. The etiquette was that you shouldn't just play music for itself – there needed to be a reason, a justification for it. You needed to be either celebrating something, or entertaining guests. Then you would get your drum out.

That was the *daireh*, the jingling frame-drum with which Afghan women accompany themselves when they sing.

In *Three Women of Herat*, her charming and meticulously observed account of this cross-cultural journey, Doubleday describes how she broke down the barriers. 'I had opted for the women's world, and made a positive choice to be where they are. This meant accepting some of the limitations of purdah,' she writes. 'There was no point in feeling outraged by customs such as veiling, as this would have emphasised our differences.' It was both surprising and salutary to discover, she adds, 'that being invisible is addictive'.

The three women of the title, all married Muslim mothers, became her close friends. One became her music teacher, another her tutor in the intricacies of Shia ritual and the rules of family life, while in the third she noted the profoundly damaging psychological effects which can result from having to live in purdah. In her account Doubleday had to protect them with pseudonyms.

37 Veronica Doubleday being taught a song by her beloved tutor
Zainab Herawi.

'Shirin' was the leader of an all-woman band calling themselves the Minstrels. Performing at weddings, and going from house to house at festival
times like barber-musicians, they were, like all those of their calling, socially
despised; if they felt they'd been underpaid, they would noisily shame their
patrons. Doubleday learned seventy songs, complete with texts, under Shirin's
tutelage. But she was hampered by the fact that female Afghan musicians
weren't taught, as male musicians were, with the aid of technical terms based
on Indian classical music. 'Shirin had no precise terminology through which
musical concepts could be expressed,' she writes. 'Nor, unlike male professionals, did they have any system of notation.' Initially a pupil and observer,
Doubleday was deemed to have fledged after singing on Radio Kabul with
Baily's accompaniment. She was invited to join the band, and even occasionally to lead it, which gave her an exhilarating feeling akin to that of driving
a car. 'I slipped easily into my new identity,' she says. 'Farahnaz, the musician
girl, veiled and dressed like a Herati, but made attractive with eye make-up,
lipstick, and rouge. By then the veil had become second nature to me, and I
always wore Herati dresses and loose trousers. I didn't look noticeably foreign.'
Nor did she sound it: the self-accompanied songs she sings on a CD recorded

by John Baily – *Heart to Heart: Afghan Songs of Love and Marriage* – are delivered with an artless vibrato-free directness pretty well indistinguishable from the real Herati thing. Her official back-story had been that she came from Iran, but a different and hurtful story had also begun circulating: that Baily was hard up, and was sending his wife out with this disreputable bunch to earn their daily bread.

Hurtful, too, were some of the side-effects of her purdah: 'I felt uncomfortable singing for men, highly conscious of their admiration, and aware that I was granting a rare, almost erotic, delight. The fact that the words of the songs concerned desire and romantic longing emphasised a singer's identity as a sex object when viewed by men. I had become infected with a Herati sense of shame.' And as time went on, that gnawed at her: 'I needed to get home, to see which aspects of my Herati self would wash away like make-up, and which were indelibly impressed upon me.'

* * *

Their two-year residence, plus subsequent visits, furnished Baily and Doubleday with material for a major study of Afghan music which is still ongoing. In 1988 Baily published *Music of Afghanistan: Professional Musicians in the City of Herat*, which is now a key text. In 2015 he published *War, Exile, and the Music of Afghanistan: The Ethnographer's Tale* – that being both a history and a stock-taking account of Afghan music since the defeat (but not the demise) of the Taliban. Baily observes, not at all facetiously, that the Taliban's *tarana* songs themselves deserve research: 'They are real music – there actually is a Taliban musical aesthetic.'

Baily's films focus on individual musicians: for example, we follow the *rubab* player Amir Jan Herati as he rehearses, plays at weddings, takes us to his infant daughter's grave, and visits a shrine where he weeps for all he has lost. But they also flesh out the recovery projects which Baily, operating from the Afghanistan Music Unit he set up at Goldsmiths College in London, has helped to bring about. With the support of the Aga Khan Trust for Culture he established a school in Kabul for talented young Afghan musicians which has gone so well that a second school has now opened in Herat. Meanwhile the musicologist Ahmad Sarmast has founded the Afghanistan National Institute of Music in Kabul, blazing a trail for others to follow: it's a co-educational vocational music school, and its Ensemble Zohra Afghan Women's Orchestra now tours the world. Many of this orchestra's members are orphans with a street-kid background. 'I asked Ahmad Sarmast why he had placed such emphasis on recruiting orphans,' says Baily. 'And he replied that they hadn't any families to get in the way.' Social prejudice against musicians, particularly female ones, still runs deep. 'There may be a shortage of career opportunities for young musicians in Afghanistan, but we are at least helping create a generation who know about music.'

Perhaps the most poignant testimony to the importance of what Baily and Doubleday have done for Afghan music comes in a lullaby recorded by 'Shirin' – real name Zainab Hairawi – at her house in Herat in 1977. She prefaced it with a speech to Doubleday, who was about to leave for home: 'I'll sing a lullaby so Zeri Jan will fall asleep, eh, Veronica? So that, God willing, when you have a child – a son or a daughter – you'll sing it to sleep. You'll sit next to your baby boy or baby girl's cradle. Only promise you'll remember me, thinking that Zainab used to lull her baby like this, and here I am singing to my baby just as she did. So learn it, won't you!' Zainab Hairawi died in 1985. 'Remember me.'

Sources

John Baily's *Music of Afghanistan: Professional Musicians in the City of Herat* and *War, Exile, and the Music of Afghanistan* are key texts; the latter comes with four of Baily's filmed reports on a DVD. Simon Broughton's BBC film *Breaking the Silence* – made in 2002, just after the Taliban had been defeated – is a moving testament to the resilience of Kabul's musicians. Veronica Doubleday's beautifully written *Three Women of Herat* brings female Herati society into brilliant close-up, while her CD *Heart to Heart* gives her own take on its music. *Radio Kaboul: Hommage aux compositeurs afghans* reflects the artistry of Mahwash and Kabuli urban music during its brief golden age; *The Traditional Music of Herat* and *Afghanistan: Female Musicians of Herat* do the same for that city.

Bibliography, recordings, documentaries, and online sources

Baily, John, *Music of Afghanistan: Professional Musicians in the City of Herat* (Cambridge: Cambridge University Press, 1988)

Baily, John, *Songs from Kabul: The Spiritual Music of Ustad Amir Mohammad* (Farnham: Ashgate, 2011)

Baily, *John, War, Exile, and the Music of Afghanistan: The Ethnographer's Tale* (Farnham: Ashgate, 2015)

Doubleday, Veronica, *Three Women of Herat* (London: Jonathan Cape, 1988)

Afghanistan: Female Musicians of Herat, Naïve, D 8285

Afghanistan: The Traditional Music of Herat, Auvidis D 8266

Ghazals afghans: Poèmes d'amour séculiers et sacrés, Mahwash, Accords Croisés AC 118

Radio Kaboul: Hommage aux compositeurs afghans, Accords Croisés ACC100

Breaking the Silence: Music in Afghanistan, dir. Simon Broughton, BBC, 2002

Ustad Rahim: Herat's rubab maestro, www.therai.org.uk

38 Pioneer folklorist Mitrofan Piatnitsky with the peasant choir he founded in 1910.

19

Out of the womb of Russia

Riches awaiting rediscovery

In 1911 a group of folklorists set out from St Petersburg to comb the Russian shtetls for Jewish songs and chants. Inspired by Nikolai Rimsky-Korsakov and led by the playwright Shloyme Ansky – author of *The Dybbuk* – they wanted to record this oral tradition before it evaporated for good. The resulting collection of cylinders was so impressive that the incoming Bolsheviks decreed the work should continue, and they put their own man in charge. Moisei Beregovsky was a loyal Stalinist but an excellent folklorist, and until his deportation to Siberia in 1949 he recorded and meticulously transcribed several thousand more songs and texts. When he was released in 1955 the cylinders had disappeared, and it was generally assumed that his unique archive had been destroyed.

Forty-four years later Israel Adler, professor of musicology at the Hebrew University of Jerusalem, announced a discovery. The director of the National Library in Kiev had come to see him about photocopying manuscripts. 'And seeing our cylinder collection, he mentioned that he too had some cylinders, which the American Library of Congress had looked at without much interest. Could this be the Beregovsky collection? I jumped on the first available plane to Kiev, and discovered that it was.'

Even leaving aside the awkward matter of past pogroms, the course of the ensuing affair was bumpy, with Kiev raising endless obstacles to the digitisation of the recordings Jerusalem wanted. While Adler's aim was to make the archive available to scholars all over the world, Kiev's aim was to make a profit. But as a Berlin-born *Ost-Jude*, Adler took this sort of thing for granted. 'Whenever things seem discouraging, I listen again to these marvellous recordings,' he told me. 'Then I am re-inspired.' To illustrate the point, he played some examples: a Bartókian country song with driving rhythms; a dance sounding as if it was straight out of *Fiddler on the Roof*; and an austerely beautiful liturgical chant. When the latter was broadcast on Haifa Radio, Adler said, a middle-aged Israeli rang in to say that he recognised the voice of the cantor: his own grandfather.

One thing which the early Soviet cultural commissars did get right – initially at least – was their support for traditional folk music. They took their cue from the work of the conductor/song collector Mitrofan Piatnitsky, whose celebrated peasant choir had in the early years of the twentieth century alerted the urban bourgeoisie to the musical riches of the forests and steppes. Under the Soviets every village had its choir, and every district its elite vocal, instrumental, and dance ensemble. With flutes and fiddles, horns and accordions, each had its own sound and style. They were routinely recorded, but most of those recordings are now gathering dust in private collections and city archives, still awaiting rediscovery.

However, Russian folk music became denatured when the Soviets started professionalising and politicising it, ironing out its dissonances and erasing both its bawdiness and its religious fervour. Yet during the last three decades of the twentieth century it enjoyed a revival of sorts; this was thanks to a campaign led by the charismatic conductor and song collector Dmitri Pokrovsky, who picked up the torch which political pressures had forced Piatnitsky to put down.

Pokrovsky died aged fifty-two in 1996, but in a series of interviews with his American collaborator Theodore Levin he explained his rationale, and outlined his extraordinary career as he fell out of favour, and back into it again following shifts in the Soviet political wind. His initial ambition had been to conduct opera, but when the Gnessin Institute, where he was a student, opened its doors to folklore during the Khrushchev thaw, he began to lead song-collecting expeditions to villages, covering huge distances on foot.

His particular focus was on how singers produced their sound. Different kinds of singing had to be developed in different acoustic conditions, he said. 'Forest, steppe, river valleys, mountains – they all have different acoustics, and folk singers use their mouth and throat differently from how academic singers do, because of the acoustic demands.' He began using equipment which allowed him to see aspects of sound on a screen, and he assembled his own ensemble, none of whom were professional singers, and sent them out on the road to research and perform. He was now an accredited state folklore specialist, charged with the duty to support local amateur groups. He put up with the official stipulation that a substantial part of their folklore would have to be what he called 'fakelore': 'Thirty percent had to be songs about the Soviet system, and how great it is, about collective farms, tractors, and so on.'

Accidentally caught up in a protest demonstration, Pokrovsky and his choir found themselves at one point cast as a dissident underground ensemble, which did wonders for their street cred. Yet at the same time the KGB smiled on them and supported their tours – the reason being that, in contrast to the

39 Musicians at a carnival in Petrograd in 1919.

big choirs, they were cheap, and more than happy to sing in remote places where they could collect uncontaminated new material. They appeared on television, recorded a disc, and trained other groups to find and sing their own local material. 'We created a new kind of person,' said Pokrovsky. 'A singing folklorist.'

At that time, he said, they were the only professional group presenting Russia's real folklore. Until their emergence, what masqueraded as Russian folk culture was really just a Russian variant on Western culture. Tchaikovsky and Rachmaninov were European composers who used Russian material, but they were working according to the rules of European academic music, and the big state folklore troupes were doing the same. Pokrovsky's ideological models were the Mighty Handful – Musorgsky, Borodin, Cui, Balakirev, and Rimsky-Korsakov. 'We didn't sing *Russian* folk songs,' he said. 'We sang

Smolensk songs, Belgorod songs, Don Cossack songs. We and our audiences were far from being nationalists.' 'Russian' folk song, he said, was either an abstraction, or an artificial creation by composers.

Pokrovsky was acutely aware that the enemy was not only to be found in what he called 'Potemkin' village ensembles portraying happy and strong Russians singing and dancing in the healthy and wealthy Russian state: 'There are also ensembles doing authentic folk music who represent what is essentially a fascist position. They say the music I do is too sophisticated – that the *narod* [people] don't understand it.' His aim was to present the art of what he termed the village intelligentsia: subtle and complex polyphony which he wanted to reclaim by supporting its revival in its natural habitat.

* * *

In 2009 Melodiya released a survey of Russian folk music, taking in calendar songs and joke songs, ballads and work songs, wedding songs and laments from every corner of the country. Little of this music traded on rustic charm: most had a gritty social purpose. The most striking song in this collection came from a wedding ritual in Vologda called 'seating the bride', which had by chance also been observed by one of Shloyme Ansky's colleagues back in 1905. 'After the girls had braided the bride's hair,' he wrote,

> the bridesmaids and older women came to seat the bride. She was led into a special room where she was helped to get dressed and do her make-up. Then she was led into the wedding chamber where the *badkhn* [the wedding jester] and the musicians were impatiently waiting for her. While the women sat the bride down on a chair and unbraided her hair, the badkhn intoned a melancholy rhyming poem. All wept bitterly, especially the bride, who remained in this pose, surrounded by elderly women and with a handkerchief pressed to her eyes, until the groom appeared.

A Russian village wedding ceremony is a symbolic ritual which can last weeks, with the groom's family theatrically cast as robbers, and the father haggling over the sum they must pay. The words on the Melodiya disc translate as follows:

> O father, what have you done? I knew nothing of this. I will have to live among strangers, far from home. Sit down with me, my dear ones, I am so young, come close and help me undo my braids. Your blue flowers are blooming in the field, but mine is standing by the wayside, ready to leave you all. What will it be like, to live among strangers, far from my mother?

To call this recording dramatic would be an understatement – it sounds like the prelude to an execution. Against a steady ground-bass in Georgian-style triads and parallel thirds, the soloist's high-pitched lament sounds deranged, as she pleads for help from a chorus who impassively repeat that she must go through her 'ordeal'.

And here Pokrovsky re-enters the story: the recording of Stravinsky's *Les noces* which he and his ensemble released in 1994 put a new gloss on both Stravinsky's musical source material, and that wedding ritual itself. Stravinsky famously denied that he'd borrowed from folk sources for this work, apart from one factory song. Pokrovsky and his singers travelled to villages in the south and west of Russia where Stravinsky himself had gathered songs and melodies, in an attempt to prove his assertion wrong, and to find texts and tunes which comprised the folk underpinnings of *Les noces*. Case proven, one thinks, as chorus after chorus in the Stravinsky is shown to have local roots; the Pokrovsky Ensemble's recording of *Les noces* itself is wrapped in a garland of songs whose liberated ebullience is even more exciting than what

40 Dmitri Pokrovsky and his ensemble on a visit to Boston, USA, in 1988.

Stravinsky created out of them. Thus was *Les noces* reunited with the Russian world in which it was set.

One of the groups on the Melodiya disc came from a village called Podserednieje, close to the present Ukrainian border. In 2018 in London I once chanced to hear songs from that village sung by two Polish musicologists named Monika Walenko and Justyna Piernik and their performance was captivating, with some songs rough, some tender, some jokingly sarcastic.

Half of the CD which this concert was designed to promote consisted of recordings by the choir, East Warsaw, of which these women were members. The richness of their heterophony within a narrow pitch-range, and the swirling momentum of their songs for circle dances with individual voices breaking cover in improvised whoops, had arresting power. The other half of the CD was recordings made with the villagers themselves. The songs were the same, but these versions – with atmospheric embellishments from honking geese, crowing cocks, and children crowding round – felt very different. In contrast to the youthful grace of the Poles, here one could sense hard-won wisdom in the gnarled, forceful voices, which sometimes stopped each other to correct slips of tuning or memory.

The songs themselves had preserved a childlike innocence, as in their welcome to spring: 'On our street, fresh grass is growing like beautiful silk. Come on, girls, let's dance on it. Let's grab bad-tempered wives, bring them out to join their husbands.' Preparations for a wedding were evoked by a word-painting as calm as the effusion from Vologda had been wild: 'There's a lime tree in the meadow, its leafy branches spread wide. Under it is a wooden table, at which a beautiful girl sits. Her name is Maryushka, and she's weaving a carpet as a gift to her father.' In these songs love could also become a bitter memory, as when a young soldier went off to war: 'Oh, my dark sweetheart, have you forgotten our love? We will never embrace again, never meet again. Our country has parted us for ever.'

There was clearly a story behind this CD. It turned out to have originated when Walenko and her friends chanced to hear some recordings made by a Soviet musicologist who had been attracted by Podserednieje's reputation as 'the singing village'. Word about the choir had spread West, with the villagers being invited to star in a Smithsonian Folk Life festival.

The standard Soviet way of song collecting was to select a village, record its songs, then move on quickly with few questions asked. But the Poles decided to get to know their quarry, and made a film of daily life in the village. Grindingly poor and intensely religious, Podserednieje had intense civic pride; nobody saw anything strange in the fact that the church bell should be sounded with a hammer, or that the blade of a scythe should make a serviceable musical instrument and give a merry twang. And everybody sang. 'We have three hundred and sixty five songs,' boasted the head of the community centre. 'Nobody ever needed to organise a festival – these things just happened.' 'My mother would never spin in silence,' said a woman with a mouthful of gold teeth. 'She would always sing as she spun.' The women of the choir paraded in elaborate head-dresses, the men in belted white shirts and high boots; their polyphony had pumping energy and absolute precision, their voices firm and clean with no vibrato.

By the time of the Poles' first visit in 1992 the Soviet empire had crumbled, but official attitudes had not: the Poles were stopped in mid-recording, taken to the police station, and expelled from the country for not having permission to record. Returning with permission the next year, they embarked on a deep study, getting the singers, who were now mostly old women, to deliver each song many times. This was because their heterophony was constantly changing. 'We learned the boundaries of the style,' said Walenko. 'How far you can go in any given direction.' How many parts would there be? 'As many as you like. As many parts as there are singers. We haven't done transcriptions, because they would have been too approximate. It's all on a modal scale, between the Western minor and major, different when you go up and when you come down.' Moreover, the old singers tuned not by pitch but by timbre. 'Speaking for myself,' Walenko went on, 'as I know this music so well by heart, notations would be meaningless. And in any case it's improvised – no two performances are the same. I have learned so many variants that I can now make my own. The CD is our work in progress, an interim document. The more we do this music, the better we do it. But it must be heard live.'

When the Poles had got on top of the repertoire they joined forces with the local choir to celebrate the festival of the Holy Trinity, but everyone was aware that the music was slipping away. Some of the singers on the original recordings had been born in the nineteenth century, and by the time Walenko and her friends had finished their work in 2014, only six remained alive; even fewer will be alive today. 'Younger people know the songs,' says Walenko. 'But they can't sing them as they need to be sung.'

What is this music's future? 'We will pass it on,' says Walenko. 'The question of who owns traditional music is complicated – you can only own your personal version of it.' There is still work to do in analysing their recordings, but now that politics has turned Russia into a hostile environment for researchers like Walenko and her friends, they won't be going back to record any more. 'Something has come to an end,' she says ruefully. Yet at the same time something else has begun: as we saw in London, old music is being made new.

Sources

Theodore Levin's chapter in *Retuning Culture* is both an in-depth interview with Pokrovsky and a chronicle of the fluctuating fortunes of Russian folk music in the twentieth century; the Pokrovsky Ensemble's recording of *Les noces* is revelatory. *Ławeczka* combines village renditions of Podserednieje songs with the ethnomusicologists' versions. The Melodiya CD *Russian Music* has no musicological information, but is still fascinating.

Bibliography, recordings, and documentaries

Levin, Theodore, 'Dmitri Pokrovsky and the Russian Folk Music Revival Movement', in Mark Slobin, ed., *Retuning Culture: Musical Changes in Central and Eastern Europe* (London: Duke University Press, 1996), 14–36

Folk Music Anthology: Russian Music, MELCD 3001640
Ławeczka (The Bench), East Warsaw Ensemble, double CD, 2014
Les noces, Pokrovsky Ensemble, Elektra Nonesuch 7559-79335-2

From Podserednieje with Love, dir. Tomasz Knittel and Jagina Knittel, 2015

20

Three-in-one

The Georgian way

'I WAS BORN twice,' said the great Russian bass Fyodor Chaliapin. 'In Kazan I opened my eyes to life, and in Tbilisi to music.' The city where he began his career in 1894 may have had a thriving operatic scene, but what made it one of the most musical cities on earth – and still does today – was its unique polyphony.

On my first visit to Tbilisi I went up to the fourth-century Narikala fortress, symbol of the nation's independence, where I found a group of young men with tear-stained faces, clutching bottles of vodka and singing a slow choral lament. This was their way of mourning a friend who had just died in a car crash, and would I like to join them for a shot?

It being a Sunday, I then walked down to Sioni Cathedral, past magazine vendors selling classical sheet music. In the surrounding streets impromptu circles of middle-aged gents were singing folk songs in immaculate three-part counterpoint. Inside the cathedral, amid a blur of bells, candles, incense, and more tear-stained faces, three choirs – one male, one female, one mixed – were taking it in turns to ramp up religious fervour with a non-stop stream of the three-part harmony which the eleventh-century Georgian philosopher Ioane Petritsi had compared to the Holy Trinity.

This was in 1997, before capitalism had discovered Tbilisi, and when it was still effectively a Soviet city. In those days, every Georgian adult could join in complex three-part drinking songs with an accuracy which no amount of liquor could damage – the music was hard-wired into their DNA. And when I watched a children's choir being taught a new song full of awkward jumps and dissonances, I sensed the truth of that: within an hour, without a score, they had not only mastered it, but had each learned all three parts. This was a society in which the distinction between amateur and professional singers scarcely existed. Although young Georgians now listen to the same pop music as millennials do everywhere else, you can still count on this polyphonic facility in all Georgians over fifty.

That musical three-in-one is an over-simplification. Georgian polyphony, which is as perfectly evolved as North Indian raga, takes a multiplicity of forms; the only safe generalisation is that Georgians never sing in unison. When there are three voices, the top is regarded as second in importance to the middle one, which begins and leads the song; the bass, which is often sung by a group, is in no way looked down on, as witness the local saying, 'The song is adorned by the bass, the garden by the red apple.' Georgians sometimes liken their part-singing to *aelebra* – the harmonious singing of a flock of birds – and nowhere is this better exemplified than in the vertiginous four-part counterpoint of the harvest songs – in a style much admired by Stravinsky – to be found in the Black Sea province of Guria. Here the top voice is a crazy yodel, beneath which is a drone, below which is the leading voice, plus a bass which is melodically very active. The improvisation in such songs creates its spell by simultaneously obeying two contrary principles: each part develops horizontally within consonant thirds and fifths, but the vertical coordination of different parts is based on the ruggedly dissonant intervals which Georgians particularly love – seconds, fourths, and ninths. The work songs feel as though carved from rock, the ploughing songs have a meditative beauty, the lullabies are ineffably sweet; some songs respond to the rough-hewn poetry of their texts with the sudden force of thunder and lightning.

As a bridge between Europe and Asia, Georgia had preserved its identity despite a long series of Muslim invasions, as well as through the Tsarist Russian hegemony; it triumphantly retained its own language under Soviet rule, helped by the fact that Stalin was a Georgian. Until industrialisation supplanted the crafts on which many of its traditional songs were based, Georgia's folk music was never a threatened species; whether for weddings, or laments, or healing sessions, or above all for feasting, Georgians had a song for every activity, and every event in the life-cycle.

Georgia's sacred music, whose roots are thought to go back to the dawn of Georgian Christianity in the fourth century CE, works on the same polyphonic principles as its secular equivalent; it's sometimes almost impossible to distinguish one from the other. But the sacred music took a big hit under Communism. As in other parts of the Soviet empire, priests in Georgia were either shot or sent to Siberia, and their churches were converted to other uses. And it was under such conditions that a remarkable Georgian song collector carried out his crowning exploit. Father Ekvtime the Confessor had been born in the remote Racha region in 1865, and as a young man in Tbilisi joined a book club distributing free copies of Orthodox texts and chants. Ordained to the priesthood in the year of the Bolshevik revolution, he was arrested for subversion, then released for lack of evidence, and embarked on the clandestine task of gathering ancient hymns and transcribing them into staff notation. When the persecution of Christians was at its height he buried thirty-four volumes of manuscripts, and deposited them at the Georgian state museum when the political pressure had eased; they lay there in a vault until their rediscovery in 1988. It's largely thanks to Father Ekvtime that this medieval choral efflorescence is now again in full bloom.

The first folklorist to record a comprehensive collection of Georgian songs was Anzor Erkomaishvili, who with his Rustavi Ensemble produced a series of CDs in the 1990s. These immaculately polished concert performances generated a backlash: Erkomaishvili's conservatoire colleague Edisher Garakanidze launched a rival choir called Mtiebi ('Dawn'), which worked on very different principles.

'Initially,' Garakanidze told me,

> we didn't want to create a formal ensemble – we just wanted to sing together, and who better to sing with than one's friends? We didn't look for accomplished singers – it's no accident that I am the only trained musician in the group. Indeed, I envy my friends' freedom from academic convention. And as with any village group, our members double up as instrumentalists and dancers – we want to restore the natural unity of singing and dancing.

Mtiebi made a point of song collecting in every corner of the country, and of joining in village festivals and improvising on stage, but they didn't pretend to be villagers: it was a long time before they gave in to showbiz pressure and donned traditional costumes with bullet-and-dagger accoutrements. But the key difference between Mtiebi and Rustavi was musical. Where Rustavi had simplified the complex traditional scales and ironed out microtonal dissonances, Mtiebi didn't tamper with the original tonal untidiness, and the results were raw and earthy.

Garakanidze was killed with his wife and daughter in a car crash in 1998; his son Gigi, who died sixteen years later of injuries sustained in the same crash, took over the leadership of Mtiebi, but Edisher Garakanidze's influence continues to be profound. He had also set up a children's ensemble named Amer-Imeri – the children's choir to which I referred above – some of whose original members now sing with Mtiebi. Meanwhile other Georgian groups are pursuing his policies, and offshoot ensembles have sprung up in Europe, America, and Japan; it's no surprise that people all over the world should be addicted to the physical thrill of singing in the Georgian style.

But the most important offshoot of Garakanidze's work was the foundation of Mtiebi's sister-choir, the all-female Mzetamze who have ploughed a unique furrow. The six Tbilisi musicologists who comprise it stress the significance of their name, which translates as 'sun of suns' – a matriarchal title echoing a line

41 Georgian song collector Edisher Garakanidze with his young singers in Tbilisi.

from one of the ring-dance songs they have recorded: 'The sun lay down and bore the moon'. In traditional Georgian society, men and women reign over separate domains – only men sing the table songs, for example. But the songs which Mzetamze sing have been collected from all over Georgia and from exiled Georgian communities in Turkey, and they show the female domains to be many and varied. Milking and spinning have their songs, sometimes laced with barbs addressed to errant males ('Would that my spindle should break/ Would that he should break his neck'). Cradle songs are not mere lulling exercises: in Georgia the moment of falling asleep is seen as fraught with danger from evil spirits, which must be warded off with a *sotto voce* twist in the song. Songs to heal sick children are addressed to spirits from beyond the Black Sea, who must be obeyed without question and placated with gifts of sweets. Mzetamze can't illustrate it on a CD, but one of their drought songs used to be performed by singers fording a river in harness, like oxen ploughing a field.

Laments are a quintessentially female preserve: to have a funeral graced by a celebrated professional mourner whose performance is interlarded with sobs is a sought-after honour. Mzetamze give a moving example of this, with a text which is heart-rending in its candid directness: 'Don't furrow your brow with wrinkles/ Let no tears fall from those beautiful eyes/ In the black land of the dead/ Don't be afraid, my beloved daughter.' With their combination of beauty and strangeness, wildness and wit, the vibrantly dark-toned songs on the CDs which Mzetamze have released represent a high point of the song-collecting art.

Sources

Joseph Jordania's chapter on Georgian music in *The Garland Encyclopedia of World Music* is an authoritative guide to this unique tradition, while Ted Levin's liner note for *Georgian Voices* is a fine pocket distillation; tracks on that CD include a ploughing song rendered with mesmerising beauty by the tenor Hamlet Gonashvili. The field recordings by Michael Church in *Songs of Survival* offer a conspectus of all Georgia's folk styles, sacred and secular; *Ensemble Mzetamze Volumes 1 and 2* are riveting compilations.

Bibliography and recordings

Jordania, Joseph, 'Georgia', in Timothy Rice, James Porter, and Chris Goertzen, eds, *The Garland Encyclopedia of World Music: Europe* (London: Routledge, 2002)

Georgian Voices: The Rustavi Choir, Elektra Nonesuch 7559-79224-2
Mtiebi: Traditionelle Gesänge aus Georgien, Edition Musikay, 398055552-6
Songs of Survival: Traditional Music of Georgia, recordings by Michael Church, Topic Records TSCD935D
Traditional Georgian Women's Songs: Volume 1, Ensemble Mzetamze, Face Music Switzerland FM 50016
Traditional Georgian Women's Songs: Volume 2, Ensemble Mzetamze, Face Music Switzerland FM 50030

42 The *mbela* one-string bow is said to have been invented by the Pygmies.

21

Small is beautiful

Pygmy polyphony

GYÖRGY LIGETI'S EIGHTIETH-BIRTHDAY bash at the Barbican was characteristically provocative. The stage was shared in turn – and on strictly equal terms – by pianist Pierre-Laurent Aimard playing Ligeti's ferociously complex *Etudes*, and by some singer-drummer Pygmies brought in from the rainforests of the Congo. No allowances were made for the latter: it became immediately clear that, despite their dramatically differing provenance, these musics were, in terms of melodic and rhythmic sophistication, on a par; the segues between them seemed so unforced that they might have been designed to go together.

The founder of this feast was a French-Israeli ethnomusicologist named Simha Arom, for whom the concert marked the culmination of a forty-year crusade. That had begun when, as a visiting horn player hired to create a brass band in the Central African Republic, he had looked out of his hotel window in Bangui and heard some Pygmy musicians in the garden below. 'It was a shock,' he told me in 2003. 'It was a polyphony which made my spine tingle. How could these people play such complex music without a conductor? For me, that was as deep a musical experience as first hearing the music of Bartók. I sensed that this music existed in us all, like some Jungian archetype.'

He got to know the musicians, learned their language, and began to analyse how they made their music. 'I noticed that they knew instantly when a wrong note was played. That meant they had rules. And if you have rules, you have a theory. But their theory was implicit – they didn't know they had one, because they couldn't express it in words. I made it my job to discover that theory, to establish the grammar of their music.' To notate it, he first recorded the full ensemble, then played the tape through headphones to each musician in turn, getting them to perform their particular part for him to record. Meanwhile Ligeti had come to adore this intricately layered music thanks to some recordings he'd heard by the British anthropologist Colin Turnbull. Under its influence Ligeti had written similarly constructed pieces for Aimard to play, and the Barbican concert was the hall's birthday present to him.

Discovering the Pygmies – and their music – had been going on for a very long time. The earliest known reference was not Homer's famous battle between the Pygmies and the cranes in the *Iliad*, but a record of an expedition sent from Egypt in the Fourth Dynasty – predating the Pyramids – to discover the source of the Nile. When the leader of the expedition reported that he had found some tiny forest people who sang and danced to their god, he was instructed to bring some home, and his ruler was delighted with their performance. Many centuries later, Pompeian mosaics indicated a detailed knowledge of the Pygmies, but thereafter they receded into myth, with a thirteenth-century cartographer depicting them as one-legged troglodytes. It was only in the mid-twentieth century that they came back into focus: Colin Turnbull's book *The Forest People*, published in 1961, was the first serious and sympathetic analysis to be made of the mores of an Mbuti Pygmy community, for whom singing was an essential part of everyday life.

The musical event which most intrigued Turnbull was the *molimo*, in which two hollowed-out tree trunks served as trumpets which were noisily paraded round the encampment by a group of young men; this happened whenever a misdemeanour had occurred, or when there was something to celebrate. But it was only after months of acculturation – and after queasily allowing his hosts to carve deep tribal scars into his face – that Turnbull could induce them to explain, with engaging simplicity, what the *molimo*, which they referred to as 'the animal of the forest', actually meant.

'The forest is father and mother to us,' he translated them as saying.

And like a father or mother it gives us everything we need – food, clothing, shelter, warmth, affection. So when something big goes wrong, like illness, or a bad hunt, or a death, it must be because the forest is sleeping, and not looking after its children. So what do we do? We wake it up. We wake it up by singing to it, and we do this because we want it to awaken happy. Then everything will be well and good again. And when our world is going well, then also we sing to the forest, because we want it to share our happiness.

One of Turnbull's recordings is of a *molimo* chant which rings out joyfully in immaculate polyphony, until brought to a halt by a deafening roll of thunder.

Turnbull had approached Pygmy music as a social phenomenon: it was only with Simha Arom's researches, which began ten years later, that it went under the musicological microscope. Arom's initial aim was to disprove a notorious assertion by Curt Sachs, one of the sages of early ethnomusicology, that 'African polyrhythm is beyond analysis'. Arom's quest took him to a forty-member encampment of Aka Pygmies in the Central African Republic. Originally nomadic, this group spent the rainy half of the year hunting in the forest, and the dry season camped on the edge of villages where they worked

228

as labourers. At first Arom saw no traces of hierarchy in the community, but he gradually realised that its life was rigorously organised. He also realised that its music exhibited organised characteristics, each participant having relative autonomy but working within strictly observed rules.

The music was primarily vocal, with added percussion from drums, pairs of knife-blades, clapping, and occasionally one- or two-string musical bows. The singing had a leader, but once underway it became a collective affair, with all members of the community – men, women, and children – playing an equal part. Songs did not end in a precise way – one would merge into another, depending on when individual singers wanted to move on. Anyone who wanted could occupy the musical foreground, then retire into the background again. When the singers got tired, a song would simply dissolve, reversing the process by which it had begun.

There were no nuances in the dynamics, no variations in tempo, and there were usually only four singing parts, but since each part involved yodelling, and could be varied in an infinity of ways, the effect was of a dense web of sound. In terms of form, Arom described the music as 'ostinato with variations' – cyclical music founded on a principle similar to that of the European passacaglia. Dubbing it 'a polyphony of consonances', he observed that there were points of consonance at the fifth and the octave, with passing dissonances everywhere else. This, he said, mirrored the principles of the medieval European music known as *ars nova*: his Aka singers employed the melodic device known as the *cantus firmus*, and, just as medieval European musicians had a horror of the tritone – 'the Devil's interval' – so the Aka had a horror of unison.

If by chance they found themselves in unison, there would be an immediate divergence of pitches, since for them a unison, with its coercive symmetry and its lack of colour and tension, was as much to be dreaded as silence. And their rhythms obeyed a similar principle: symmetry was avoided by dividing the singers into two groups, one following an 11-beat cycle and the other a 13-beat one, but both being contained within the same over-arching cycle of 24 beats. This music may have had a repetitive surface, but through overlapping melodic lines and asymmetrical rhythms it gave an impression of unpredictability, and of being in a state of perpetual evolution. Children were encouraged to learn these techniques by imitation, as soon as they could walk.

Arom's recordings are fascinating, and to European ears humbling, because they reveal so high a degree of contrapuntal artistry. A lullaby caressingly sung by two girls in their leaf hut reminds me of one recorded in the Solomon Islands, but the communal lament sung over a corpse has a cathedral-like grandeur. Whether it's a children's game or a hunting chant creating a horizon of yodels, whether it's to launch a search for honey or to make mischief by making that search a metaphor for the pleasures of sex, each song has its own purpose and character, and is delivered with spot-on precision. This music represents a serenely self-contained world of custom, ritual, and belief.

Arom's personal charisma, coupled with the allure of the music he had brought to light, attracted student disciples. Prominent among those was Susanne Fürniss, now one of the directors of the Langues, Musiques, Société laboratory in Paris, and an authority in her own right on Central African music. But her route towards this specialism was, as is so often the case with song collectors, serendipitous. As a violinist and choir conductor she had been marked out for a classical career. Then lightning struck: she was listening to a lecture on the origins of music at the Hamburg Conservatoire when one of the examples played happened to be an Aka recording by Arom. 'It came as a physical shock,' she recalls. 'I knew immediately that I wasn't going to write my end-of-year thesis on Mozart or on any other European composer.' She abandoned her course and spent a year immersed in African musicology, hunting out Pygmy recordings wherever she could find them. After reading Arom's writings she went to Paris to study with him, and as part of her doctorate on Aka scales was sent out to work in the Central African Republic. She recalls the moment a little man came running out of the forest to embrace Arom: 'I'd heard his recorded voice thousands of times, singing and speaking, and I'd even subjected it to acoustic analysis, and suddenly there he was in front of me!' The fieldwork she began there led her to make the first-ever record of Aka instrumental music, which complemented Arom's one of the singing.

Wood, bark, and leaves were the prime materials from which these Pygmy instruments were made: almost everything came from the forest. Strings predominated, with zithers, harps, and several varieties of musical bow; flutes and lamellophones (variants on the thumb piano) were common, with cooking pots serving as resonators. A flute was made from the hollow stem of a pawpaw leaf, and as it had no finger-holes (and therefore gave just one note) players added their own sung notes, yodelling to create variety.

The two-string bow consisted of a stick, a length of creeper, and a big arrowroot leaf: the stick was bent into a U, the creeper was stretched to form two strings, and the leaf acted as a resonator which was amplified by a cooking pot placed under it; the upper string was tapped with the right forefinger, the lower one was plucked with the left thumb. In the one-string bow the musician's mouth served as the resonator, with the string being struck with a twig. Harmonics were created by changes in the shape and volume of the mouth cavity. Meanwhile the ground bow, which the children played, could not have been simpler: its resonator was a hole in the ground covered with a bark soundboard; a string was tied to a flexible branch stuck in the ground and attached to the middle of the soundboard.

The songs about hunting and conjugal matters which Fürniss collected are bewitching in their sweetness and their vivid sense of place. On the first track, where the singers are accompanied by the *bogongo* harp-zither, we also hear a tree being felled, while the second is punctuated by children's shouts. The main function of the *bogongo* is to accompany love songs. As Fürniss writes, a harmonious sex life and good luck in the hunt are the twin Pygmy goals: 'A happy camp is a camp which is rich in both children and game.' What's most striking is the delicacy of these chants, even a provocatively horny one whose lyric translates as 'I want you right now – come, even if you haven't had a wash'. A song called 'Sleep now, master of the penis' apparently had its female audience in fits of laughter, as did the suggestive 'Her loincloth has slipped aside'. But this music could be didactic, too: a song entitled 'The separation of

43 Women play the *engbitti* two-string bow.

the married couple' expresses grave regret that a couple are no longer getting on. Each song creates a landscape in which voices near and far – some little more than a murmur – are skilfully interwoven.

Civil war and political chaos in the Central African Republic forced Fürniss to abandon her observation of Aka mores, and in 1999 she transferred her researches to a Baka Pygmy community in neighbouring Cameroon. Semi-nomadic like the Aka, the Baka too were able to trade on their deep knowledge of the forest, and on their authority as controllers of its spiritual forces for therapeutic or magical purposes. Fürniss's new research focused on circumcision rituals, revealing among other things the extent to which the international arms market had polluted this remote culture: the make-believe guns brandished by circumcised Pygmy boys were modelled on the weapons they saw in specialist magazines which circulated even in the heart of the rainforest.

But the traditional process by which Pygmy males achieve manhood is now being disrupted. Elephant-hunting was the crucial element, but the law now forbids it; it still goes on, but furtively and in silence, without the associated rituals. Ritual songs for healing and mourning are still sung as they always were, but songs casting benign spells for the hunt have lost their social function. And at the risk of sounding like a Luddite, Fürniss lists other enemies of traditional music. Electricity and alcohol top her charge-sheet: the arrival of cassettes and CDs means that Pygmies no longer have the old urge to sing, while drunkenness impairs their ability to sustain their complex musical forms. And she draws attention to an unexpected threat: American evangelists, particularly Pentecostalists, whose cultural colonisation is accompanied by the prohibition of rituals which they see as the work of the Devil. They haven't got to the Pygmies yet, but they're on their way.

Fürniss has spent the last two decades compiling a French-Aka dictionary and working with a team on a multi-volume Pygmy Encyclopaedia, but she's no advocate of Pygmy music as museum-culture: 'That way lies sclerosis.' Girls still play the two-string musical bow, but harps and guitars (often homemade) are replacing the soft-toned *bogongo*. Both the Aka and Baka are now increasingly sedentary: when their way of life loses its nomad forest character, so inevitably must their music.

As with other musics under threat of extinction, Aka music has received UNESCO's 'intangible cultural heritage' accolade, though that confers prestige with no cash. More significant are the accolades conferred on Aka and Baka music by European and American musicians. For a reworking of 'Watermelon Man' the African American pianist Herbie Hancock's drummer Bill Summers blew into a bottle to imitate the singing/whistle-playing he'd heard on a Pygmy recording made by Simha Arom; British and Belgian pop musicians have exploited other Pygmy effects. By far the most successful exploiters have been Deep Forest, a group led by the French musicians Michel Sanchez and Eric Mouquet whose first album – melding sampled Pygmy voices and new-age techno effects – scooped the pool in terms of both critical acclaim and commercial success.

But this was sentimental, soft-focus stuff, as the lyric to the title track makes clear: 'Somewhere, deep in the jungle, are living some little men and women. They are our past, and maybe, maybe they are our future.' Only a small fraction of the enormous proceeds from album sales went back to the little men and women who had been their inspiration. By contrast, the British enthusiasts Martin Cradick and Su Hart have harnessed their knowledge of Baka culture to a cottage industry which they have christened Baka Beyond, and this really has brought benefits for the Africans. Two of their Baka records present the real thing, while a third presents it in gently Westernised form, with the proceeds from sales going back to Cameroon; the pair have helped the Baka set up a recording studio in the rainforest.

There are now just 900,000 Pygmies spread across eleven countries of Central Africa. Since the future of their music is in doubt thanks to war, ebola, the coronavirus, and all the elements of modernity, we must be grateful to Turnbull, Arom, Fürniss, and their song-collecting colleagues for catching it so gracefully on the wing, and for highlighting its unique qualities. We should also be grateful to György Ligeti for creating works which trade on those qualities, and for his neat encapsulation of the paradoxical nature of Pygmy polyphony: 'What we witness in this music is a wonderful combination of order and disorder, which in turn produces a sense of order on a higher level.'

And whatever happens to Pygmy culture in the future, it has in its present form a profound truth to teach us. This is most perceptively expressed by Dave Abram and Jerome Lewis in an essay for the *Rough Guide to World Music*:

> Moving around the rainforest paths, where dense vegetation prevents you from seeing very far, hearing becomes the primary sense. In the absence of visual pointers, the Pygmies find their way by tuning into auditory landmarks: to the sound of particular trees, to the flow of a river or to noises from different encampments, and by calling to one another, often over long distances. It's not surprising, therefore, that forest-dwellers become skilled listeners at a very early age. This uncanny sensitivity to sound perhaps explains the Pygmies' highly developed musical ability. Good group musicianship is, after all, ninety percent listening.

Sources

Colin Turnbull's *The Forest People* is the ideal starting point, with Susanne Fürniss's ethnomusicological publications (see the Bibliography) opening up further avenues. But the best routes in are the liner notes to Simha Arom's *Centrafrique* and Fürniss's *Aka Pygmies*, which provide detailed musical commentaries; *African Rhythms* is the CD of the Barbican performance; Turnbull's *Music of the Rainforest Pygmies* gives a flavour of the music he originally heard. *Spirit of the Forest* is Baka Beyond's musical mission statement.

Bibliography and recordings

Abram, Dave and Jeromoe Lewis, 'Pygmy Music: Forest Songs from the Congo Basin', in Simon Broughton, Mark Ellingham, and Jon Lusk, eds, *The Rough Guide to World Music* (London: Rough Guides, 2006), 304–12

Fürniss, Susanne, 'Recherches ethnomusicologiques en Afrique centrale', *Analyse musicale*, vol. 75 (2014), 84–90

Fürniss, Susanne, 'The Adoption of the Circumcision Ritual Beka by the Baka-Pygmies in Southeast Cameroon', *African Music*, vol. 8, no. 2 (2008), 94–113

Hagège, Lucille and Susanne Fürniss, 'The Story behind the Music', *CNRS International Magazine*, vol. 9 (October 2007)

Leclair, Madeleine and Susanne Fürniss, 'Profession: Pygmologue – Entretien avec Susanne Fürniss', *Cahiers d'ethnomusicologie*, vol. 28 (2015) 229–49

Turnbull, Colin M., *The Forest People* (London: Jonathan Cape, 1961)

African Rhythms, Pierre-Laurent Aimard and Aka Pygmies, Teldec 8573 86584-2

Aka Pygmies: Hunting, Love, and Mockery Songs, recordings by Susanne Fürniss, Ocora C56II39

Centrafrique: Musical Anthology of the Aka Pygmies, recordings by Simha Arom, Ocora C 56II7I/72

Music of the Rainforest Pygmies, recordings by Colin M. Turnbull, Lyrichord LLST 7157

Spirit of the Forest, field recordings and studio embellishments by Martin Cradick for Baka Beyond, Hannibal HNBC1377

22

It's a physical thing

A Persian musician relocates the *radif*

ON STAGE, ELSHAN Ghasimi cuts a graceful figure with her *tar* lute; in her playing and in her commentary, every phrase is invested with deep thought and grave authority. She was born in Isfahan in 1981, two years after the Islamic revolution. 'The first music I heard was by the leading masters of the Persian classical tradition,' she told me in 2019.

> They were all members of the Chavosh Institute, which had been set up to defend Persian classical music against attacks from the revolutionary guards. I loved that music, so when I went for my first lessons at the age of eight with Majid Vasefi, I copied it on my miniature *setar* lute. When I was eleven I graduated to the bigger *tar*, and I was sent to the Honarestane

44 Iranian *tar* virtuoso Elshan Ghasimi (born 1981).

Musighi conservatoire, where I was taught by Fariborz Azizi. And whatever he told me to do, I did.

Persian classical music is framed by a suite-form known as the *radif*, within which modes known as *dastgah*s and melodic units called *gusheh*s are component parts. Between the ages of twelve and seventeen, Elshan played her *tar* all day, every day, but there was a problem:

> Iranian masters don't usually reveal the secrets of the theory behind certain dastgahs until they believe you are ready – and for them being ready meant knowing the associated literature, and even the associated mathematics. Only then would they initiate you into the secrets – when you had earned the right to know them. But to play the radif properly, you need to understand the complicated system on which it is based. And that means, in practical terms, to understand how you can progress from one mode to another. They let me imitate them, without explaining why they were doing what they were doing. I would listen and listen, and sometimes I would understand – in a sudden flash – how a particular transition could be made. I remember once intentionally playing a wrong succession of gushehs, making a wrong transition to a different dastgah, and my tar master didn't stop me. I said, 'You are my teacher, so surely you must correct me' – but still he wouldn't.

To illustrate her point, she demonstrates the beginning of a *dastgah* on her *tar*, explaining that certain awkward intervals are forbidden in the classical style. She then draws a circle, marking points along its circumference:

> Each step is a gusheh, and you can't miss out a step in that circle. But at certain points you can make a transition to another scale, another dastgah. All this must take place slowly – if I am playing for an hour, I don't go through more than three dastgahs, as you have to digest the effect of each in turn. Young players today don't always recognise these rules, so if I am teaching them, and if I see that they have thirsty eyes, I reveal the secrets.

At twenty she joined the Iranian International Orchestra, formed under the guidance of the enlightened minister of culture Mohammad Khatami. With a melange of classical and modern instruments they played a melange of classical and modern works, though with six *tars* playing a musical line originally designed for one, the effect was in her view unsatisfactory. Her next step – after the orchestra had been closed down under the philistine Ahmadinejad regime – was to move to Azerbaijan.

Her parents had both come from Tabriz, an Iranian city where Azeri is spoken, and she had grown up bilingual. And she remembered her grandmother's Azeri songs: 'She used to just murmur them, but I loved them, and I decided to research them.' She also decided to learn to play the Azeri *tar*, which is smaller than the Iranian one: it's held to the chest rather than kept in the lap, and, under the tutelage of Ramiz Quliev, she fell in love with that too. 'I had planned to spend just one month in Baku, to learn about the songs, and then come back.' However, invited to enrol in the Baku Conservatoire as a PhD student, she started to learn *mugam*, which was Azerbaijan's equivalent of the *radif*, and she stayed in Baku for four years.

As with the *radif*, this music also depended on learning the modes. 'And it opened a new door in my mind. This was partly the effect of the instrument on my body. The wood of the Iranian tar is thick, it's a heavy instrument. The Azeri tar is lighter, the wood is thinner, and the sound comes through your breast-bone, creating a strong internal resonance in your body. It's a physical thing.'

But the music itself was a revelation too. Azerbaijan was originally part of Iran before Russia seized most of it in the nineteenth century; Iran kept the remainder, which included Tabriz. And while the Islamic revolutionaries disrupted Persian classical music, no such thing happened in Azerbaijan. The Soviets may have adapted *mugam* to their own revolutionary purposes, but there was no period of enforced musical silence there, so, as Elshan points out, the old *mugam* tradition was not temporarily lost.

Since they have a common root, there are many similarities between Azeri *mugam* and the Iranian *radif*, but in Elshan's opinion Azeri music retains the purity of Persian classical music as it must have existed in the nineteenth century. 'It's true that Azeri musicians have added a lot of their own ornamentation,' she says. 'But if you remove that ornamentation, you are left with the backbone of the music, its essence, which reflects the true Persian heritage. I believe the purest expression of the radif can be found more easily in Azerbaijan than it can in Iran. This may sound surprising, but it's my theory, based on my experience, and I am sure it is true.' A modest aperçu in the grand scheme of things, but yet another way in which unexpected musical discoveries can be made.

Bibliography

Nooshin, Laudan, *Iranian Classical Music: The Discourses and Practice of Creativity* (Farnham: Ashgate, 2015)

45 Yang Yinliu (1899–1984), the father of Chinese song collecting.

23

Plucking the winds

Chinese village music today

SOME REGARD YANG Yinliu as the Chinese Bartók. Others think it would be more appropriate to describe Bartók as the Hungarian Yang Yinliu. Yet Yang's work is all but unknown outside China. Search the English-language internet and you'll find very little on him, apart from a couple of book chapters, a photo of him playing his bamboo flute, and a bibliography of the books, transcriptions, articles, talks, and research findings which were the residue of his phenomenally productive life. The scope of that bibliography takes the breath away.

Born in 1899 and brought up in the last years of the Qing dynasty, Yang started learning instruments from priests of the Daoist faith which was, and still is, dedicated to the pursuit of the Three Treasures: compassion, frugality, and humility. As a precocious six-year-old he joined an elite music society, becoming adept on the *qin* zither and the *pipa* and *sanxian* lutes; he later learned to sing falsetto for *kunju* opera. He studied English, and Western music theory, and became a lifelong Christian, something about which, after 1949, he wisely kept quiet. Invited to head a Chinese music institute in America, he declined, saying 'I can do nothing if I leave Chinese soil, where Chinese music lives'.

Until the mid-Thirties almost all his musicological energies were devoted to adapting English Christian hymns for Chinese consumption, but, appointed professor of Chinese history in Beijing in 1936, he immersed himself in cutting-edge German musicology, and then in the folk music of China. In the Forties, while his friends were joining the Communist resistance, he embarked on a concise history of Chinese music in all its ritual and recreational forms. When revolution came, he cannily wrapped up his musical ideas in the politically correct jargon of the time, and was rewarded with the directorship of the Music Research Institute in Beijing.

His book was circulated in draft form from 1944 but had to go through many political revisions before, with much virtuous talk about the 'exploited labouring masses', it was properly allowed to see the light of day. Yang was also roundly criticised during the 1958 Anti-Rightist Campaign, and was induced to sum up his criminality in cringing terms: 'I was imbued with a sense of idealism, my thoughts coloured by abstractions and theoretical issues. As a result, I wrote a very poor book ... I have gradually realized that an important factor in my inability to thoroughly analyse issues on music was because I did not understand the "particularity of contradictions" in society, and its interconnectedness to other contradictions.'

In the Cultural Revolution of the Sixties he and his colleagues were made to suffer, just as the peasants were made to suffer, as representatives of the hated 'Four Olds'. Yang was paraded in front of his students wearing a dunce's cap and a sign round his neck proclaiming his crimes; he was confined to the 'cow-shed' for the re-education of intellectuals. In the camp where he was sent for further re-education, he furtively went on with his research: for musicologists, exile to the countryside paradoxically offered a wealth of opportunities for song collecting.

He ended his career peacefully after the Maoist persecution had dissipated, but, nearly four decades after his death in 1984, he still awaits the global recognition which is his due. His whole purpose had been, as the musicologist Peter Micic puts it, to rescue Chinese music history from the clutches of the imperial scribes, and to subject it to analytical rigour. The devotion he inspired in his pupils was sweetly caught in an encomium from one of them: 'Yang Yinliu was a large tree with luxuriant foliage and branches reaching high into the sky. I can only caress each branch and leaf with my hands. Yang was a bridge between ancient and modern, Chinese and foreign. I'm still walking across the bridge that Yang built.'

Yang's work is now being continued by teams of Chinese researchers; one of its leading international advocates is the British ethnographer Stephen Jones, whose entry into this arcane world was prompted by a Damascene moment. Jones was trained as an orchestral violinist, but while studying at Cambridge he fell under the spell of the scholar Laurence Picken, whom he assisted on a magisterial history of music from the Tang period, and in 1986 Jones went to Beijing to research that music further.

'I was entirely classically oriented,' he says. 'I had no idea about living folk music in China, any more than most other people in the West did at that time.' In his first week, however, he chanced to hear some *sheng-guan* wind-ensemble music played by elderly ex-monks of the famous Zhihua temple, and it blew his mind. 'That sound will always stay with me,' he says. 'The soulful *guanzi* [double-reed pipe], the darting *dizi* [flute], the sturdy *sheng* [mouth organ], the halo of the *yunluo* [gong-set] piercing the bright Beijing sky above the green and yellow roof tiles of the temple.' From that moment on, he lost all interest in speculations about how the music of the ancient past might have sounded: now his business was with the music of the present. And he's taken a mischievous pleasure in challenging two groups of academics: the scholars of religion whose interest lies in ancient manuscripts rather than in performance, and the ethnomusicologists who treat rituals as what he calls 'reified sound-objects', rather than as facets of an all-embracing culture.

Jones never met Yang Yinliu, but he did have a fortuitous connexion with him. It was Yang's recordings of the Zhihua temple monks back in 1953, plus the celebrated monograph he wrote on its *sheng-guan* style, which first sparked musicological interest in that teasingly intricate art form. Moreover, a field trip inspired Yang to launch a massive musical research project, in which Jones has played a key role. In 1956, despite encroaching collectivisation, Yang and his team documented all kinds of music-making in the southern province of Hunan; after the end of the Cultural Revolution his blueprint was expanded on an industrial scale, in the monumental *Anthology of Folk Music of the Chinese Peoples* sponsored by the Ministry of Culture. This took decades of labour by countless local scholars: each province had to produce its own bundle of tomes covering folk song, narrative song, opera, instrumental music, and dance; the published material was only ten per cent of what had been collected. Abrupt political change after the Maoists had been tamed brought its own problems: fieldworkers had to steer a careful course past local officials, who themselves had to watch their step. Some villagers, encouraged by cultural cadres to perform their rituals, were then promptly arrested for doing so by the political-correctness police. Other villagers were reluctant to give interviews in the presence of cadres, fearing that anything they said might incriminate them, as in the days of the Cultural Revolution; 'enticing the snake out of its hole' was the evocative name for this Maoist method of entrapment.

Jones's own survey focused on the amateur ritual association of a village just south of Beijing called Gaoluo. And there, making regular visits over fifteen years, he wrote a remarkable study of one ensemble's embattled past and turbulent present. Its title was *Plucking the Winds* – a Chinese phrase for song collecting – and Jones's research method was the antithesis of the go-in/record/get-out approach which Chinese musicologists mockingly stigmatise as 'gazing at flowers from horseback'. Jones went for total immersion in everything, from sleeping on the platformed brick-bed of his village hosts, to qualifying as a fully fledged member of their ensemble in which he played gongs and mouth organ. He couldn't fully comply with the Communist rule of the Three Togethers – eating, living, and working together – but he made a good stab at it, as resident photographer, communal cigarette-supplier, and occasional donor of new instruments. The rigours of existence in Gaoluo have

241

46 The Gaoluo music association playing to celebrate New Year in 1998, with Stephen Jones third from right.

probably softened a bit since his book was published in 2004, but what he uncomplainingly put up with in terms of hygiene and the basics of life makes the jaw drop.

Ritual – including vocal liturgy – has always been central to Chinese village life. The twenty-strong members of the South Gaoluo Music Association were all amateurs; slow and stately music like theirs was only heard in villages (it was no longer played by the priests of urban temples), and Jones likens the situation to Europeans only hearing Bach performed by local church groups. He draws the Bach analogy again when describing the way the players relish the grandeur of their ritual percussion suite, and the twists and turns of their ancient melodies.

One of Jones's aims has been to document the Maoist period while there are still survivors to interview. And the big conclusion he draws from his research is the unchanging durability of this ritual music. Tracing the Gaoluo association's lineage back to the imperial period, he points to what they endured while still bravely flying their flag. After the collapse of the Qing dynasty came the Republic and warlord eras, during which the villagers were prey to murderous bandits and kidnappers. Then came the horrors of the Japanese invasion, and of the civil war which followed that; Maoism brought three years of famine and well-publicised oppressions of its own. The musical and cultural traditions kept alive by China's embattled peasantry have been one of the few things providing some semblance of social stability.

Jones has other irons in the fire. He has documented the shawm bands which are China's commonest form of instrumental music. Village calendrical rituals are known as 'red and white joyous business' – red for the living (notably weddings), white for funerals; whereas the ritual groups perform mainly for the latter, the shawm bands also play for weddings and shop-openings. And these bands are known as 'blowers and drummers' for good reason: their gritty music is by turns exuberant and anguished, with the screaming of the shawms – oboes with a flared bell – penetrating everything. With circular breathing, two play continuously in heterophony, and the volume can be deafening.

While the ritual groups perform at the centre of the ritual arena, the shawm bands blow and bang outside the gate. As Jones observes, they've always been at the bottom of the social pile: 'Virtual outcasts, they were traditionally illiterate bachelors, opium smokers, begging in the slack season, associated with theft and violence.' Until recently they were also often disabled, and sometimes blind. But their playing can be intense and complex – suggesting Ming-dynasty bebop, as Jones puts it. He got to know one shawm-band family well, noting that although they were a profoundly dysfunctional group – with

47 Stephen Jones with the Hua family shawm band playing at a funeral in 2001.

two brothers on shawm and drum who were barely on speaking terms – they still played in perfect ensemble.

There are no such dysfunctions among the Li family Daoists in Shanxi, of whom Jones has made a filmed portrait to show how tenaciously rituals persist, despite the scorched-earth cultural policies of Maoism and the subsequent invasion by commercial pop. The Lis are a hereditary group of 'household' Daoists who hire themselves out to families wishing to mark key events with the correct rituals. And the way the Li family interpret their duties, 'correct' is very much the word. The voluminous scriptures announcing a person's departure to the after-life are meticulously copied by hand; the ritual documents that Li Manshan writes at funerals are eventually burned; the angle and direction at which a coffin is lowered into the earth is determined with almanac, compass, and twine as fastidiously as any foundation-stone positioned by a hard-hatted Western surveyor with a theodolite.

Eighth-generation Daoist Li Manshan speaks regretfully of what has been lost since the 1950s. He points to the mound of earth which is all that's left of his village's main temple, and he details the rites which the Eliminating Superstition campaign obliterated, with picturesque titles like Roaming among the Lotuses, Smashing the Hells, and Dispatching the Pardon. In the old days he and his group were employed for three functions – temple rites, 'thanking the earth' rites, and funerals, but now it's only funerals.

There's a calm sweetness in the way these musicians go about their work, a peaceful sense of communion with a spirit world to which they connect both musically and through writing ritual documents and decorating coffins. 'Human life is like a lantern,' they chant over a coffin, 'the wind is its greatest fear.' Burning incense and hell-money, and laying out elaborate feasts – little pyramids of everything – they enact the complex rites which must take place between death and burial, their gentle voices mingling with the sound of oboe, mouth organ, hand-drum, small cymbals, and conch. The purpose of it all is to safely deliver the soul of the deceased, and to invite all the 'orphan souls' of the world to join the benediction. In one of the most startling scenes of Jones's film, the Daoists play in procession on their way to the 'soul hall'. As they pass, villagers crowd round a truck with pop singers dancing provocatively to electronic keyboard and drum kit, yet the Daoists take it all in their stride.

What strikes one most is the richness and integrity of this still-thriving culture. Most villagers in China know nothing of the *qin* zither, the *pipa* lute, or any other instruments of their country's classical tradition, which is now ring-fenced by UNESCO's 'intangible cultural heritage' designation. Conversely, China's city dwellers know nothing about their parallel rural musical traditions. Musically speaking, the divide between metropolis and countryside is absolute.

The Gaolou music association which Jones befriended wanted him to record everything in their repertoire, so concerned were the musicians to preserve it. But since fifty per cent of the Chinese people still live in villages, and since most still regard at least some of the ancient rituals as an essential adjunct to the well-lived life, the short-term future of Chinese village music seems assured. However, the villages are steadily emptying. And when China's all-seeing digital surveillance system wraps even the remotest hamlets in its lethal embrace – as it surely will – what will happen to that music, in the longer term, is anyone's guess. The Uyghur genocide, which started with the suppression of their music, is a terrible portent. Jones and his colleagues have got their snapshots of village music just in time.

Sources

Peter Micic's chapter in *Lives in Chinese Music* offers an efficient short biography of Yang Yinliu. Stephen Jones's books offer an ideal introduction to the past and present of Chinese folk music. *Folk Music of China* is a magisterial study of the main traditions; *Plucking the Winds* takes the reader inside the life of one particular band; *Ritual and Music of North China* lifts the curtain on a musical strand which is almost unknown outside academe. Jones's blog www.stephenjones.blog is capacious and wide-ranging, and includes links to his films, of which https://stephenjones.blog/the-film/ portrays a Daoist family at work through two decades.

Bibliography

Jones, Stephen, *Folk Music of China* (London: Clarendon Press, 1995)
Jones, Stephen, *Plucking the Winds: Lives of Village Musicians in Old and New China* (Leiden: Chime Foundation, 2004)
Jones, Stephen, *Ritual and Music of North China: Shawm Bands in Shanxi* (Aldershot: Ashgate, 2007)
Micic, Peter, 'Gathering a Nation's Music: A Life of Yang Yinliu', in Helen Rees, ed., *Lives in Chinese Music* (Urbana: Illinois University Press, 2009), 91 ff.

48 Ahn Sook-Sun in a *p'ansori* performance: a typical scene.

24

Voice, handkerchief, fan

New life for Korea's p'ansori

AHN SOOK-SUN, FOR South Koreans a Living Human Treasure, makes her theatrical entrance borne aloft like a little doll by two assistants who plant her centre-stage with reverential care. At first she cuts a frail figure in her voluminous dress. Her voice – something between a gurgle and a yodel – seems to come from far away, but she's soon weaving a spell with a story about two brothers. The elder is an anarchic ne'er-do-well who kicks disabled people and pisses in the communal wine; the younger is so caring that he mends a swallow's broken leg; virtue is eventually rewarded, and a message of brotherly love affirmed.

Accompanied by a drummer who also acts as her narrative feed, Ahn evokes not only the brothers but also their entire village: the stiff little doll becomes a commanding figure. Her gestures are grave and stately, and she uses her fan to suggest everything from feminine modesty to murderous aggression. In her driving, rhythmic chant one senses a kinship with Kyrgyz recitations of the *Manas* epic; the repressed passion in her voice is reminiscent of the sound-world of Japanese *Noh*. She may be telling a Confucian morality tale, but she punctuates it with poker-faced asides which have her audience in stitches: much of her story is pure slapstick. In the course of her first gruelling hour, she takes just one sip of water: for a septuagenarian grandmother, Ahn's stamina and authority are remarkable.

This is *p'ansori*, Korea's home-grown answer to opera, and a form of epic story-telling which goes back four centuries; its name conflates the words for 'meeting place' and 'song', and its original purpose was social commentary, morally improving and politically satirical. It was initially a quasi-shamanic art practised by men, with women coming into the frame in the late nineteenth century. In 1964 it was declared an Intangible Cultural Property, and in 2003 UNESCO added it to its list of protected musics. Ahn is one of her country's leading exponents of this art, and after her performance she gives me a brief sketch of her credo and career.

We met in London in 2019. It's a shock to see her close-up – a little old lady whose self-effacing demeanour wouldn't earn her a second glance in the street. She was born in 1949 in the city of Namwon, the birthplace of *p'ansori*, and at nine she started taking lessons in it. 'But I was alone in my enthusiasm – everyone else I knew regarded it as a dusty relic of the past,' she tells me through an interpreter. 'I set out to acquire all the techniques – I trained so hard that my teacher feared I might injure myself, make myself ill.' A child prodigy, she joined a group of older musicians to give performances in private homes, there being no suitable public stages at the time. 'And when, later, I joined the National Theatre of Korea and watched other masters at work, I understood that p'ansori was a great art form. And I had a sudden moment of clarity – that I could create my own p'ansori, do it my way. My performances now are never the same. Some days I focus on the drama, some days the music is the main thing, and sometimes it's the virtuosity. I improvise a lot.'

In musical terms the techniques she had to master consisted of a complex system of melodic modes and rhythmic patterns; the punishing things were physical, given that the solo singer – whose vocal range needs to be at least three octaves – must somehow evoke massed battles, storms at sea, and armies of extras. As the British ethnomusicologist (and *p'ansori* performer) Anna Yates-Lu has pointed out, 'all they have is their fan, their voice, and their handkerchief. They traditionally seek out waterfalls against which to match their power, to develop the husky tone their art demands: it's achieved by intentionally scarring the vocal cords, tearing their throat muscles to make them bigger. They believe you have to suffer to sing well.'

Ahn certainly believes this, but she also draws inspiration from those water-falls: 'Some are thunderous, but others whisper gently: it can be the sound of the wind, or of ordinary people talking. It can be the sound of sadness, or anger. Imitating their sounds became a spiritual journey for me.' Then, dreamily, she expands on text and subtext, and on that spiritual dimension.

> Even if the audience can't understand the language, they can hear the emotions. All you have, and all you need, are the three elements – the singer, the percussionist, and the audience to respond. The challenge is to convey the meaning beneath the banter. When p'ansori is at its best you can feel your heart stop beating. It doesn't express the simplified emotions of pop music – it's about the complexity of human feelings, particularly suffering. It's the complete expression of your soul.

Ahn may be speaking in a muted monotone, but as she makes this speech she radiates visionary intensity.

In her long career Ahn has consistently pushed out the boundaries of her art form, creating her own *p'ansori* stories and melding them with other styles.

She's also encouraged younger singers – notably the charismatic Jun-Su Kim, whose androgynous performances have made him a *p'ansori* pop-idol – to give the art form contemporary relevance. When South Korea's president was impeached for corruption in 2016, satirical *p'ansori* accounts of the case appeared on YouTube; *p'ansori* competitions go on all over the country, as Japan's competitions for *min'yo* folk singers do, and as do the bardic *eisteddfod* tradition in Wales and the proliferating variants on 'Britain's Got Talent'. As the demotic counterpart to Korea's ceremonial court music, *p'ansori* is a unique art form, and thanks to Ahn, Jun-Su, and their friends, it's being saved from extinction, and developed in new directions.

Until North was separated from South in 1945, *p'ansori* had belonged to the entire peninsula, and ideologues of the new government of the North initially tried to make it conform to their new political orthodoxy. But in a speech on literature and art in 1964, the Dear Leader Kim Il Sung cast it into outer darkness. 'P'ansori does not inspire the people, nor arouse them to struggle,' he declared. 'It is utterly ridiculous to imagine soldiers rushing into battle inspired by p'ansori.' And he attacked the typically rasping *p'ansori* voice: 'Koreans generally have beautiful voices, and it's really terrible to hear a good-looking girl make hoarse sounds … That hoarse noise should definitely be eliminated.'

Keith Howard, the leading Western authority on Korean music, doubts whether *p'ansori* has a future in the North. And Ahn admits that in today's commercialised musical hurly-burly it speaks to a niche audience, and even in the South must be fought for: 'P'ansori has many ancestors, and it may not have so many descendants. There were once twelve standard p'ansori epics, but now there are only five. But it will never die.' At the end of our talk she takes my hand in both of hers with such tenderness that it might have been that swallow with the broken leg.

Sources

Keith Howard's *Preserving Korean Music* sets *p'ansori* efficiently in its social and historical context, as does at greater length the same author's excellent *Songs for 'Great Leaders'*.

Bibliography

Howard, Keith, *Preserving Korean Music: Intangible Cultural Properties as Icons of Identity* (Farnham: Ashgate, 2006)

Howard, Keith, *Songs for 'Great Leaders': Ideology and Creativity in North Korean Music and Dance* (London: Oxford University Press, 2020)

49 Kodo in action with the *miya-daiko* drums.

25

'My whole body was singing'

Kodo and the *taiko* drum

INSTRUMENTAL REVIVALS CAN crop up in unlikely places: the power-house behind the current *taiko* craze – mushrooming on every continent – is to be found on the ruggedly windswept island of Sado in the Sea of Japan. In medieval times, Sado was a place of exile to which shoguns consigned their political enemies, one of whom was the fourteenth-century dramatist Zeami Motokiyo, the father of Noh theatre. 'When I go there,' said the Japanese director Yukio Ninagawa, as he presented *The Tempest* as a Noh rehearsal on Sado, 'I hear the voices of the dead.'

Sado is beautiful in summer, but in winter it's a desolate place whose inhabitants scratch a meagre living from fishing and rice-growing. Since labouring in the paddy-fields holds no charms for the young, they now routinely migrate to the mainland cities. Yet young people of a different, somewhat masochistic stamp are queuing up to enrol for a two-year *taiko* drumming apprenticeship on Sado, and are ready to endure rigours reminiscent of a Siberian penal colony to do so.

Fancy starting your day at 6.00am with a six-kilometre run up and down a steep mountain path – no rests allowed, and no walking, in all weathers including snow? Thereafter your day will be rigidly timetabled, with relentless drilling on drums interspersed with intensive training in a wide range of performance arts, until you tumble into bed from exhaustion at 10.00pm. There's no TV in your dormitory, and you're not allowed to smoke, drink alcohol, or have sex. And how are your woodwork skills? You'll need some, because you must fashion your own drumsticks from the hardwood block you're given at the outset. And will you miss your mobile? There's just one landline shared with everyone else which you're allowed to use when you feel a bit lonesome and want to call home. Residents at Her Majesty's prisons have it cushy in comparison.

Kodo is the name of the company which these apprentices – now increasingly female – hope to join after they graduate, but with a mandatory probationary year, followed by a further weeding-out, most don't make the final cut. Although it's by no means the only professional company focusing on *taiko* drumming, Kodo is the best-known internationally. And its innovative aesthetic has spawned imitators, while several of its home-grown stars have gone on to found companies of their own.

For the Japanese the *taiko* – 'fat drum' – has a legendary origin. It began with Amaterasu, goddess of the sun, being lured from her cave by the sound of another goddess dancing on top of an empty sake barrel. The earliest historical evidence of its introduction to Japan from China dates from the sixth century CE, and it has had multiple functions. These include providing the soundtrack for temple rituals, and for sending messages over long distances: Atsushi Sugano, director of the Kodo cultural foundation, claims that on a still day the big drums can be heard three miles away. The sound of *taiko* is the heart of a summer festival, and it was also used for firing up combatants in war; in the sixteenth century, different patterns of beat were used to order an advance or a retreat, to summon an ally or pursue an enemy. Moreover, *taiko* drumming has always been integral to *gagaku* court music, and to the theatres of Noh and Kabuki.

Taiko drums come in many shapes and sizes, from the sharply resonant little *shime-daiko*, to the barrel-shaped *miya-daiko* for which the players lie back in an Easy Rider position and grip the drum between their calves, to the giant *odaiko* which is hollowed out of a single block of wood, and which can weigh 400 kilos and be two metres in diameter. It was only in the 1950s that the contrasts in their timbres were exploited to create a concert art, thanks to a jazz musician named Daihachi Oguchi inventing an ensemble style known as *kumi-daiko*. And the timing was right: the popularity of *taiko* had languished during Japan's self-hating post-war years, but with a modernising society rapidly losing its links with traditional culture, *taiko* came to be a symbol of continuity.

It was *kumi-daiko* which a visionary musicologist named Den Tagayasu taught at the summer school he set up on Sado in 1970, adopting as the house style a muscular tradition unique to Sado called *ondeko* ('demon drumming'). Some students stayed on to form a permanent commune which Den christened Ondekoza; their purpose was to reinvigorate Japan's regional musical forms, and take them round the world. Members followed a ferociously Spartan regime, limbering up for their assault on the drums by running twenty kilometres every day; in 1975 they astonished the crowd at the Boston Marathon by picking up their drumsticks at the finishing line, and launching without pause into a thunderous riff.

But Den grew cranky, and after ten gruelling years there was a schism, with most of the group seceding en masse and renaming themselves Kodo. And in this name there was a felicitous double meaning: its written characters mean 'drum child', but an infinitesimally different stressing of the second syllable will give you the character which means 'heartbeat'. The company regard this accidental ambiguity as a symbolic blessing from the gods.

When I visited Kodo in 1993 I was assured that the rigours of the Den era had given way to a mellower life-style, but I didn't see much sign of that – the daily run, with nobody exempt, started at 5.30am, and you could smell the asceticism in the air. Returning in 2019, I was struck by how little had changed in the intervening time, including the personnel. I had remembered Chieko Kojima as a bewitching dancer, and Yoko Fujimoto as a compelling singer of *min'yo* folk songs, and here they were again, still charismatic in their sixties and pursuing successful solo careers. 'Then Kodo was a family,' says Chieko. 'Now it's a real company, where everyone is respected as an artist, whether they are a drummer, singer, or dancer.'

Here too were Motofumi Yamaguchi – in 1993 the company's democratically elected artistic director – now happily officiating as its lead flautist, and Eiichi Saito, at fifty-six another of the company's veterans, who in his spare time leads *taiko* workshops for elderly people fighting off dementia.

And by 2019 things really had mellowed. Company members no longer had to do the cooking and cleaning; they were now allowed to marry, and to sleep in flats in town rather than in a dormitory. But the *shime-daiko* players still had to tighten the tuning ropes on their drums each day – a job which takes two people twenty strenuous minutes – and there was no let-up in the life of the apprentices, whose cooking and cleaning duties scarcely left them time to eat. The way they laid out their personal chopsticks between meals reflected their instinctive communal discipline better than any words could convey: each pair, beautifully carved to a design by its owner, was lined up with the others in a formation as immaculate as the drummers' presence on stage. The young Swiss woman I persuaded to give me a few words over her shoulder – while she served her turn as cook – wouldn't have wanted to be anywhere else: 'It's tough, but I love it, even the morning runs.' After graduating she planned to take the *taiko* message round the world. Not everyone stays the course: social media is a drug some can't live without.

The company's rehearsal room is full of mirrors in front of which they bend, stretch, arch, and tense as dancers do, and when a performance starts you realise why. Unlike Western drummers, who operate from the wrist, these men and women drum with their whole body, often in punishing positions. Back injuries used to be the commonest reason for quitting the game, but they're now much reduced, thanks to anatomically intelligent training. With the *odaiko* you feel the sound as a thump in the chest and a pulsing through the soles of your feet, and you begin to appreciate the rich sound-world which can be created by one perfectly placed stroke on that giant combination of wood and hide.

Legacy, the programme with which Kodo were touring the world in 2020 until Covid-19 brought them to a halt, is a majestic showcase for their communal art. It's a kaleidoscopic sequence of pieces in which choral and *min'yo* interludes, or pieces for bamboo flute plus *koto* zither, oil the transitions between the set-piece drumming works, each of which is a musical drama deserving to be taken as seriously as any piece by Steve Reich. Beautifully lit, with the male performers in their trademark bandanas and *fundoshi* loincloths, it's a feast for the eyes as well as a celebration of virtuosity.

And I am as entranced by the physical drama as I am by the musical one: the men attacking the *miya-daikos* with quasi-murderous intent; the women's left hands flashing faster than the eye could register as they pummel both ends of their double-headed drums; the line of Buddha-like *shime-daiko* players conjuring up shimmering sonic worlds. These begin with a delicate susurration, the sticks propelled by nothing more than their own weight; then they bring the volume up to a boil which makes the hall shake, before embarking on an antiphonal conversation where each drummer takes his or her turn in the limelight. The arrival of the *odaiko* – reverently prayed to, before it is played – marks the grand climax of an evening which, though often extremely loud, never once hurts the ears.

One of the pieces consists of a shamanic dance from Mongolia, accompanied by an oboe and two six-foot horns: the Kodo aesthetic is nothing if not eclectic. Their policy is to reach out to other cultures, and is best exemplified by the Earth Celebration which they stage on Sado every August. This is where they collect and share melodies and ideas, collaborating with drummers and singers from Burundi, South Africa, Korea, Vietnam, India, and Trinidad. Their current collaboration is with the avant-garde French-Canadian director Robert Lepage, whose Cirque du Soleil aesthetic will, they hope, meld productively with their own. As the young Kodo drummer Ryotaro Leo Ikenaga puts it: 'We are now creating a new identity for the company, and we can take risks because we know we always have our core to come back to, the essential classical Kodo aesthetic. The tree remains strong.'

Taiko drumming may be rooted in Shinto and Zen, but Kodo's often lighthearted art has no explicit connexion with religion, or with the fanaticism of the Den years – indeed, they wince at any mention of 'demon' or 'kamikaze'. Defections, when they occur, tend to be amicable: some players eventually find the Kodo style too restricting, and cross over into jazz and other forms as their erstwhile hand-cymbal virtuoso Ryotaro Kaneko has done; he is now a star in his own right.

But at the deepest level Kodo's art is indeed religious. Why else would they not consign their broken drum-sticks to the waste bin, but instead burn them ceremonially as sacred objects? There's a sacramental seriousness in everything they do. Seventy-year-old Yoshikazu Fujimoto, who has spent his entire adult life first with Ondekoza and then with Kodo, speaks with profound reverence for his encounters with the giant drum: 'Before I start drumming, I pray, "Please let me play you". And I am told, "OK, you may play me". We become one. And as I play, I feel at peace. I become the sound.'

When I ask Ryotaro Leo Ikenaga about his earliest musical experience, he gives a mystical reply: 'It came when I was three. I was under a cherry blossom tree, and the leaves were fluttering in the spring wind. I know this may not sound like music to Westerners.' And as with many other Kodo players, his dreams are musical: 'In my best dream I was falling through space in bright light, and singing very loudly.' He looks down at his muscular forearms: 'I was singing with every limb. My whole body was singing.'

Sources

There is no history of Japanese drumming as such, but David W. Hughes's *Traditional Folk Song in Modern Japan* sets it efficiently in its wider context. Yoko Fujimoto has just released a CD entitled *Yume no Utsutsu* which might best be described as a love song to Sado and its culture, with traditional lullabies and songs for every season; her delicately inflected folk-singing is supported by drumming and birdsong.

Bibliography and recordings

Hughes, David W., *Traditional Folk Song in Modern Japan* (Folkstone: Global Oriental, 2008)
Yume no Utsutsu, Yoko Fujimoto with Kodo drummers, Otodaiku Co, OD-023

50 Keepers of the flame: a traditional dance at a Bon festival in Kanagawa, Japan, in 2015.

26

'Intangible cultural heritage'

UNESCO's lengthening list

WHEN TRADITIONAL MUSIC is politically useful, its preservation becomes government policy. Japan, perennially obsessed with preserving its cultural uniqueness, led the field in this respect with its Law for the Protection of Cultural Properties in 1950. Its 35-year occupation of Korea inspired a similar decree in that country; Taiwan followed suit, and there were parallel movements elsewhere. 'Living treasures', or their equivalent, were singled out and celebrated in Thailand, the Philippines, France, and Romania; in Uzbekistan and Kyrgyzstan; in Latvia, Lithuania, and the Czech Republic; and in Vietnam and the Lao Republic; 'perishing professions' like music and theatre became protected in Poland. But it was UNESCO – which in 1961 had begun sponsoring recordings of traditional music – which turned all this into a global campaign.

Prompted by Egypt's flooding of the Abu Simbel temples as well as by Venice's ecological plight, UNESCO's 1964 Venice Charter established the principle of protection for buildings, from which it was but a short step to the protection of 'intangibles'. It issued a mission statement arguing that cultural heritage should be protected, including 'the works of its artists, architects, musicians, writers, and scientists, and also the work of anonymous artists, expressions of a people's spirituality, and the body of values which give meaning to life'. It then broadened the issue to take account of the damage caused by 'colonialism, armed conflict, foreign occupation and the imposition of foreign values: all these have the effect of severing a people's links with – and obliterating the memory of – its past.' Wise words, which could make a perfect epigraph for this book. In 2003 UNESCO agreed the Convention for Safeguarding of the Intangible Cultural Heritage, and in 2008 it began listing the genres to be defined and enshrined.

It has not all been music: Kirkpinar oil-wrestling and Croatian gingerbread craft have been among the genres singled out, as has, preposterously, the 'French restaurant meal', but the musical choices in the project's first year could not be faulted. Uzbek-Tadjik *shashmaqom*, Pygmy polyphony, and Iraqi *maqam* had all been on the danger list, and all were indeed treasurable. In 2009 an additional list was created for genres 'in need of urgent safeguarding', with Vietnamese *ca trù* singing – one of the most delicately calibrated styles in the world, and definitely in need of protection – as its first element. Nominations in the following years came thick and fast, with Tibetan opera, the Iranian *radif,* Japanese *gagaku*, Portuguese *fado*, Greek *rebetiko*, and Dominican *merengue* all being added to the pile.

But where folklore is concerned, UNESCO should tread carefully. An eighteenth-century Easter ritual revived in 2019 in the Polish town of Pruchnik had a straw 'Jew' with hooked nose and *payot* sidelocks dragged through the streets, beaten with sticks, and burnt at the stake: in a country with anti-Semitism newly rampant, this was hardly a thing to celebrate. In the same year in Belgium, UNESCO was petitioned to remove its 'intangible heritage' blessing from a carnival, one of whose stock characters was a 'savage' in blackface wearing a chain round his neck and a ring through his nose; two weeks later a similar row broke out over Morris dancers in blackface at a carnival in the Yorkshire town of Settle. At a Croatian village carnival last year, a gay couple were burnt in effigy.

Another worm in the UNESCO bud is aggressive nationalism. When the People's Republic of China was consolidating control of its 'autonomous regions' in the 1950s, the Uyghur 'twelve muqam' – the classical music of Xinjiang – became one of the minority art forms selected for preservation. And when UNESCO launched its list, China proudly announced its ownership of Uyghur music, and was not gainsaid (China's current activities in Xinjiang no longer include the promotion of Uyghur music). Moreover China, which easily tops the international league in terms of the number of its listed 'intangible heritage' genres, has also laid claim to *Arirang* folk song (which belongs to Korea), and to the *Manas* epic (which indisputably belongs to Kyrgyzstan).

No money accompanies the UNESCO accolade, so unless governments are provoked into responding with increased subsidy, struggling art forms just have to struggle on. But an interesting profit-and-loss account of governmental heritage schemes in East Asia – and the UNESCO scheme in particular – is to be found in the essays of Keith Howard's *Music as Intangible Cultural Heritage*.

From Matt Gillan in Okinawa comes an unequivocal thumbs-up: thanks to enthusiastic state support, traditional arts are flourishing there as never before. The *sanshin* lute, long the national emblem, is now itself a protected species, in that such historically important instruments may not be exported; the Japanese government's requirement that secondary schools must include traditional Japanese music in the curriculum has given the *sanshin* a further boost.

In an essay on the heritage movement in China, Helen Rees notes the remarkable resurgence of the *qin* zither, both as an instrument for professionals and as a recreational pursuit, often in tandem with literature and calligraphy. She also notes that folk songs are now revealingly referred to by the Chinese as 'original ecology' songs. Two-thirds of a large sample of undergraduate essays she examined chose to focus on the death of local musics: the West's Extinction Rebellion movement has many sympathisers in China.

Some essays in Howard's book underline problematic aspects of the UNESCO operation. Howard's own report from Korea focuses on a long-running dispute between Confucian groups and the Korean Office of Cultural Properties, over which versions of the country's sacrificial rites are truly authentic. Earlier versions, officially enshrined, have been challenged by later versions which differ in everything from costumes and choreography to the correct dates for observance, and whether the celebrants should drink wine or tea. The vigour of this seemingly arcane dispute is testimony to the enduring power which these rites still possess for a nation whose embrace of modernity is only skin-deep.

The Yi womenfolk of Sichuan have traditionally made a two-leafed bamboo mouth harp called a *hxohxo* for their menfolk to play, and an essay in Howard's volume by Olivia Kraef chronicles its rescue from near-oblivion thanks to a concerted publicity campaign, after the local prefecture decreed that it should be their prime cultural-heritage item. But Kraef also touches on a theme which runs through much of the book: the unwelcome side-effects of officially promoted 'ethnic tourism'. According to Ying-fen Wang, who writes about the *nanguan* music of Taiwan, state sponsorship of that refined ensemble art has been little short of disastrous. Until the state started to subsidise and promote it, says Wang, *nanguan* was a pastime for cultivated amateurs. The last thirty years may have seen its professionalisation, she says, but the music itself has been theatricalised and vulgarised.

She winds up by calling the entire heritage industry into question: 'It is time for the state to stop using nanguan as a tool for soft diplomacy, for promoting cultural tourism and the heritage industry, and as a way to prove itself part of the international community by responding to UNESCO's call for the preservation of heritage.' There are musicians and musicologists in many parts of the world who would regretfully echo that sentiment.

But many more would cheer UNESCO to the rafters for the uncompromising clarity of its credo: 'To be kept alive, intangible cultural heritage must be relevant to the community, continuously recreated, and transmitted from one generation to another.' The old museum-culture approach has been replaced by something dynamic: leading practitioners are now being encouraged to pass on their skills, and to experiment with new forms. And in the case of Central Asian *shashmaqom*, for example, this policy has been successful. Twenty years ago it was on the musical equivalent of life-support, but thanks to a UNES-CO-backed initiative by the Aga Khan Trust for Culture, plus the fact that Uzbekistan and Tajikistan are now both brandishing it as part of their national heritage, this music now looks fit enough – well almost – to emerge from intensive care, and make its way unaided.

The most subtle analysis of the issues discussed in this chapter comes from the musicologist David Hughes in *Music as Heritage: Historical and Ethnographic Perspectives*. Hughes's unique insights into Japanese *min'yo* folk music derive from his unusual career: not only has he followed the fortunes of specific singers (and songs) over several decades, he's also appeared on stage and TV in Japan as a charismatic *min'yo* singer, and as a *min'yo* competition judge.

Taking as his text the Japanese maxim 'Folk song is the heart's home town', Hughes charts the trajectories of seven songs, and asks what role local 'preservation societies' and government recognition might have played – or might yet play – in their survival. In some cases the songs have withered on the vine because the last singers who knew them have died; with Western music's hegemony establishing itself ever more firmly among the young, the *min'yo* audience grows ever older (though with Japan's population steadily ageing, that is no great problem). And as the manual trades on which songs were founded die – for example, threshing with flails – so inevitably do the songs. But they can still remain emotional rallying-points for those who have grown up with them. As one member of a preservation society tells Hughes, apropos the threshing song of a village near Tokyo: 'Young folks today haven't experienced suffering. We [elders] know what it's like to do manual labour, and the experience is valuable in building good human beings.'

When folk songs become standardised, notated, and turned into art music, their original spirit and energy can be lost. Japanese songs which in their original context would have been unaccompanied are given instrumental and vocal backing on television; those which were originally sung in unison are tricked out with backing choruses. Hughes notes that a female singer of the rousing Yodo River boat song fails to pass muster in a competition because she has *shakuhachi* accompaniment and lacks what one judge describes as the necessary 'stinking mud' timbre.

Hughes's most surprising case study concerns a graceful *shakuhachi*-accompanied song from a small town on Hokkaido entitled 'Esashi Oiwake'. It was sung by herring fishermen in the nineteenth century, but when the industry departed and a new railway bypassed the town, recession set in; town officials decided to make the song their anthem for urban renewal. They made its singers wear formal dress, and insisted that they stick to a standardised version which was notated down to the smallest ornamental curlicue; in 1977 the song was designated a Hokkaido Prefectural Intangible Folk Cultural Property. Its now-annual contest draws hundreds of entrants from all over the country, who must first pass through preliminary competitions; the Esashi Oiwake Association has 159 branches and 3,600 members, and its contest (along with the related museum) attracts 25,000 visitors; a teacher is on hand to help tourists learn the song. No need here for a UNESCO designation: civic pride has done the job.

Hughes concludes that there are limits to what subsidy can do to preserve songs which don't have a spontaneous groundswell of communal support. Teaching folk songs at home or in school may help, and he stresses the value of that: they deepen historical awareness, and strengthen local identity. But as to whether UNESCO recognition is the grail, Hughes remains agnostic. It could, he says, be as much a burden as a blessing.

Sources

UNESCO's ever-lengthening list of protected musical forms is regularly updated on the internet; Keith Howard's *Music as Intangible Cultural Heritage* and Norton and Matsumoto's *Music as Heritage* offer a useful *tour d'horizon*.

Bibliography

Howard, Keith, ed., *Music as Intangible Cultural Heritage: Policy, Ideology, and Practice in the Preservation of East Asian Traditions* (London: Routledge, 2012) [chapters by Matt Gillan, Helen Rees, Keith Howard, Olivia Kraef, and Ying-fen Wang]

Hughes, David W., 'Safe-guarding the Heart's Home Town', in Barley Norton and Naomi Matsumoto, eds, *Music as Heritage: Historical and Ethnographic Perspectives* (London: Routledge, 2019)

51 Calabrian tuna fishermen singing as they turn the capstan,
photographed by Alan Lomax in 1954.

27

Going, going...

Disappearing musics

IF THIS BOOK has an underlying theme, it's the need to catch music before it disappears: this is what drives all song collectors. Two centuries ago the German collector Ludolf Parisius wrote: 'Whoever wants to collect from the mouth of the people should hurry; folk songs are disappearing one after another.' Writing in 1940, Béla Bartók ringingly declared: 'One day all folk music will have been swept away.' Meanwhile Percy Grainger was pointing to the force which many people today regard as the destroyer of indigenous music: 'We see on all hands the victorious on-march of our ruthless Western civilisation, and the distressing spectacle of the gentle but complex native arts, wilting before its irresistible simplicity.' Soon, he said, folk music in Europe would be dead.

These predictions were in some senses wrong – folk music still thrives in many forms – but in other senses they were also right. They were right about the consequences of Westernisation, industrialisation, and urbanisation; they were right about the musical losses following the death of villages.

Look at the songs which Alan Lomax collected in the Fifties in Spain, Portugal, Italy, and the Bahamas. A great many of them had evolved as integral facets of manual work: the Bahaman sponge fishermen's polyphonic spirituals, the salt-miners' songs in Sicily, the stone-cutters' songs in Liguria; threshing and harvest songs, songs to accompany the making of shoes, or pots and pans for the kitchen. Consider the shirt-making and glove-sewing songs which Cecil Sharp collected in Somerset, or the sea shanties he collected on a quay beside the Bristol Channel. Consider the song which the ploughmen sang, and Komitas transcribed, while mounted on their twelve-ox leviathan in the Armenian province of Lori. Many of these songs had a structure reflecting the ritualised movements of the work they accompanied: they had no existence independently of the trade of which they formed an integral part.

All this work is now done by machines. Take away the physical activity, and you take away the meaning of the song, its purpose, its force; you neuter it. Very few of the peasant songs which Alan Lomax collected in Europe sixty years ago are sung today, except as folklore lovingly preserved in aspic. They're gone, because the reasons for their existence are gone.

The issue is often less a matter of individual songs than of entire lifestyles. Theodor Strehlow, dedicated to the study of Aboriginal music and poetry, was only exaggerating a little when he wrote: 'I am recording *the sunset of an age* that will never return – every act that I see is being performed for the last time, and the men who are with me have no successors. When they die, they will take all their knowledge to the grave with them – except that part which I have recorded.' Eighty years ago the Canadian composer Colin McPhee, who recovered musical forms in Bali which had almost died out, modestly claimed that he'd 'succeeded in helping prolong the past. To delay it, even for a day, was my one wish.'

A hundred years ago the pioneering American collector Alice C. Fletcher noted the ubiquity of music in Omaha Indian culture: 'There is not a phase of life that does not find expression in song. Religious rituals are embedded in it, the reverent recognition of the creation of the corn, of the food-giving animals, of the fructifying sun, is passed from one generation to another.' Yet her sad conclusion, after decades of fieldwork, was this: 'The Omahas as a tribe have ceased to exist; therefore there can be no speculation upon any future development of Omaha Indian music'. Henceforth, she declared, her business had to be not the anatomy of music, but its archaeology.

One could attempt an inventory of lost musics, starting with the recordings in Wergo's box celebrating the centenary of the Berlin Phonogramm-Archiv. What tourist in present-day Ibiza would imagine that within living memory its villages echoed at Christmas with male-voice carols growled in a unique throat-trill style? Visitors to Malta before its culture became Europeanised would have been treated to *ghana* competitions in bars, with male falsettists vying to deliver impromptu rhymed verses with a killer punch. I would be amazed if it were still possible to hear the immaculate call-and-response song which Friedrich Weiss recorded from some boatmen in Sichuan in 1912.

But you never know with 'lost' songs: there's often somebody, somewhere, rediscovering and performing them. However, certain generalisations are widely agreed to be true, chief of which is that where villages decant their inhabitants into cities, folk music dies. This applies to most of Western Europe, and much of North America. Whole musical categories have disappeared, from work songs to lullabies, from calendar songs (celebrating the seasons and religious festivals) to songs marking key moments in the life-cycle (births, comings of age, marriages, deaths). Only in those regions where village traditions still flourish does folk music still thrive: in India, Pakistan, Turkey, and Iran; in much of Africa and South America; and also in China, where, despite a nation-wide rush to the cities, fifty per cent of the inhabitants still live in villages. But as our chapter on contemporary Chinese village music indicates, folk music's purchase on life can be tenuous.

Moreover, war and persecution are taking their toll, with China's policy of obliterating Uyghur culture in all its forms setting a dreadful precedent. Religious zealots in Mali and Senegal now have musicians in their sights. And with ongoing anarchy in Syria, Iraq, and Libya, exponents of the Middle East's most venerable musical traditions have had to take refuge abroad. Who would now go looking for Jewish liturgical chants in Yemen?

And how much longer will local amateurs go on singing complex Albanian Lab polyphony? How much longer will Vietnamese *ca trù*, the exquisite chamber music of Hanoi, continue to be sung? At present these art forms – both on UNESCO's list – depend for their support on foreign enthusiasts. With every year that passes, the catalogue of musical disappearances noted in this book will lengthen.

Sources

Books and articles

Abram, Dave and Jerome Lewis, 'Pygmy Music: Forest Songs from the Congo Basin', in Simon Broughton, Mark Ellingham, and Jon Lusk, eds, *The Rough Guide to World Music* (London: Rough Guides, 2006), 304–12

Amiot, Jean-Joseph-Marie, *Mémoire sur la musique des Chinois, tant anciens que modernes* (Paris: 1779)

Asch, Moses and Alan Lomax, eds, *The Leadbelly Songbook* (New York: Oak Publications, 1962)

Baily, John, 'John Blacking and his Place in Ethnomusicology', *Yearbook for Traditional Music*, vol. 22 (1990), xi–xxi

Baily, John, *Music of Afghanistan: Professional Musicians in the City of Herat* (Cambridge: Cambridge University Press, 1988)

Baily, John, *Songs from Kabul: The Spiritual Music of Ustad Amir Mohammad* (Farnham: Ashgate, 2011)

Baily, John, *War, Exile, and the Music of Afghanistan: The Ethnographer's Tale* (Farnham: Ashgate, 2015)

Baring-Gould, S., *Further Reminiscences: 1864–1894* (London: John Lane The Bodley Head Ltd, 1925)

Bate, Jonathan, *John Clare: A Biography* (London: Picador, 2003)

Bird, John, *Percy Grainger* (London: Paul Elek, 1976)

Blacking, John, *Venda Children's Songs* (Johannesburg: Witwatersrand University Press, 1967)

Bluestein, Gene, 'Moses Asch, Documentor', *American Music*, vol. 5, no. 3 (Autumn 1987), 291–304

Bowles, Paul, *The Sheltering Sky* (London: Penguin, 1949)

Bowles, Paul, *Their Heads Are Green* (London: Abacus, 1990)

Bowles, Paul, *Without Stopping: An Autobiography* (London: Peter Owen, 1972)

Bragg, Billy, *Roots, Radicals and Rockers: How Skiffle Changed the World* (London: Faber, 2017)

Brennan, Ian, *How Music Dies (or Lives)*, New York: Allworth Press, 2016

Brocken, Michael, *The British Folk Revival* (London: Ashgate, 2003)

Callimachi, Scarlat, *Demetrius Cantemir* (Bucharest: Meridiane, 1966)

Carlin, Richard, *Worlds of Sound* (New York: Collins, 2008)

Chalmers, Kenneth, *Béla Bartók* (London: Phaidon, 1995)

Cohen, Ronald D., ed., *Alan Lomax: Selected Writings 1934–1997* (New York: Routledge, 2003)

Cole, Douglas, *Franz Boas: The Early Years, 1858–1906* (Seattle: University of Washington Press, 1999)

Cooley, Timothy J., 'Folk Music in Eastern Europe', in Philip V. Bohlman, ed., *The Cambridge History of World Music* (Cambridge: Cambridge University Press, 2013), 352–70

Cooper, David, *Béla Bartók* (London: Yale University Press, 2015)

De Lisle, Tim, *Lives of the Great Songs* (London: Penguin, 1994)

Demény, János, ed., *Béla Bartók Letters* (London: Faber, 1971)

Densmore, Frances, 'The Study of Indian Music in the Nineteenth Century', *American Anthropologist*, vol. 29, issue 1 (1927), 77–86

Djajadiningrat, Madelon and Clara Brinkgreve, 'A Musical Friendship: The Correspondence between Mangkunegoro VII and the Ethnomusicologist Jaap Kunst, 1919 to 1940', in Bart Barendregt and Els Bogaerts, eds, *Recollecting Resonances* (Leiden: Brill, 2014), 179–201

Doubleday, Veronica, *Three Women of Herat* (London: Jonathan Cape, 1988)

Du Halde, J. B., *Description géographique, historique, chronologique, politique et physique de l'empire de la Chine et de la Tartarie chinoise* (Paris: 1735)

During, Jean, *Musiques d'Asie Centrale* (Paris: Cité de la Musique, 1998)

Ellis, Catherine J., *Aboriginal Music Making: A Study of Central Australian Music* (Adelaide: State Libraries Board of South Australia, 1964)

Engel, Carl, *The Literature of National Music* (London: Novello, 1879)

Fauser, Annegret, *Musical Encounters at the 1889 Paris World's Fair* (New York: University of Rochester Press, 2005)

Fillmore, John Comfort, 'Report on the Structural Peculiarities of the Music', in Alice C. Fletcher, *A Study of Omaha Indian Music*, introduction by Helen Myers (Lincoln, NE: University of Nebraska Press, Bison Books, 1994)

Fletcher, Alice C., *A Study of Omaha Indian Music*, introduction by Helen Myers (Lincoln, NE: University of Nebraska Press, Bison Books, 1994)

Fox Strangways, A. H., *Cecil Sharp* (London: Oxford University Press, 1933)

Fürniss, Susanne, 'The Adoption of the Circumcision Ritual Beka by the Baka-Pygmies in Southeast Cameroon', *African Music*, vol. 8, no. 2 (2008), 94–113

Fürniss, Susanne, 'Recherches ethnomusicologiques en Afrique centrale', *Analyse musicale*, vol. 75 (2014), 84–90

Gillies, Malcolm, *Bartók Remembered* (London: Faber, 1990)

Gillies, Malcolm, ed., *The Bartók Companion* (London: Faber, 1993)

Gillies, Malcolm, David Pear, and Mark Carroll, eds, *Self-Portrait of Percy Grainger* (Oxford: Oxford University Press, 2006)

Grainger, Percy, 'The Impress of Personality in Unwritten Music', *Musical Quarterly*, vol. 1, no. 3 (July 1915), 416–35

Hagège, Lucille and Susanne Fürniss, 'The Story behind the Music', *CNRS International Magazine*, vol. 9 (October 2007)

Harker, Dave, *Fakesong: The Manufacture of British 'Folksong', 1700 to the Present Day* (Milton Keynes: Open University Press, 1985)

Hill, Barry, *Broken Song: TGH Strehlow and Aboriginal Possession* (Vintage, Knopf: Sydney, 2002)

Howard, Keith, *Preserving Korean Music: Intangible Cultural Properties as Icons of Identity* (Farnham: Ashgate, 2006)

Howard, Keith, *Songs for 'Great Leaders': Ideology and Creativity in North Korean Music and Dance* (London: Oxford University Press, 2020)

Howard, Keith, ed., *Music as Intangible Cultural Heritage: Policy, Ideology, and Practice in the Preservation of East Asian Traditions* (London: Routledge, 2012) [chapters by Matt Gillan, Helen Rees, Keith Howard, Olivia Kraef, and Ying-fen Wang]

Hughes, David W., 'Safe-guarding the Heart's Home Town', in Barley Norton and Naomi Matsumoto, eds, *Music as Heritage: Historical and Ethnographic Perspectives* (London: Routledge, 2019)

Hughes, David W., *Traditional Folk Song in Modern Japan* (Folkstone: Global Oriental, 2008)

Ingólfsson, Árni Heimir, *Jón Leifs and the Musical Invention of Iceland* (Bloomington: Indiana University Press, 2019)

Jacknis, Ira, 'Beyond Boas? Re-assessing the Contribution of "Informant" and "Research Assistant"', in *Franz Boas and the Music of the Northwest Coast Indians, From Constructing Cultures Then and Now* (Washington, DC: Arctic Studies Centre, Smithsonian Institution, 2003)

Jones, Stephen, *Folk Music of China* (London: Clarendon Press, 1995)

Jones, Stephen, *Plucking the Winds: Lives of Village Musicians in Old and New China* (Leiden: Chime Foundation, 2004)

Jones, Stephen, *Ritual and Music of North China: Shawm Bands in Shanxi* (Aldershot: Ashgate, 2007)

Jordania, Joseph, 'Georgia', in Timothy Rice, James Porter, and Chris Goertzen, eds, *The Garland Encyclopedia of World Music: Europe* (London: Routledge, 2002)

Karpeles, Maud, *Cecil Sharp – His Life and Work* (London: Routledge, 1967)

Komitas, *Armenian Sacred and Folk Music*, translated by Edward Gulbekian, introduction by V. N. Nersessian (London: Curzon, 1998)

Krader, Barbara, 'Vasil Stoin, Bulgarian Folk Song Collector', *Yearbook of the International Folk Music Council*, vol. 12 (1980), 27–42

Kuyumjian, Rita Soulahian, *Archaeology of Madness: Komitas, Portrait of an Armenian Icon* (Princeton, NJ: Gomidas Institute, 2001)

Lam, Ching-Wah, 'A Highlight of French Jesuit Scholarship in China: Jean-Joseph-Marie Amiot's Writings on Chinese Music', *CHIME: Journal of European Foundation for Chinese Music Research*, nos. 16–17 (2005), 127–47

Leclair, Madeleine and Susanne Fürniss, 'Profession: Pygmologue – Entretien avec Susanne Fürniss', *Cahiers d'ethnomusicologie*, vol. 28 (2015) 229–49

Lemny, Stefan, *Les Cantemir: l'aventure européenne d'une famille princière au XVIIIe siècle* (Paris: Complexe, 2009)

Levin, Theodore, 'Dmitri Pokrovsky and the Russian Folk Music Revival Movement', in Mark Slobin, ed., *Retuning Culture: Musical Changes in Central and Eastern Europe* (London: Duke University Press, 1996), 14–36

Levin, Theodore, *The Hundred Thousand Fools of God: Musical Travels in Central Asia* (Bloomington: Indiana University Press, 1996)

Levin, Theodore, *Where Rivers and Mountains Sing* (Bloomington: Indiana University Press, 2006)

Levin, Theodore, Saida Daukeyeva, and Elmira Köchümkulova, eds, *The Music of Central Asia* (Bloomington: Indiana University Press, 2016)

Lewisohn, Jane, 'Conservation of the Iranian Golha Radio Programmes and the Heritage of Persian Classical Poetry and Music', in Maja Kominko, ed., *From Dust to Digital: Ten Years of the Endangered Archives Programme* (Cambridge: Open Book Publishers, 2016), 587–616

Lloyd, A. L., *Folk Song in England* (London: Paladin, 1967)

Lomax, Alan, *The Land Where Blues Began* (New York: Knopf, 1993)

Lomax, Alan, Woody Guthrie, and Pete Seeger, *Hard-Hitting Songs for Hard-Hit People* (New York: Oak Publications, 1967)

Lomax, John A., *Adventures of a Ballad Hunter* (Austin: University of Texas, 2017)

Lomax, John A., *Negro Folk Songs as Sung by Lead Belly* (New York: Macmillan, 1936)

Lomax, John A. and Ruth Crawford Seeger, *Our Singing Country: Folk Songs and Ballads* (New York: Macmillan, 1941)

MacMahon, Bernard and Alison McGourty with Elijah Wald, *American Epic* (New York: Touchstone, 2017)

McNutt, James C., 'John Comfort Fillmore: A Study of Indian Music Reconsidered', *American Music*, vol. 2, no. 1 (Spring 1984), 61–70

McPhee, Colin, 'The Five-tone Gamelan Music of Bali', *Musical Quarterly*, vol. 35, issue 2 (April 1949), 250–81

McPhee, Colin, *A House in Bali* (London: Periplus Publishers, 2000)

McPhee, Colin, *Music in Bali: A Study in Form and Instrumental Organisation in Balinese Orchestral Music* (Boston: Da Capo Press, 1976)

Marett, Allan, *Songs, Dreamings, and Ghosts: The Wangga of North Australia* (Middletown, CT: Wesleyan, 2005)

Mead, Margaret, 'The Anthropology of Franz Boas', *American Anthropologist*, vol. 61, no. 5, part 2 (1959)

Melvin, Sheila and Cai Jindong, *Rhapsody in Red: How Western Classical Music Became Chinese* (New York: Algora, 2004)

Micic, Peter, 'Gathering a Nation's Music: A Life of Yang Yinliu', in Helen Rees, ed., *Lives in Chinese Music* (Urbana: Illinois University Press, 2009), 91 ff.

Miller, Jeffrey, ed., *In Touch: The Letters of Paul Bowles* (London: Flamingo, 1995)

Müller-Wille, Ludger, ed., *Franz Boas: Among the Inuit of Baffin Island, 1883–84* (Toronto: University of Toronto Press, 2016)

Myers, Helen, ed., *Ethnomusicology: Historical and Regional Studies* (New York: Norton, 1993)

Nettl, Bruno, 'North American Indian Musical Styles', *Memoirs of the American Folklore Society*, vol. 45, 1954

Nettl, Bruno and Victoria Lindsay Levine, 'Amerindian Music', *New Grove Dictionary of Music and Musicians* (London: Macmillan, 2001)

Nooshin, Laudan, *Iranian Classical Music: The Discourses and Practice of Creativity* (Farnham: Ashgate, 2015)

O'Neill, Sean, 'The Boasian Legacy in Ethnomusicology: Cultural Relativism, Narrative Texts, Linguistic Structures, and the Role of Comparison', in Regna Darnell, Michelle Hamilton, Robert L. A. Hancock, and Joshua Smith, eds, *The Franz Boas Papers*, vol. 1 (Lincoln, NE, and London: University of Nebraska Press, 2015), 129–60

Oja, Carol J., *Colin McPhee: Composer in Two Worlds* (Washington, DC: Smithsonian, 1990)

Oliver, Paul, *The Story of the Blues* (London: Barrie and Jenkins, 1969)

Park, Mungo, *Travels in the Interior Districts of Africa*, London: John Murray, 1816

Polansky, Larry, ed., *Ruth Crawford Seeger's 'The Music of American Folk Song' and Selected Other Writings* (London: University of Rochester Press, 2001)

Racy, Ali Jihad, 'Historical Worldview of Early Ethnomusicologists: An East-West Encounter in Cairo, 1932', in Stephen Blum, Philip V. Bohlman, and Daniel M. Neuman, eds, *Ethnomusicology and Modern Music History* (Chicago: Illinois University Press, 1991), 68–91

Ratliff, Ben, *Every Song Ever: Twenty Ways to Listen in an Age of Musical Plenty* (New York: Picador, 2016)

Riggs, Kirsty K., 'Bartók in the Desert: Challenges to a European Conducting Research in North Africa in the Early Twentieth Century', *Musical Quarterly*, vol. 90, issue 1 (March 2007), 72–89

Roud, Steve, *Folk Song in England* (London: Faber, 2017)

Roud, Steve and Julia Bishop, *The New Penguin Book of English Folk Songs* (London: Penguin, 2012)

Salvador-Daniel, Francisco, *The Music and Musical Instruments of the Arab, with an Introduction on how to appreciate Arab music*, translated by Henry George Farmer (London: William Reeves, 1914)

Sarkissian, Margaret and Ted Solis, *Living Ethnomusicology: Paths and Practices* (Champaign, IL: University of Illinois Press, 2019)

Shepard, Leslie, *The Broadside Ballad: A Study in Origins and Meaning* (Newton Abbot: David & Charles, 1973)

Sorrell, Neil, *A Guide to the Gamelan* (London: Faber, 1990)

Strehlow, TGH, *Aranda Phonetics and Grammar, Sydney*, Oceania Monograph 7 (Sydney: University of Sydney, 1944)

Strehlow, TGH, *Journey to Horseshoe Bend* (Sydney: Angus and Robertson, 1969)

Strehlow, TGH, *Songs of Central Australia* (Sydney: Angus and Robertson, 1971)

Suchoff, Benjamin, ed., *Bartók: Turkish Folk Music from Asia Minor* (London: Princeton University Press, 1976)

Suchoff, Benjamin, ed., *Béla Bartók Essays* (London: Faber, 1976)

Suchoff, Benjamin, ed., *Béla Bartók: Studies in Ethnomusicology* (London: University of Nebraska Press, 1997)

Suchoff, Benjamin, ed., *The Hungarian Folk Song, By Béla Bartók* (Albany: State University of New York Press, 1981)

Suff, David, *Three-score and Ten: A Voice to the People* (London: Topic, 2009)

Sultanova, Razia, *From Shamanism to Sufism: Women, Islam, and Culture in Central Asia* (London: I. B. Tauris, 2011)

Szwed, John, *The Man Who Recorded the World* (London: Arrow Books, 2010)

Taruskin, Richard, *Stravinsky and the Russian Traditions*, vol. 2 (Oxford: Oxford University Press, 1996)

Thompson, Flora, *Lark Rise to Candleford* (Oxford: Oxford University Press, 1945)

Thwaites, Penelope, ed., *The New Percy Grainger Companion* (Woodbridge: Boydell, 2010)

Trotsky, Leon, *Literature and Revolution* (Chicago: Haymarket, 2005)

Turnbull, Colin M., *The Forest People* (London: Jonathan Cape, 1961)

Wald, Elijah, *The Blues: A Very Short Introduction* (Oxford: Oxford University Press, 2010)

Widdess, Richard, *Dapha: Sacred Singing in a South Asian City* (London: Ashgate, 2013)

Recordings

Afghanistan: Female Musicians of Herat, Naïve D 8285

Afghanistan: The Traditional Music of Herat, Auvidis D 8266

African Rhythms, Pierre-Laurent Aimard and Aka Pygmies, Teldec 8573 86584-2

Aka Pygmies: Hunting, Love, and Mockery Songs, recordings by Susanne Fürniss, Ocora C561139

Bali 1928 – Anthology: The First Recordings, World Arbiter 2018

Borderlands: Wu Man and Master Musicians from the Silk Route, Smithsonian Folkways SFWCD 40529

Centrafrique: Musical Anthology of the Aka Pygmies, recordings by Simha Arom, Ocora C 561171/72

Chine: Musique Ouighoure: Muqam Nava, Ocora C 560253

Folk Music Anthology: Russian Music, MELCD 3001640

Georgian Voices: The Rustavi Choir, Elektra Nonesuch 7559-79224-2

Ghazals afghans: Poèmes d'amour séculiers et sacrés, Mahwash, Accords Croisés AC 118

Indonésie-Bali: Hommage à Wayan Lotring, Ocora France B07XW8DX6H

Istanbul: Dimitrie Cantemir 1673–1723, Hespèrion XXI, directed by Jordi Savall, Alia Vox AVSA9870

Jola: Hidden Gnawa Music in Brussels, Muziekpublique, 2020

Ławeczka (The Bench), East Warsaw Ensemble, double CD, 2014

Les noces, Pokrovsky Ensemble, Elektra Nonesuch 7559-79335-2

Komitas: Seven Songs, Lusine Grigoryan, piano, ECM New Series 2514 481 2556

Mademoiselle, voulez-vous danser?, Smithsonian Folkways SFWCD 40116

Mtiebi: Traditionelle Gesänge aus Georgien, Edition Musikay 398055552-6

Music of Central Asia Vol. 4: Bardic Divas, Smithsonian SFWCD 40523

Music of Central Asia Vol. 5: Song and Dance from the Pamir Mountains, The Badakhshan Ensemble, Smithsonian Folkways SFWCD 40524

Music of Central Asia Vol. 8: Rainbow, Kronos Quartet with Alim and Fargana Qasimov and Homayun Sakhi, Smithsonian Folkways SFWCD 40527

Music of Morocco from the Library of Congress, Dust to Digital DTD-46

Music of the Rainforest Pygmies, recordings by Colin M. Turnbull, Lyrichord LLST 7157

Ouzbekistan, Turgun Alimatov, Ocora C 560086

Radio Kaboul: Hommage aux compositeurs afghans, Accords Croisés ACC100

Seven Sisters, Don Kipper TUGCD1114

Sing We Yule, Joglaresa JOG007

Songs from the Steppes: Kazakh Music Today, recordings by Michael Church, Topic Records TSCD929

Songs of Survival: Traditional Music of Georgia, recordings by Michael Church, Topic Records TSCD935D

Spirit of the Forest, field recordings and studio embellishments by Martin Cradick for Baka Beyond, Hannibal, HNBC1377

Stravinsky: Les noces, Pokrovsky Ensemble, Electra Nonesuch Explorers 7559 79335-2

Tengir-Too: Mountain Music of Kyrgyzstan, Smithsonian Folkways SFWCD 40520

Traditional Georgian Women's Songs: Volume 1, Ensemble Mzetamze, Face Music Switzerland FM 50016

Traditional Georgian Women's Songs: Volume 2, Ensemble Mzetamze, Face Music Switzerland FM 50030

Vision and Revision: The First 80 Years of Topic Records, Topic Records TXCD597

Yume no Utsutsu, Yoko Fujimoto with Kodo drummers, Otodaiku Co, OD-023

Documentaries and films

Breaking the Silence: Music in Afghanistan, dir. Simon Broughton, BBC, 2002

From Podserednieje with Love, dir. Tomasz Knittel and Jagina Knittel, 2015

The Songs from the Depths of Hell, BBC World Service documentary, 2019

Online sources

domnasamiou.gr

Ustad Rahim: Herat's rubab maestro, www.therai.org.uk

Index

Page numbers in *italic* refer to illustrations.